# LIGHT
# COOKING
## for TWO

Library of Congress Catalog Card Number: 94-74029
ISBN: 0-8487-1434-2

Manufactured in the United States of America
First Printing 1995

Editor-in-Chief: Nancy J. Fitzpatrick
Senior Foods Editor: Katherine M. Eakin
Senior Editor, Editorial Services: Olivia Kindig Wells
Art Director: James Boone

***Light Cooking for Two***

Editor: Anne C. Chappell, M.S., M.P.H., R.D.
Foods Editor: Deborah Garrison Lowery
Copy Editor: Holly Ensor
Editorial Assistant: Lisa C. Bailey
Text Consultants: Helen Anne Dorrough, R.D.;
      Christin Loudon, R.D.
Director, Test Kitchens: Kathleen Royal Phillips
Assistant Director, Test Kitchens: Gayle Hays Sadler
Test Kitchen Home Economists: Susan Hall Bellows,
      Christina A. Crawford, Iris Crawley, Michele Brown Fuller,
      Elizabeth Tyler Luckett, Angie Neskaug Sinclair, Jan A. Smith
Recipe and Menu Developers: Patricia Coker; Helen Anne
      Dorrough, R.D.; Susan McEwen McIntosh, M.S., R.D.;
      Susan Reeves, R.D.
Senior Photographer: Jim Bathie
Photographer: Ralph Anderson
Senior Photo Stylist: Kay E. Clarke
Photo Stylist: Virginia R. Cravens
Senior Production Designer: Larry Hunter
Designer: Mary Grace Wright
Production and Distribution Director: Phillip Lee
Production Manager: Gail Morris
Associate Production Manager: Theresa L. Beste
Production Assistant: Marianne Jordan

Cover: *Blushing Pears in Chocolate Sauce* (page 168)
Back cover: *Salad Niçoise* (page 76), *Grasshopper Parfaits* (page 178),
      *Beef and Vegetable Kabobs* (page 82)
Pictured at right: *Quick Vegetarian Chili* (page 155)

# LIGHT COOKING for TWO

Oxmoor
House®

# CONTENTS

Dips, spreads, slushes, ciders—find a host of recipes for cozy, great beginnings.

Main dish or on the side. You'll make these salads again and again.

A loaf, biscuits, or sweet breakfast breads just for you. Here's an ovenful of freshly baked and scaled-down selections.

Meat, fish, fowl, or meatless entrées make the main event. These top-billed entrées are the ticket to memorable meals.

# The Way to Cook for Two

**We've taken the guesswork out of healthy cooking for two. Here's a complete guide to cooking smaller amounts.**

No more leftovers. No more scribbling mathematics in the recipe margins to cut the amounts down to size for the two of you. If you want recipes with smaller servings, all your recipe needs are met in this book. Here's how:

- All the recipes make exactly two servings.

- The pantry guide on page 9 shows how to stock your shelves to make cooking for two more convenient.

- Shopping tips on pages 10 and 11 tell you how to buy just the amount of food you need so that leftover food doesn't go to waste in your refrigerator.

Are your meals becoming monotonous or not as much fun as when you have a guest or two? If so, try a few of our secrets for making meals what they're meant to be—a time to enjoy delicious, healthy food and good company (even if you're dining alone!) in a relaxing atmosphere.

- Cook together. Let your child or partner help with simple cooking tasks. You do the cooking one night while your partner creates unique garnishes. Then swap assignments the next night.

- Have a picnic in January—in front of the fireplace on a favorite quilt.

- Eat out. Out of the kitchen, that is. Try eating breakfast on the deck, dinner on the coffee table, or lunch in rocking chairs on your front porch.

- Bring out your dining best. Polish the silver, dust the crystal, and serve an elegant meal on your best china.

- Color the table. Use placemats, tablecloths, napkins, or even a single fresh flower to paint your table, and your mood, a little brighter.

- Cater to your whims. Maybe it's a plate with painted ants marching around the rim, handmade pottery with a design you think is neat, or a funky plate pattern that's too pricey to buy a whole set. Splurge on a set of two, and pull them out for dining when you get the urge to be different.

# Nutrition Information at Your Fingertips

Put away your calculator. In addition to designing recipes that serve two, we give you the nutrition facts you want to know for each recipe. Every recipe is analyzed for:

Calories
Percent Calories from Fat
Fat
Saturated Fat
Carbohydrate
Protein
Cholesterol
Sodium

## Extra, Extra! Exchanges

In addition to nutrient values, we provide exchange list values for those who use them as a guide for planning meals. Exchange lists have been developed to help people on calorie-controlled diets plan healthy meals.

All foods within a certain group contain approximately the same amount of nutrients and calories, so one serving of a food from a food group can be substituted or exchanged for one serving of any other item in the list. The exchange values are based on the *Exchange Lists for Meal Planning* developed by the American Diabetes Association and The American Dietetic Association and are similar to the exchange lists used by weight-control programs.

Exchange values are provided for every recipe in *Light Cooking for Two* so that you can use these recipes in your own meal pattern. For example, if your meal plan for supper is the following:

2 Starch Exchanges,
3 Meat Exchanges, and
1 Vegetable Exchange,

you could choose the Turkey Fajitas on page 100. One serving of the fajita recipe counts as 2 Starch, 3 Lean Meat, and 1 Vegetable. Or, you could have Hot-and-Spicy Pork Burritos (page 228) or Shepherd's Pie (page 207). All three of these recipes have the same exchange values. The choice is yours!

The nutritional analysis appears beside each recipe as in the sample below.

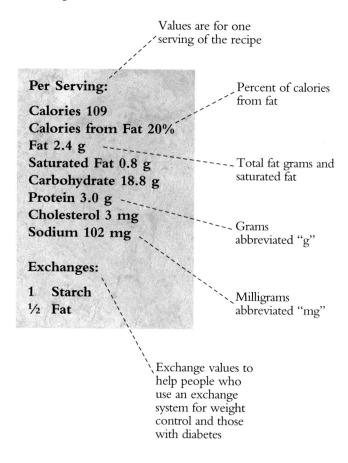

Values are for one serving of the recipe

**Per Serving:**

Calories 109
Calories from Fat 20%
Fat 2.4 g
Saturated Fat 0.8 g
Carbohydrate 18.8 g
Protein 3.0 g
Cholesterol 3 mg
Sodium 102 mg

**Exchanges:**

1   Starch
½   Fat

Percent of calories from fat

Total fat grams and saturated fat

Grams abbreviated "g"

Milligrams abbreviated "mg"

Exchange values to help people who use an exchange system for weight control and those with diabetes

## How We Got the Numbers

The nutritional values come from a computer analysis based on information from the U.S. Department of Agriculture and the following guidelines:

• When a range is given for an ingredient, the lesser amount is calculated.

• Some alcohol calories evaporate during cooking; the analysis reflects the remaining amount.

• When a marinade is used, only the amount of the marinade absorbed by the food is used in the calculation.

• Garnishes and optional ingredients are not included in the calculation.

# Stocking Up

You'll find cooking and menu planning easier when your kitchen is stocked with plenty of basic items.
Keep these staples on hand, and then shop for fresh ingredients as you need them.
Use the chart below as a guide for what to keep on hand.

## KEEP IN THE PANTRY

### Baking Supplies

Baking powder
Baking soda
Brown sugar
Cocoa, unsweetened
Cornstarch
Flour
Sugar

### Condiments and Sauces

Barbecue sauce, no-salt-added
Fruit spreads
Honey
Ketchup, reduced-calorie
Mustard
Pasta sauce, low-fat,
    low-sodium
Salsa or picante sauce
Soy sauce, low-sodium
Vinegar
Worcestershire sauce,
    low-sodium

### Dairy Products

Evaporated skimmed milk
Nonfat dry milk powder

### Fruits and Vegetables

Dried fruit
Canned fruit packed in juice
Canned vegetables, no-salt-added

### Herbs/Spices/Flavorings

Almond extract
Basil
Chili powder
Cinnamon
Cumin
Dill
Garlic powder
Ginger
Herb-and-spice blend, salt-free
Lemon pepper, salt-free
Marjoram
Oregano
Paprika
Parsley
Pepper
Rosemary
Tarragon
Vanilla extract

### Miscellaneous

Bouillon granules
Broth, canned, no-salt-added or
    low-sodium
Chicken, canned, packed in broth
Gelatin, unflavored
Peanut butter, reduced-fat
Tuna, canned, packed in water

### Pasta/Grains, Legumes

Angel hair (cappellini)
Beans, dried
Bulgur
Couscous
Jumbo shells
Lasagna
Macaroni
Noodles
Rice, white and brown
Rice mixes, low-sodium
Spaghetti

### Salad Dressings/Oils

Nonfat mayonnaise
Nonfat salad dressings
Vegetable cooking spray
Olive oil
Vegetable oil

## KEEP IN THE REFRIGERATOR

Nonfat cream cheese
Cheese, reduced-fat Cheddar and
    other semi-firm cheeses
Parmesan cheese
Ricotta cheese, lite and nonfat
Eggs
Egg substitute
Bottled minced garlic
Bottled minced ginger
Bottled lemon juice
Reduced-calorie margarine
Skim milk
Nonfat sour cream alternative
Nonfat yogurt

## KEEP IN THE FREEZER

Fruit juice concentrates
Nonfat or low-fat ice cream
Nonfat or low-fat frozen yogurt
Onion, chopped
Pepper, green, chopped
Vegetables, loose-pack

# BUYING THE RIGHT SIZE

The best way to avoid leftovers is to not buy too much food in the first place. Supermarkets and food product manufacturers have responded to the growing number of small households by offering products packaged in smaller, more convenient sizes. Even fresh foods, which you can buy in amounts you need, are available at supermarket salad bars, bakeries, and delicatessens.

Don't know whether a can of your favorite vegetable comes in a smaller, more convenient size than the size you usually buy? Then check the chart below to save yourself time, money, and leftovers. The items listed are the smallest packages or cans of the type ingredients available. If your supermarket doesn't offer a product in the size you'd prefer, check with your store manager and request it.

**Beverages**
Fruit juices, boxed (4.23 ounces)
Fruit juices, canned (6 ounces)
Sparkling apple juice (10 ounces)
Sparkling cider (6.3 ounces)
Liqueur (50 milliliters)
Wine (6 ounces)
Soft drinks (1 liter or 20 ounces)

**Canned Fruit**
Applesauce, unsweetened (3.9 ounces)
Apricot halves in juice (8¼ ounces)
Fruit cocktail in juice (4½ ounces)
Diced peaches in juice (4½ ounces)
Diced pears in juice (4½ ounces)
Pineapple tidbits in juice (4½ ounces)

**Canned Fish**
Salmon (3¼ ounces)
Tuna in water (3 ounces)

**Canned Vegetables (no-salt-added)**
Whole-kernel corn (8¾ ounces)
Green beans (8 ounces)
Sweet peas (8½ ounces)

**Cereals, Crackers, and Cookies**
Animal crackers (2 ounces)
Bagel chips, fat-free (5 ounces)
Breadsticks, fat-free (4½ ounces)
Cookies, reduced-fat cream sandwich (1.7 ounces)
Cookies, reduced-fat (5½ ounces)
Crackers, saltine (4 ounces)
Crackers, whole grain, fat-free (6½ ounces)
Graham crackers (5¼ ounces)
Graham snacks, cinnamon (5 ounces)
Vanilla wafers (3½ ounces)

**Dairy Products**
Cottage cheese, nonfat (8 ounces)
Cottage cheese, 1% fat (12 ounces)
1% low-fat cottage cheese (8 ounces)
Cream cheese, nonfat (8 ounces)
Egg substitute (4 ounces)
Fruit-flavored nonfat yogurt (4.4 ounces)
Skim milk (½ pint)
Evaporated skimmed milk (5 ounces)
Nonfat sour cream alternative (8 ounces)

**Desserts**
Frozen yogurt, low-fat and nonfat (1 pint)
Gelatin dessert (4 ounces)
Pudding, low-fat (4 ounces)

**Meats**
Reduced-fat baked ham (5 ounces)
Low-fat luncheon meats (8 ounces)
Turkey breast, roasted (5 ounces)

**Produce**
Broccoli flowerets (8 ounces)
Broccoli coleslaw (8 ounces)
Cauliflower flowerets (12 ounces)
Shredded red cabbage (8 ounces)
Peeled or shredded carrots (8 ounces)
Celery slices (12 ounces)
Coleslaw (8 ounces)
Gourmet salad (6, 8, or 10 ounces)
Italian salad (10 ounces)

**Snacks**
Cereal bars, reduced-fat (1.3 ounces)
Corn chips, low-fat (4 ounces)
Granola bars, fat-free (6 ounces)
Tortilla chips, no-oil, baked (7 ounces)

# Cooking The Right Amount

| Food | Amount for Two Servings |
|---|---|
| **Meat** | |
| Beef, pork, lamb, or veal, boneless | 8 ounces |
| Beef steak with bone | 10 ounces |
| Game | 8 ounces |
| Ground meat | 8 ounces |
| Lamb or veal chops with bone | 10 ounces |
| Pork chops with bone | 12 ounces |
| **Poultry** | |
| Chicken or turkey breast, boneless | 8 ounces |
| Chicken breast or thigh with bone | 12 ounces |
| Chicken legs | 4 medium |
| Chicken or turkey, diced, cooked | 1 cup |
| Cornish hen | 1 pound |

| Food | Amount for Two Servings |
|---|---|
| **Fish and Seafood** | |
| Fish fillets or steaks | 8 ounces |
| Fresh lump crabmeat | 8 ounces |
| Fresh scallops or oysters | 8 ounces |
| Salmon, tuna, or crab, canned | 8 ounces |
| Shelled shrimp or crayfish | 8 ounces |
| **Grains and Rice (uncooked)** | |
| Bulgur | ⅓ cup |
| Couscous | ⅓ cup |
| Oats | ½ cup |
| Polenta | ⅓ cup |
| Rice, brown, long-grain, wild | ⅓ cup |
| Rice, quick-cooking | ½ cup |

# Pasta Pointers

When the recipe calls for cooked pasta, it's up to the cook to decide what kind or shape of pasta to use. Remember that you can interchange dry pastas of similar sizes and shapes when you measure them by weight instead of by the cup. The following chart will help you know how much dry or cooked pasta is just right for two. If you enjoy fresh pasta, 3 ounces of fresh uncooked refrigerated pasta serves two.

| Pasta | Amount for Two Servings | | Pasta | Amount for Two Servings | |
|---|---|---|---|---|---|
| | Dry | Cooked | | Dry | Cooked |
| Fettuccini | 4 ounces | 2 cups | Corkscrew macaroni | 4 ounces | 2 cups |
| Linguine | 4 ounces | 2 cups | Elbow macaroni | 4 ounces | 2 cups |
| Spaghetti | 4 ounces | 2 cups | Shell macaroni | 4 ounces | 2 cups |
| Vermicelli | 4 ounces | 2 cups | Rigatoni | 4 ounces | 2 cups |

# PERFECT PAN SIZE

You don't need a lot of special equipment to make the recipes in *Light Cooking for Two*, just smaller pans and baking dishes. When we tested the recipes for this book, we found the cooking containers below to be the most useful.

 These 5- x 7- x 1½-inch casseroles are just the right size for entrées or side dishes.

 Small baking pans are handy for baking cakes and breads. Look for 4- x 2- x 1½-inch or 6- x 3- x 2-inch loafpans, 6- x 6-inch square or 6-inch round pans.

 Soufflé dishes, ramekins, and gratin dishes are good for baking vegetable dishes, layered desserts, and casseroles.

 Four-inch pie pans and tartlet pans make dessert baking for two convenient.

 Two-cup freezer/microwave dishes with lids make it easy to freeze and reheat.

 Four-inch and 6-inch springform pans are handy for baking small cheesecakes.

 A small wok or a stir-fry pan is good for quick, fat-free stir-frying. You can also use a 6-inch or an 8-inch nonstick skillet.

 Four-inch angel food cake pans are just the right size for baking individual cakes.

# How Long Will It Keep?

When you're shopping and cooking for two, you may often have extra food to store. Use this chart to know how to store commercially frozen, packaged foods and home-frozen foods in the freezer without sacrificing texture or flavor. If you store it longer, the food is safe, but it might not taste as good.

**Bread**

| | |
|---|---|
| Quick breads | 3 months |
| Yeast breads | 3 months |
| Yeast dough | 1 month |

**Cheese**

| | |
|---|---|
| Soft | 2 weeks |
| Hard | 3 months |

**Desserts**

| | |
|---|---|
| Cakes, angel food | 2 months |
| Cakes, pound | 6 months |
| Cookies | 1 month |
| Fruit pies, unbaked | 6 months |
| Ice cream or sherbet | 1 month |

**Eggs**

| | |
|---|---|
| Whites | 12 months |
| Yolks | 12 months |

**Fish**

| | |
|---|---|
| Fatty fish (perch, trout, bass) | 3 months |
| Lean fish (cod, flounder, halibut) | 6 months |
| Shellfish | 3 months |

**Frozen Fruit**

| | |
|---|---|
| Apples | 12 months |
| Berries | 12 months |
| Cherries | 12 months |
| Citrus fruit | 4 to 6 months |
| Melons | 12 months |
| Nectarines | 12 months |
| Peaches | 12 months |
| Pears | 12 months |
| Plums | 12 months |

**Margarine** — 9 months

**Meats and Poultry**

| | |
|---|---|
| Beef, Lamb, and Veal | |
|     roasts, uncooked | 9 months |
|     steaks, uncooked | 9 months |
|     ground, uncooked | 3 months |
|     all cuts, cooked | 3 months |
| Pork | |
|     roasts, uncooked | 6 months |
|     chops, uncooked | 6 months |
|     ground, uncooked | 3 months |
|     all cuts, cooked | 3 months |
| Poultry | |
|     breast, thigh, and | |
|       leg pieces, uncooked | 6 months |
|     boneless pieces, uncooked | 6 months |
|     all cuts, cooked | 1 month |

**Frozen Vegetables**

| | |
|---|---|
| Asparagus | 8 to 12 months |
| Beets | 8 to 12 months |
| Black-eyed peas | 8 to 12 months |
| Broccoli | 8 to 12 months |
| Brussels sprouts | 8 to 12 months |
| Cabbage | 8 to 12 months |
| Carrots | 8 to 12 months |
| Cauliflower | 8 to 12 months |
| Corn | 8 to 12 months |
| Green beans | 8 to 12 months |
| Green peas | 8 to 12 months |
| Lima beans | 8 to 12 months |
| Peppers | 6 months |
| Spinach | 8 to 12 months |
| Summer squash | 8 to 12 months |
| Winter squash | 8 to 12 months |
| Turnip greens | 8 to 12 months |
| Turnips | 8 to 12 months |

Cheddar-Jack Cheese Ball (page 17), Roasted Red Pepper
Dip (page 18), Tangy Cranberry Coolers (page 30)

# OPENERS

Create a first impression with a frosty fruit sipper or a spicy dip.
Then forget leftovers—these appetizers cater to parties of two.

# Cheese Sticks with Marinara Sauce

**Per Cheese Stick with 1½ Teaspoons Sauce:**

Calories 65
Calories from Fat 43%
Fat 3.1 g
Saturated Fat 1.7 g
Carbohydrate 4.1 g
Protein 5.2 g
Cholesterol 10 mg
Sodium 159 mg

**Exchanges:**

½ Medium-Fat Meat
1 Vegetable

½ (8-ounce) block reduced-fat Monterey Jack cheese
1 egg white, lightly beaten
¼ cup fine, dry breadcrumbs
  Olive oil-flavored vegetable cooking spray
1 tablespoon chopped sweet red pepper
1 tablespoon chopped fresh parsley
1 tablespoon chopped onion

½ (8-ounce) can no-salt-added tomato sauce
½ teaspoon chopped fresh oregano
½ teaspoon chopped fresh basil
½ teaspoon chopped fresh thyme
¼ teaspoon garlic powder
⅛ teaspoon sugar
⅛ teaspoon salt
⅛ teaspoon pepper

Cut cheese crosswise into 4 (1-ounce) slices. Cut each slice in half lengthwise. Dip cheese sticks into egg white; dredge in breadcrumbs. Repeat coating procedure once, using remaining egg white and breadcrumbs. Place cheese sticks on a baking sheet coated with cooking spray. Freeze 30 minutes.

Coat a small saucepan with cooking spray. Place over medium heat until hot. Add red pepper, parsley, and onion; sauté 3 minutes or until tender. Stir in tomato sauce and remaining ingredients; bring to a boil. Cover, reduce heat, and simmer 10 minutes, stirring occasionally. Remove from heat, and set aside.

Remove cheese sticks from freezer, and coat with cooking spray. Bake at 450° for 5 minutes or until cheese begins to soften. Serve immediately with tomato sauce mixture. Yield: 8 cheese sticks and ¼ cup plus 2 tablespoons sauce.

The use of reduced-fat cheese in these three cheese appetizers keeps the fat content significantly lower than that of traditional cheese appetizers. Note that the total fat for each appetizer is about 3 grams or less per serving.

# CHEDDAR-JACK CHEESE BALL

¼ cup Neufchâtel cheese, softened
1 tablespoon plain nonfat yogurt
¼ cup (1 ounce) shredded reduced-fat Cheddar cheese
¼ cup (1 ounce) shredded reduced-fat Monterey Jack cheese
½ teaspoon minced onion
½ teaspoon prepared horseradish
¼ teaspoon Dijon mustard
Dash of ground red pepper
1 tablespoon nutlike cereal nuggets
2 teaspoons chopped fresh parsley
24 fat-free crackers

Combine Neufchâtel cheese and yogurt, stirring until smooth. Add Cheddar cheese and next 5 ingredients; stir well. Cover and chill at least 2 hours.
Shape cheese mixture into a ball. Wrap in wax paper, and chill.
Combine cereal nuggets and parsley. Roll cheese ball in cereal mixture just before serving. Serve with fat-free crackers. Yield: ½ cup.

Per 1 Tablespoon and 3 Crackers:

Calories 71
Calories from Fat 38%
Fat 3.0 g
Saturated Fat 1.8 g
Carbohydrate 6.7 g
Protein 4.2 g
Cholesterol 10 mg
Sodium 138 mg

Exchanges:

½ Starch
½ Medium-Fat Meat

# SHRIMP-CHEESE SPREAD

2 cups water
3 unpeeled large fresh shrimp
¼ cup nonfat cottage cheese
2 tablespoons Neufchâtel cheese, softened
1 teaspoon Dijon mustard
1 tablespoon shredded reduced-fat Cheddar cheese
1 tablespoon finely chopped fresh parsley
1 teaspoon finely chopped jalapeño pepper
24 Melba rounds

Bring water to a boil in a medium saucepan; add shrimp, and cook 3 to 5 minutes or until shrimp turns pink. Drain well; rinse with cold water. Peel and devein shrimp. Finely chop shrimp, and set aside.
Position knife blade in a miniature food processor bowl; add cottage cheese, Neufchâtel cheese, and mustard. Process 1 minute or until smooth, stopping once to scrape down sides. Transfer mixture to a small bowl. Stir in shrimp, Cheddar cheese, parsley, and jalapeño pepper. Cover and chill thoroughly. Serve with Melba rounds. Yield: ½ cup.

Per 1 Tablespoon and 3 Melba Rounds:

Calories 59
Calories from Fat 31%
Fat 2.0 g
Saturated Fat 0.8 g
Carbohydrate 6.4 g
Protein 4.1 g
Cholesterol 13 mg
Sodium 163 mg

Exchanges:

½ Starch
½ Lean Meat

# Roasted Red Pepper Dip

1  medium-size sweet red
   pepper
3  tablespoons Neufchâtel
   cheese, softened
1  teaspoon white wine vinegar
½  teaspoon prepared
   horseradish
⅛  teaspoon salt
⅛  teaspoon ground red pepper
24 fat-free crackers

Cut pepper in half lengthwise; remove and discard seeds and membranes. Place pepper halves, skin side up, on a baking sheet; flatten pepper halves with palm of hand. Broil pepper 5½ inches from heat (with electric oven door partially opened) 15 to 20 minutes or until charred. Place in ice water until cool. Remove from water; peel and discard skins.

Place roasted pepper, cheese, and next 4 ingredients in container of an electric blender; cover and process until smooth, stopping once to scrape down sides. Transfer mixture to a small bowl; cover and chill thoroughly. Serve with fat-free crackers. Yield: ½ cup.

# Ricotta Pesto Bites

¼  cup lite ricotta cheese
2  tablespoons grated Parmesan
   cheese
2  tablespoons finely chopped
   fresh basil leaves
1  tablespoon minced celery
1  tablespoon nonfat sour
   cream alternative
¼  teaspoon garlic powder
⅛  teaspoon salt
⅛  teaspoon pepper
⅛  teaspoon ground thyme
4  large fresh spinach leaves
1  cup water
   Vegetable cooking spray

Combine first 9 ingredients in a small bowl, stirring with a fork until blended. Set aside.

Remove and discard stems from spinach leaves. Bring water to a boil in a small saucepan. Cook spinach leaves, one at a time, in boiling water 15 seconds. Place leaves on paper towels to drain.

Coat 4 (1¾-inch) miniature muffin pan cups with cooking spray. Line each cup with a spinach leaf, covering bottom and sides of cup, allowing leaf to overhang. Spoon cheese mixture evenly onto spinach leaves. Fold leaves over to enclose cheese mixture. Bake at 350° for 20 minutes. Carefully remove from pan. Serve warm. Yield: 4 appetizers.

# SUN-DRIED TOMATO BRUSCHETTA

4 (1-ounce) slices French bread
   (½ inch thick)
¼ cup sun-dried tomatoes
1 teaspoon olive oil
1 tablespoon minced onion
1 tablespoon minced green
   pepper

2 tablespoons water
1 tablespoon dry white wine
¼ teaspoon garlic powder
¼ teaspoon dried basil
   Dash of ground red pepper
2 teaspoons freshly grated
   Parmesan cheese, divided

Place bread slices on an ungreased baking sheet. Bake at 450° for 5 minutes or until lightly browned.

Place tomatoes in a small saucepan; cover with water. Bring to a boil; cook, uncovered, 2 minutes. Drain well. Cut tomatoes into very thin slices; set aside.

Add oil to pan; place over medium-high heat until hot. Add onion and green pepper; sauté until tender. Stir in sliced tomato, water, and next 4 ingredients. Bring to a boil; reduce heat, and simmer, uncovered, 5 minutes or until liquid is absorbed. Spread tomato mixture evenly over toasted bread slices. Sprinkle ½ teaspoon cheese on each slice. Yield: 4 appetizers.

**Sun-Dried Tomato Bruschetta**

**Per Appetizer:**

Calories 122
Calories from Fat 19%
Fat 2.6 g
Saturated Fat 0.6 g
Carbohydrate 20.9 g
Protein 4.0 g
Cholesterol 2 mg
Sodium 285 mg

**Exchanges:**

1½ Starch
½ Fat

# Radish Rosette Canapés

4 (¾-ounce) slices reduced-calorie white bread
2 tablespoons light process cream cheese product, softened

2 tablespoons minced green onions
2 radishes, finely shredded

Cut 2 rounds from each slice of bread, using a 2-inch biscuit cutter. Reserve excess bread for another use. Place rounds on a baking sheet; broil 5½ inches from heat (with electric oven door partially opened) 1 to 2 minutes on one side or until golden. Let cool.

Combine cream cheese and green onions. Spread cheese mixture evenly on untoasted sides of bread rounds. Top each with 1 teaspoon radish, lightly pressing into cheese mixture. Yield: 8 appetizers.

**Per 4 Appetizers:**

Calories 76
Calories from Fat 30%
Fat 2.5 g
Saturated Fat 1.4 g
Carbohydrate 9.0 g
Protein 3.7 g
Cholesterol 8 mg
Sodium 193 mg

**Exchanges:**

1   Starch
½   Fat

# Oriental Vegetable Wontons

2 tablespoons rice wine vinegar
1 tablespoon low-sodium soy sauce
¼ teaspoon garlic powder
⅛ teaspoon ground ginger
2 tablespoons chopped fresh broccoli
2 tablespoons chopped cabbage

1 tablespoon chopped onion
1 tablespoon chopped fresh mushrooms
1 tablespoon fresh bean sprouts
½ teaspoon garlic powder
6 fresh or frozen wonton skins, thawed
Vegetable cooking spray

Combine first 4 ingredients, stirring well; set aside.

Position knife blade in food processor bowl, and add broccoli and next 5 ingredients. Process until mixture is minced, scraping sides of processor bowl once.

Place vegetable mixture evenly on top corner of each wonton skin. Fold top point of wonton skin over filling; tuck point under filling. Roll once toward center, covering filling and leaving about 1 inch unrolled at bottom of skin. Moisten remaining corners with water; bring corners together, and overlap, pressing ends together to seal securely.

Cook wontons in boiling water 3 minutes or until tender. Drain; coat wontons with cooking spray, and arrange on 2 serving plates. Serve with vinegar mixture. Yield: 6 appetizers.

**Per 3 Appetizers:**

Calories 92
Calories from Fat 9%
Fat 0.9 g
Saturated Fat 0.1 g
Carbohydrate 16.7 g
Protein 3.2 g
Cholesterol 2 mg
Sodium 338 mg

**Exchanges:**

1   Starch

# Veggie Quesadillas

Butter-flavored vegetable
    cooking spray
½ cup finely shredded cabbage
¼ cup finely chopped fresh
    mushrooms
2 tablespoons finely chopped
    sweet red pepper
2 tablespoons finely shredded
    carrot

1 tablespoon minced onion
⅛ teaspoon ground celery seed
    Dash of salt
2 (6-inch) flour tortillas
¼ cup (1 ounce) shredded
    reduced-fat sharp Cheddar
    cheese

Coat a small nonstick skillet with cooking spray; place over medium-high heat until hot. Add cabbage and next 6 ingredients; sauté 5 minutes or until vegetables are tender.

Spoon vegetable mixture over 1 tortilla; spread to within ½ inch of edge. Sprinkle with cheese, and top with remaining tortilla.

Coat skillet with cooking spray; place over medium-high heat until hot. Add quesadilla, and cook 2 minutes on each side or until lightly browned. Remove from skillet; cut into 4 wedges, and serve immediately. Yield: 4 appetizers.

Per Appetizer:

Calories 89
Calories from Fat 30%
Fat 3.0 g
Saturated Fat 1.0 g
Carbohydrate 11.6 g
Protein 3.9 g
Cholesterol 5 mg
Sodium 173 mg

Exchanges:

1 Starch
½ Fat

# Creole Meatballs

¼ pound ground round
2 tablespoons frozen egg
    substitute, thawed
1 tablespoon dried onion flakes
1 teaspoon prepared
    horseradish
¼ teaspoon dry mustard
    Vegetable cooking spray
½ teaspoon reduced-calorie
    margarine
1 tablespoon finely chopped
    green pepper

1 tablespoon finely chopped
    onion
¼ teaspoon garlic powder
⅛ teaspoon salt
⅛ teaspoon ground red pepper
½ cup no-salt-added tomato
    sauce
1 (2½-ounce) jar sliced
    mushrooms, drained

Combine first 5 ingredients in a small bowl, stirring well. Shape mixture into 8 meatballs. Arrange meatballs on rack of a broiler pan coated with cooking spray. Broil 5½ inches from heat (with electric oven door partially opened) 10 to 12 minutes or until done, turning once. Set aside; keep warm.

Heat margarine in a small saucepan over medium-high heat until margarine melts. Add green pepper and next 4 ingredients; sauté until onion is tender. Stir in tomato sauce and mushrooms; cook until thoroughly heated. Add meatballs, and stir until coated. Serve immediately. Yield: 8 meatballs.

Per Meatball:

Calories 36
Calories from Fat 30%
Fat 1.2 g
Saturated Fat 0.3 g
Carbohydrate 2.6 g
Protein 3.8 g
Cholesterol 9 mg
Sodium 73 mg

Exchanges:

½ Lean Meat
½ Vegetable

# MINIATURE CHILI PIES

**Per Appetizer:**

Calories 61
Calories from Fat 28%
Fat 1.9 g
Saturated Fat 0.7 g
Carbohydrate 9.3 g
Protein 3.0 g
Cholesterol 6 mg
Sodium 153 mg

**Exchanges:**

½  Starch
½  Medium-Fat Meat

1  ounce lean ground chuck
1  tablespoon minced onion
1  tablespoon water
2  teaspoons ketchup
½  teaspoon all-purpose flour
½  teaspoon ground cumin
¼  teaspoon garlic powder
⅛  teaspoon chili powder

3  tablespoons low-fat biscuit
   and baking mix
¼  teaspoon chili powder
2  teaspoons skim milk
   Vegetable cooking spray
2  teaspoons shredded reduced-
   fat Cheddar cheese

Cook ground chuck and onion in a small saucepan over medium heat until browned, stirring until meat crumbles. Drain and pat dry with paper towels. Wipe drippings from saucepan with a paper towel. Return beef mixture to saucepan. Stir in water and next 5 ingredients. Cover and cook over low heat 5 minutes, stirring frequently.

Combine baking mix, ¼ teaspoon chili powder, and milk in a small bowl, stirring well. Divide dough into four equal portions. Roll each portion between 2 sheets of heavy-duty plastic wrap into a 2½-inch circle. Place in freezer 5 minutes or until plastic wrap can be removed easily. Invert and fit dough into 4 miniature (1¾-inch) muffin pan cups coated with cooking spray; remove remaining plastic wrap.

Spoon beef mixture evenly into dough-lined muffin pan cups. Bake at 400° for 8 minutes. Sprinkle each pie with ½ teaspoon cheese. Bake an additional 2 minutes or until cheese melts. Remove from muffin pan cups, and serve immediately. Yield: 4 appetizers.

Offer a glass of Raspberry Ale (page 31) or lemon-flavored sparkling mineral water along with these meat-filled appetizer pastries.

# Fajita Potato Skins

1 tablespoon chopped onion
1 tablespoon chopped fresh
  cilantro
1 tablespoon lime juice
¼ teaspoon garlic powder
⅛ teaspoon salt
⅛ teaspoon ground cumin
⅛ teaspoon ground red pepper
2 ounces lean boneless round
  steak

2 small baking potatoes (about
  3½ ounces each)
  Vegetable cooking spray
¼ cup (1 ounce) shredded
  reduced-fat Cheddar cheese
2 tablespoons no-salt-added
  mild salsa

Combine first 7 ingredients in a small bowl, stirring well.

Trim fat from steak; slice steak diagonally across grain into ¼-inch-wide strips. Add steak to onion mixture. Cover and marinate in refrigerator 2 hours.

Scrub potatoes. Bake at 400° for 35 minutes or until tender. Let cool to touch. Cut potatoes in half lengthwise. Carefully scoop out pulp, leaving ¼-inch-thick shells; set shells aside. Mash pulp.

Coat a small nonstick skillet with cooking spray; place over medium heat until hot. Add meat mixture; cook 2 minutes or until meat is browned on both sides. Add mashed potato to skillet, and cook 1 minute.

Place potato shells in a small baking dish. Spoon steak mixture evenly into shells, and top with cheese. Bake at 350° for 10 to 12 minutes or until thoroughly heated. Top evenly with salsa. Yield: 4 appetizers.

Per Appetizer:

Calories 84
Calories from Fat 24%
Fat 2.2 g
Saturated Fat 1.0 g
Carbohydrate 9.6 g
Protein 6.6 g
Cholesterol 13 mg
Sodium 134 mg

Exchanges:

½ Starch
1 Lean Meat

Fajita Potato Skins

# Roast Beef and Swiss Phyllo Roll-Ups

2 tablespoons nonfat sour cream alternative
1 tablespoon prepared horseradish
1 teaspoon Dijon mustard
2 sheets frozen phyllo pastry, thawed in refrigerator

Vegetable cooking spray
2 ounces thinly sliced lean roast beef
2 tablespoons (½ ounce) shredded reduced-fat Swiss cheese

Combine first 3 ingredients in a small bowl, stirring well. Set aside.

Place 1 sheet of phyllo on a damp towel (keeping remaining phyllo covered). Lightly coat phyllo with cooking spray. Place remaining sheet of phyllo on top of first sheet, and lightly coat with cooking spray. Fold phyllo stack in half crosswise, bringing short ends together. Lightly coat with cooking spray. Cut phyllo stack in half crosswise, making 2 phyllo rectangles.

Spread 1 tablespoon plus 2 teaspoons sour cream mixture evenly over 1 phyllo rectangle to within ¼ inch of edges. Place 1 ounce roast beef over sour cream mixture; top with 1 tablespoon Swiss cheese. Roll up phyllo, jellyroll fashion, starting with long side. Repeat procedure with remaining phyllo rectangle, sour cream mixture, roast beef, and cheese.

Place phyllo rolls, seam side down, on a baking sheet coated with cooking spray. Lightly coat tops of phyllo rolls with cooking spray. Bake at 375° for 15 minutes or until crisp and golden. Cut each roll in half diagonally. Serve immediately. Yield: 4 appetizers.

You can purchase small amounts of lean roast beef from the delicatessen at your local supermarket.

# GREEK PITAS

2 ounces lean boneless lamb
¼ teaspoon garlic powder
⅛ teaspoon dried rosemary, crushed
Dash of salt
Olive oil-flavored vegetable cooking spray

2 tablespoons chopped cucumber
2 tablespoons chopped tomato
1 tablespoon plain nonfat yogurt
2 (4-inch) pita bread rounds, cut in half crosswise

Cut lamb into ⅛-inch-wide strips; place in a small bowl. Sprinkle garlic powder, rosemary, and salt over lamb; toss to coat.

Coat a small nonstick skillet with cooking spray; place over medium-high heat until hot. Add lamb strips, and cook 5 minutes or until lamb is browned on both sides. Drain and pat dry with paper towels.

Combine cucumber, tomato, and yogurt, stirring well. Spoon lamb evenly into pita halves, and top evenly with cucumber mixture.
Yield: 4 appetizers.

Small pita bread rounds are usually found in packages of 10 or more rounds. You can store extra bread in the freezer for up to one month.

**Per Appetizer:**

Calories 64
Calories from Fat 20%
Fat 1.4 g
Saturated Fat 0.4 g
Carbohydrate 7.9 g
Protein 4.0 g
Cholesterol 9 mg
Sodium 119 mg

**Exchanges:**

½ Starch
½ Lean Meat

# CHICKEN-APPLE CROSTINI

1 ounce roasted chicken breast, skinned and finely chopped
2 tablespoons peeled, grated Granny Smith apple
1 tablespoon Neufchâtel cheese, softened

1½ teaspoons chopped green onions
Dash of garlic powder
10 garlic-flavored Melba rounds
Fresh chives (optional)

Combine first 5 ingredients in a small bowl, stirring well. Spread chicken mixture evenly on Melba rounds. Garnish with fresh chives, if desired.
Yield: 10 appetizers.

If roasted chicken is only available in whole form, you can freeze the remainder for other uses. Freeze chicken in an airtight container for up to three months. Be sure to remove all visible fat and skin from the chicken before using it in recipes.

**Per 5 Appetizers:**

Calories 105
Calories from Fat 28%
Fat 3.3 g
Saturated Fat 1.4 g
Carbohydrate 11.5 g
Protein 7.2 g
Cholesterol 17 mg
Sodium 170 mg

**Exchanges:**

1 Starch
½ Medium-Fat Meat

# MONTEREY CHICKEN POCKETS

Butter-flavored vegetable
  cooking spray
½ tablespoon chopped onion
½ tablespoon chopped green
  pepper
¼ teaspoon garlic powder,
  divided
  Dash of pepper
1 ounce roasted chicken breast,
  skinned and chopped

½ tablespoon finely chopped
  tomato
¼ cup low-fat biscuit and
  baking mix
1 tablespoon skim milk
½ teaspoon all-purpose flour
2 tablespoons (½ ounce)
  shredded reduced-fat
  Monterey Jack cheese

Coat a small nonstick skillet with cooking spray; place over medium heat until hot. Add onion, green pepper, ⅛ teaspoon garlic powder, and pepper; sauté until onion is tender. Remove from heat; stir in chicken and tomato. Set aside.

Combine baking mix, remaining ⅛ teaspoon garlic powder, and milk in a small bowl, stirring well. Sprinkle ½ teaspoon flour evenly over work surface. Turn dough out onto floured surface, and knead 4 or 5 times.

Divide dough in half; roll each portion into a 4-inch circle. Spoon chicken mixture evenly over half of each circle; sprinkle cheese evenly over each. Brush edges of circles with water; fold circles in half, and seal. Coat with cooking spray; place on a baking sheet coated with cooking spray. Bake at 350° for 10 to 12 minutes or until golden. Serve immediately. Yield: 2 appetizers.

Now you can enjoy the convenience of a biscuit and baking mix without the fat. The nonfat biscuit mix still contains about the same amount of sodium as the regular mix (480 mg per ¼ cup), so keep this in mind when you use this time-saving product.

# GINGER-MARINATED SHRIMP AND SCALLOPS

6   unpeeled large fresh shrimp
3   cups water
2   ounces bay scallops
2½  tablespoons rice wine vinegar
1   tablespoon finely chopped
     green onions

1½  teaspoons low-sodium soy
     sauce
½  teaspoon dark sesame oil
¼  teaspoon garlic powder
⅛  teaspoon ground ginger
1  cup shredded fresh spinach

Peel and devein shrimp, leaving tails intact. Bring water to a boil in a small saucepan. Add shrimp and scallops; cook 2 minutes or until shrimp turns pink. Drain well, and set aside.

Combine vinegar and next 5 ingredients in a small heavy-duty, zip-top plastic bag; add shrimp and scallops. Seal bag, and shake until seafood is well coated. Marinate in refrigerator 1 hour, turning bag occasionally.

Remove seafood from marinade, reserving marinade. Place ½ cup spinach on each serving plate. Arrange shrimp and scallops evenly on spinach. Drizzle with marinade. Yield: 2 appetizer servings.

Per Serving:

Calories 109
Calories from Fat 17%
Fat 2.1 g
Saturated Fat 0.4 g
Carbohydrate 1.4 g
Protein 19.2 g
Cholesterol 157 mg
Sodium 309 mg

Exchanges:

2½ Lean Meat

Ginger-Marinated Shrimp and Scallops

# CRAB CAKES WITH PLUM SAUCE

1   (6-ounce) can crabmeat
¼   cup plus 2 tablespoons soft
      whole wheat breadcrumbs,
      divided
2   tablespoons nonfat sour
      cream alternative
1   tablespoon finely chopped
      green onions
1   egg white
¼   teaspoon dried dillweed
⅛   teaspoon pepper
      Vegetable cooking spray
2   teaspoons reduced-calorie
      margarine
      Plum Sauce

Drain crabmeat; press crabmeat between paper towels to remove excess moisture. Combine crabmeat, 2 tablespoons breadcrumbs, sour cream, and next 4 ingredients in a medium bowl; shape mixture into 4 patties. Dredge patties in remaining ¼ cup breadcrumbs.

Coat a nonstick skillet with cooking spray; add margarine. Place over medium heat until margarine melts. Add patties, and cook 3 to 4 minutes on each side or until golden. Serve with Plum Sauce. Yield: 4 appetizers.

# PLUM SAUCE

      Vegetable cooking spray
1   tablespoon chopped purple
      onion
¾   teaspoon minced garlic
½   cup diced plums
1½ tablespoons honey
1   tablespoon lemon juice
1½ teaspoons low-sodium soy
      sauce
¼   teaspoon curry powder
¼   teaspoon ground allspice

Coat a small nonstick skillet with cooking spray; place over medium heat until hot. Add onion and garlic; sauté 1 minute. Add plums and remaining ingredients; stir well. Cook, uncovered, over medium-low heat 10 to 15 minutes or until slightly thickened, stirring occasionally. Yield: ¼ cup plus 2 tablespoons.

# CALIFORNIA SUNSHINE SLUSH

⅓ cup pear nectar
⅓ cup unsweetened orange juice
1 tablespoon sugar
1 (11-ounce) can mandarin oranges in light syrup, drained

1 (11-ounce) bottle peach-flavored mineral water
Orange slices (optional)

Combine first 4 ingredients in container of an electric blender; cover and process until smooth, stopping once to scrape down sides. Spoon mixture into a bowl; cover and freeze until firm.

Remove orange mixture from freezer 1 hour before serving; let thaw partially. To serve, break orange mixture into chunks, add mineral water, and stir until slushy. Garnish with orange slices, if desired. Yield: 3 cups.

Per 1½-Cup Serving:

Calories 176
Calories from Fat 0%
Fat 0.1 g
Saturated Fat 0 g
Carbohydrate 44.1 g
Protein 0.4 g
Cholesterol 0 mg
Sodium 46 mg

Exchanges:

3 Fruit

# PEPPERMINT ICED COFFEE

½ cup evaporated skimmed milk
10 round peppermint candies, crushed

1½ cups strong brewed coffee
Peppermint sticks (optional)

Combine milk and crushed candy in a small saucepan. Cook mixture over medium heat, stirring constantly, until candy melts.

Remove from heat, and stir in brewed coffee. Cover and chill. Serve over ice. Garnish with peppermint sticks, if desired. Yield: 3 cups.

Per 1½-Cup Serving:

Calories 140
Calories from Fat 0%
Fat 0.1 g
Saturated Fat 0.1 g
Carbohydrate 30.7 g
Protein 5.0 g
Cholesterol 3 mg
Sodium 86 mg

Exchanges:

2 Starch

# CHOCOLATE MOCHA FREEZE

¾ cup chocolate nonfat ice cream
¾ cup strong brewed coffee, chilled

2 tablespoons chocolate nonfat ice cream topping
¼ cup club soda

Combine chocolate ice cream, brewed coffee, and ice cream topping in container of an electric blender; cover and process until smooth, stopping once to scrape down sides. Add club soda, stirring gently to blend. Serve immediately. Yield: 2 cups.

Per 1-Cup Serving:

Calories 112
Calories from Fat 0%
Fat 0.0 g
Saturated Fat 0 g
Carbohydrate 26.4 g
Protein 3.4 g
Cholesterol 0 mg
Sodium 59 mg

Exchanges:

1½ Starch

# TANGY CRANBERRY COOLERS

**Per 1-Cup Serving:**

Calories 141
Calories from Fat 1%
Fat 0.2 g
Saturated Fat 0 g
Carbohydrate 35.7 g
Protein 0.6 g
Cholesterol 0 mg
Sodium 6 mg

**Exchanges:**

2½ Fruit

¾ cup cranberry juice cocktail, chilled
½ cup unsweetened apple juice, chilled
2 tablespoons fresh lime juice, chilled
1 tablespoon sugar
1 (6-ounce) can unsweetened pink grapefruit juice, chilled
Fresh lime slices (optional)

Combine cranberry juice, apple juice, lime juice, sugar, and grapefruit juice in a small pitcher, stirring well. Serve juice mixture over ice. Garnish with lime slices, if desired. Yield: 2 cups.

Tangy Cranberry Coolers

# Raspberry Ale

1 (10-ounce) package frozen
   raspberries in light syrup,
   thawed

1 (12-ounce) can light beer,
   chilled

Place raspberries in container of an electric blender; cover and process until smooth, stopping once to scrape down sides. Pour raspberry puree through a wire-mesh strainer into a bowl; press with back of spoon against the sides of the strainer to squeeze out juice. Discard pulp and seeds remaining in strainer. Cover puree, and chill thoroughly.

   Spoon raspberry puree evenly into glasses; pour beer evenly over puree, and stir well. Serve immediately. Yield: 2½ cups.

**Per 1¼-Cup Serving:**

Calories 179
Calories from Fat 1%
Fat 0.2 g
Saturated Fat 0 g
Carbohydrate 35.6 g
Protein 1.2 g
Cholesterol 0 mg
Sodium 6 mg

**Exchanges:**

½ Starch
2 Fruit

# Peach Spritzers

¾ cup sweet white wine, chilled
¾ cup peach nectar, chilled

½ cup club soda, chilled
   Fresh peach slices (optional)

Combine white wine, peach nectar, and club soda in a small pitcher, stirring well. Serve immediately over ice. Garnish with fresh peach slices, if desired. Yield: 2 cups.

Wines are now available in small bottles containing
6 ounces (¾ cup) of wine.

**Per 1-Cup Serving:**

Calories 110
Calories from Fat 2%
Fat 0.2 g
Saturated Fat 0 g
Carbohydrate 13.6 g
Protein 0.4 g
Cholesterol 0 mg
Sodium 26 mg

**Exchanges:**

1½ Fruit

# SPICED ORANGE CIDER

1  teaspoon grated orange rind
¼  teaspoon ground cinnamon
⅛  teaspoon ground allspice
2  whole cloves
1¾  cups unsweetened apple cider

½  cup unsweetened orange juice
2  (3-inch) sticks cinnamon (optional)

Place first 4 ingredients on a 4-inch square of cheesecloth or coffee filter; tie with string.

Pour cider and orange juice into a small saucepan; add spice bag. Cook over low heat 15 minutes, stirring occasionally. Remove and discard spice bag. Pour cider into mugs. Garnish with cinnamon sticks, if desired. Yield: 2 cups.

Warm up your morning with a steaming mug of cider and a slice of Glazed Orange Bread (page 50).

# MULLED WINE

½  teaspoon whole cloves
½  teaspoon whole allspice
¼  teaspoon grated lemon rind
¼  teaspoon grated orange rind

1  (3-inch) stick cinnamon
1  whole nutmeg, halved
1½  cups dry red wine
½  cup unsweetened apple juice

Place first 6 ingredients on a 5-inch square of cheesecloth or coffee filter; tie with string.

Pour wine and juice into a small saucepan, stirring well; add spice bag. Cover and cook over low heat 15 minutes, stirring occasionally. Remove and discard spice bag. Serve warm. Yield: 2 cups.

# Caramel Hot Cocoa

1 tablespoon sugar
1 tablespoon unsweetened
   cocoa

1¾ cups skim milk
2 tablespoons caramel ice
   cream topping

Combine sugar and unsweetened cocoa in a small saucepan; stir in skim milk and caramel ice cream topping. Cook, stirring constantly, over medium heat until mixture is thoroughly heated and caramel topping dissolves. Serve immediately. Yield: 2 cups.

Savor the intense flavor of chocolate with almost no saturated fat in this satisfying hot cocoa. One tablespoon of unsweetened cocoa contains only 24 calories and less than 0.5 grams of saturated fat.

Per 1-Cup Serving:

Calories 163
Calories from Fat 4%
Fat 0.7 g
Saturated Fat 0.5 g
Carbohydrate 31.5 g
Protein 8.4 g
Cholesterol 4 mg
Sodium 150 mg

Exchanges:

1 Starch
1 Skim Milk

# Viennese Coffee

1½ cups strong brewed coffee
½ cup skim milk
1 tablespoon sugar
1 teaspoon brandy extract

¼ cup frozen reduced-calorie
   whipped topping, thawed
   Ground nutmeg (optional)

Combine first 4 ingredients in a small saucepan; cook over medium heat until thoroughly heated, stirring occasionally. Pour mixture evenly into 2 serving mugs; top each serving with 2 tablespoons whipped topping. Garnish with nutmeg, if desired. Serve immediately. Yield: 2 cups.

If you're a fan of flavored coffees, try this recipe using hazelnut, French vanilla, or cinnamon-flavored coffee. It's delicious with decaffeinated coffee, too.

Per 1-Cup Serving:

Calories 77
Calories from Fat 14%
Fat 1.2 g
Saturated Fat 0.8 g
Carbohydrate 11.8 g
Protein 2.5 g
Cholesterol 1 mg
Sodium 41 mg

Exchanges:

1 Starch

Peach Scones (page 38), Whole Wheat Casserole
Bread (page 52), Carrot-Pineapple Bread (page 50)

# THE BREAD BASKET

Finally—a baker's collection of great breads. And you won't end up with a baker's dozen.

# BUTTERMILK BISCUITS

⅓ cup all-purpose flour
¼ teaspoon baking powder
⅛ teaspoon baking soda
    Dash of salt
2 teaspoons chilled reduced-
    calorie stick margarine

2 tablespoons nonfat
    buttermilk
1 teaspoon all-purpose flour

Combine first 4 ingredients in a small bowl; cut in margarine with a pastry blender until mixture resembles coarse meal. Add buttermilk, stirring with a fork just until dry ingredients are moistened.

Sprinkle 1 teaspoon flour evenly over work surface. Turn dough out onto floured surface, and knead 4 or 5 times. Roll dough to ½-inch thickness; cut into rounds with a 2½-inch biscuit cutter. Place rounds on an ungreased baking sheet. Bake at 425° for 10 to 12 minutes or until golden. Yield: 2 biscuits.

**Per Biscuit:**

Calories 107
Calories from Fat 23%
Fat 2.7 g
Saturated Fat 0.4 g
Carbohydrate 17.8 g
Protein 2.9 g
Cholesterol 1 mg
Sodium 206 mg

**Exchanges:**

1 Starch
½ Fat

# WHOLE WHEAT BISCUITS

2 tablespoons whole wheat
    flour
¼ cup all-purpose flour
½ teaspoon baking powder
    Dash of salt
2 teaspoons chilled reduced-
    calorie stick margarine

2 tablespoons plus 2 teaspoons
    skim milk
1 teaspoon all-purpose flour
    Vegetable cooking spray

Combine first 4 ingredients in a small bowl; cut in margarine with a pastry blender until mixture resembles coarse meal. Add milk, stirring with a fork just until dry ingredients are moistened.

Sprinkle 1 teaspoon flour evenly over work surface. Turn dough out onto floured surface, and knead 4 or 5 times. Roll dough to ½-inch thickness; cut into rounds with a 2½-inch biscuit cutter. Place rounds on a baking sheet coated with cooking spray. Bake at 425° for 10 to 12 minutes or until golden. Yield: 2 biscuits.

**Offer Whole Wheat Biscuits with fresh orange juice and
a Spinach and Mushroom Omelet (page 114).**

**Per Biscuit:**

Calories 119
Calories from Fat 24%
Fat 3.2 g
Saturated Fat 0.4 g
Carbohydrate 19.7 g
Protein 3.5 g
Cholesterol 0 mg
Sodium 122 mg

**Exchanges:**

1 Starch
½ Fat

# Herb-Sour Cream Biscuits

⅓ cup all-purpose flour
½ teaspoon baking powder
   Dash of salt
¼ teaspoon sugar
1 teaspoon chilled reduced-
   calorie stick margarine
⅛ teaspoon dried basil

1 tablespoon plus 2 teaspoons
   skim milk
1 tablespoon low-fat sour
   cream
1 teaspoon minced onion
1 teaspoon all-purpose flour

Combine first 4 ingredients in a small bowl; cut in margarine with a pastry blender until mixture resembles coarse meal. Stir in basil. Combine milk, sour cream, and onion, stirring well. Add to dry ingredients, stirring with a fork just until dry ingredients are moistened.

   Sprinkle 1 teaspoon flour evenly over work surface. Turn dough out onto floured surface, and knead 4 or 5 times. Roll dough to ½-inch thickness; cut into rounds with a 2½-inch biscuit cutter. Place rounds on an ungreased baking sheet. Bake at 425° for 13 to 15 minutes or until golden. Yield: 2 biscuits.

Round out a meal of vegetable soup and coleslaw<br>with these hearty herb biscuits.

**Per Biscuit:**

Calories 109
Calories from Fat 20%
Fat 2.4 g
Saturated Fat 0.8 g
Carbohydrate 18.8 g
Protein 3.0 g
Cholesterol 3 mg
Sodium 102 mg

**Exchanges:**

1 Starch
½ Fat

# Cinnamon-Currant Biscuits

⅓ cup all-purpose flour
½ teaspoon baking powder
   Dash of salt
1½ teaspoons sugar
¼ teaspoon ground cinnamon
1½ teaspoons chilled reduced-
   calorie stick margarine
2 tablespoons currants

2 tablespoons plus 1 teaspoon
   skim milk
½ teaspoon all-purpose flour
   Vegetable cooking spray
2 tablespoons sifted powdered
   sugar
½ teaspoon skim milk

Combine first 5 ingredients in a small bowl; cut in margarine with a pastry blender until mixture resembles coarse meal. Stir in currants. Add 2 tablespoons plus 1 teaspoon milk, stirring with a fork just until dry ingredients are moistened.

   Sprinkle ½ teaspoon flour evenly over work surface. Turn dough out onto floured surface, and knead 4 or 5 times. Roll dough to ½-inch thickness; cut into rounds with a 2½-inch biscuit cutter. Place rounds on a baking sheet coated with cooking spray. Bake at 425° for 10 minutes.

   Combine powdered sugar and ½ teaspoon milk, stirring well. Drizzle glaze over warm biscuits. Yield: 2 biscuits.

Complement these glazed biscuits with assorted<br>fresh fruit and cinnamon-flavored coffee.

**Per Biscuit:**

Calories 166
Calories from Fat 14%
Fat 2.5 g
Saturated Fat 0.2 g
Carbohydrate 33.7 g
Protein 3.2 g
Cholesterol 0 mg
Sodium 114 mg

**Exchanges:**

1 Starch
1 Fruit
½ Fat

# PEACH SCONES

**Per Scone:**

Calories 162
Calories from Fat 19%
Fat 3.5 g
Saturated Fat 0.7 g
Carbohydrate 29.5 g
Protein 3.4 g
Cholesterol 1 mg
Sodium 162 mg

**Exchanges:**

1   Starch
1   Fruit
½   Fat

⅔  cup all-purpose flour
½  teaspoon baking powder
¼  teaspoon baking soda
    Dash of salt
2  tablespoons sugar
1  tablespoon margarine
¼  cup plus 1 tablespoon vanilla
    low-fat yogurt
2  tablespoons chopped dried
    peaches
1  tablespoon all-purpose flour
    Vegetable cooking spray
½  teaspoon skim milk
1  teaspoon sugar
    No-sugar-added peach
    spread (optional)

Combine first 5 ingredients in a medium bowl; cut in margarine with a pastry blender until mixture resembles coarse meal. Add yogurt and peaches to flour mixture; stir just until dry ingredients are moistened.

Sprinkle 1 tablespoon flour evenly over work surface. Turn dough out onto floured surface, and knead lightly 4 or 5 times. (Dough may be slightly sticky.)

Pat dough into a 5-inch circle on a baking sheet coated with cooking spray. Cut circle into 4 wedges; separate wedges slightly. Brush milk over dough, and sprinkle with 1 teaspoon sugar. Bake at 400° for 14 to 15 minutes or until golden. Serve with peach spread, if desired. Yield: 4 scones.

Breakfast is a treat when you offer scones along with fresh
berries, yogurt, and a cup of hot tea.

# APPLESAUCE-OATMEAL MUFFINS

½ cup all-purpose flour
1 teaspoon baking powder
⅛ teaspoon salt
¼ cup quick-cooking oats, uncooked
3 tablespoons brown sugar
¼ teaspoon ground cinnamon
¼ cup skim milk
2 tablespoons unsweetened applesauce
1½ teaspoons vegetable oil
1 egg white
Vegetable cooking spray

Combine first 6 ingredients in a medium bowl; make a well in center of mixture. Combine milk, applesauce, oil, and egg white; add to dry ingredients, stirring just until dry ingredients are moistened.

Spoon batter into 4 muffin pan cups coated with cooking spray, filling each three-fourths full. Bake at 400° for 18 to 20 minutes or until golden. Remove from pan immediately. Yield: 4 muffins.

**Per Muffin:**

Calories 132
Calories from Fat 16%
Fat 2.3 g
Saturated Fat 0.4 g
Carbohydrate 24.1 g
Protein 3.8 g
Cholesterol 0 mg
Sodium 98 mg

**Exchanges:**

1½ Starch
½ Fat

Applesauce-Oatmeal Muffins

# WHOLE WHEAT HERB MUFFINS

Per Muffin:

Calories 127
Calories from Fat 28%
Fat 4.0 g
Saturated Fat 0.8 g
Carbohydrate 18.2 g
Protein 5.2 g
Cholesterol 1 mg
Sodium 286 mg

Exchanges:

1   Starch
1   Fat

| | | | |
|---|---|---|---|
| 3 | tablespoons whole wheat flour | ¼ | cup nonfat buttermilk |
| 2 | tablespoons all-purpose flour | 1½ | teaspoons vegetable oil |
| ¼ | teaspoon baking powder | 1 | teaspoon minced fresh chives |
| ⅛ | teaspoon baking soda | ⅛ | teaspoon dried basil, crushed |
| ⅛ | teaspoon salt | 1 | egg white |
| 1 | teaspoon sugar | | Vegetable cooking spray |

Combine first 6 ingredients in a medium bowl; make a well in center of mixture. Combine buttermilk and next 4 ingredients; add to dry ingredients, stirring just until dry ingredients are moistened.

Spoon batter evenly into 2 muffin pan cups coated with cooking spray. Bake at 400° for 16 to 18 minutes or until golden. Remove from pan immediately. Yield: 2 muffins.

Make a meal with Garden Vegetable-Pasta Soup (page 152), Congealed Berry Salads (page 56), and Whole Wheat Herb Muffins.

# YOGURT MUFFINS

Per Muffin:

Calories 150
Calories from Fat 18%
Saturated Fat 0.6 g
Fat 3.0 g
Carbohydrate 25.6 g
Protein 4.9 g
Cholesterol 1 mg
Sodium 193 mg

Exchanges:

1½ Starch
½   Fat

| | | | |
|---|---|---|---|
| ⅓ | cup all-purpose flour | 1 | teaspoon vegetable oil |
| ¼ | teaspoon baking powder | ¼ | teaspoon vanilla extract |
| ⅛ | teaspoon baking soda | 1 | egg white |
| | Dash of salt | | Vegetable cooking spray |
| 1 | tablespoon sugar | | |
| 3 | tablespoons vanilla low-fat yogurt | | |

Combine first 5 ingredients in a medium bowl; make a well in center of mixture. Combine yogurt and next 3 ingredients; add to dry ingredients, stirring just until dry ingredients are moistened.

Spoon batter evenly into 2 muffin pan cups coated with cooking spray. Bake at 400° for 15 to 18 minutes or until golden. Remove from pan immediately. Yield: 2 muffins.

To increase the fiber content of Yogurt Muffins, fold 2 tablespoons chopped dates into muffin batter, or sprinkle 2 tablespoons low-fat granola over muffin batter before baking.

# HUSH PUPPY MUFFINS

¼ cup yellow cornmeal
2 tablespoons all-purpose flour
½ teaspoon baking powder
⅛ teaspoon salt
  Dash of ground red pepper
2 tablespoons finely chopped
  onion

2 tablespoons skim milk
1 teaspoon vegetable oil
1 egg white, lightly beaten
  Butter-flavored vegetable
  cooking spray

Combine first 5 ingredients in a medium bowl; make a well in center of
mixture. Combine onion, milk, oil, and egg white; add to dry ingredients,
stirring just until dry ingredients are moistened.

Spoon batter into 6 miniature (1¾-inch) muffin pan cups coated with
cooking spray, filling each three-fourths full. Bake at 425° for 17 minutes
or until golden. Remove from pan immediately. Yield: 6 muffins.

Team oven-fried fish, Vinaigrette Coleslaw (page 65),
and Hush Puppy Muffins for a hearty meal.

**Per Muffin:**

Calories 45
Calories from Fat 22%
Fat 1.1 g
Saturated Fat 0.2 g
Carbohydrate 7.2 g
Protein 1.5 g
Cholesterol 0 mg
Sodium 61 mg

**Exchanges:**

½ Starch

# MEXICAN CORNBREAD

¼ cup yellow cornmeal
2 tablespoons all-purpose flour
⅛ teaspoon baking soda
⅛ teaspoon salt
½ teaspoon sugar
  Dash of garlic powder
¼ cup no-salt-added
  cream-style corn
2 tablespoons nonfat
  buttermilk
2 tablespoons frozen egg
  substitute, thawed

2 tablespoons (½ ounce)
  shredded reduced-fat
  Cheddar cheese
1 tablespoon minced green
  onions
1 teaspoon seeded, minced
  jalapeño pepper
  Butter-flavored vegetable
  cooking spray

Combine first 6 ingredients in a medium bowl; make a well in center of
mixture. Combine corn, buttermilk, and egg substitute; add to dry ingredients, stirring just until dry ingredients are moistened. Fold in cheese, green
onions, and jalapeño pepper.

Coat 2 (4- x 2½- x 1¼-inch) loafpans with cooking spray; place in oven
for 3 minutes or until hot. Remove from oven; spoon batter into pans.
Bake at 425° for 20 minutes or until golden. Yield: 2 (4-inch) loaves.

Enjoy your own mini-loaf of cornbread with a steaming
bowl of Quick Vegetarian Chili (page 155).

**Per Loaf:**

Calories 160
Calories from Fat 13%
Fat 2.3 g
Saturated Fat 0.9 g
Carbohydrate 28.1 g
Protein 7.2 g
Cholesterol 5 mg
Sodium 320 mg

**Exchanges:**

2 Starch
½ Fat

# SOUTHERN-STYLE CORN STICKS

¼   cup all-purpose flour
¼   cup yellow cornmeal
½   teaspoon baking powder
⅛   teaspoon salt
2   teaspoons sugar

¼   cup skim milk
1½  teaspoons vegetable oil
1   egg white, lightly beaten
     Vegetable cooking spray

Combine first 5 ingredients in a medium bowl; make a well in center of mixture. Combine milk, oil, and egg white; add to dry ingredients, stirring just until dry ingredients are moistened.

Coat 4 molds of a cast-iron corn stick pan with cooking spray, and place in oven for 3 minutes or until hot. Remove pan from oven; spoon batter evenly into 4 molds, filling each three-fourths full. Bake at 425° for 14 minutes or until golden. Yield: 4 corn sticks.

Southern-Style Corn Sticks

# German Apple Pancake

⅔ cup canned unsweetened
    sliced apple
2 teaspoons sugar
⅛ teaspoon ground cinnamon
¼ cup all-purpose flour
1½ teaspoons sugar
¼ cup skim milk

½ teaspoon vegetable oil
¼ teaspoon vanilla extract
1 egg, lightly beaten
    Vegetable cooking spray
1 teaspoon vegetable oil
1 tablespoon sifted powdered
    sugar

Combine first 3 ingredients in a small saucepan, stirring well. Cook over medium-heat until thoroughly heated. Drain; set aside, and keep warm.

Combine flour and sugar, stirring well. Combine milk and next 3 ingredients; add to dry ingredients, stirring well with a wire whisk. Set aside.

Wrap handle of an 8-inch nonstick skillet with aluminum foil; coat skillet with cooking spray. Add 1 teaspoon oil, and place in oven. Preheat skillet in oven at 425° for 2 to 3 minutes. Pour batter into hot skillet. Bake at 425° for 15 minutes or until puffy and browned.

Remove pancake from skillet. Top with warm apple mixture, and sprinkle with powdered sugar. Serve immediately. Yield: 2 servings.

**Serve this main-dish pancake with broiled Canadian bacon.**

Per Serving:

Calories 221
Calories from Fat 28%
Fat 6.8 g
Saturated Fat 1.5 g
Carbohydrate 34.5 g
Protein 6.0 g
Cholesterol 111 mg
Sodium 49 mg

Exchanges:

1½ Starch
1 Fruit
1 Fat

# Granola Pancakes

¼ cup plus 1 tablespoon
    all-purpose flour
¼ cup whole wheat flour
1 teaspoon baking powder
    Dash of salt
2 teaspoons sugar
¼ teaspoon ground cinnamon
¼ cup plus 2 tablespoons skim
    milk

¼ cup low-fat granola without
    raisins, crumbled
1½ teaspoons vegetable oil
1 egg white, lightly beaten
    Vegetable cooking spray
    Reduced-calorie maple syrup
    (optional)

Combine first 6 ingredients in a medium bowl; make a well in center of mixture. Combine milk, granola, oil, and egg white; add to dry ingredients, stirring just until dry ingredients are moistened.

For each pancake, pour ¼ cup batter onto a hot griddle or skillet coated with cooking spray; spread batter to a 4-inch circle. Cook pancakes until tops are covered with bubbles and edges look cooked; turn pancakes, and cook other side. Serve with reduced-calorie maple syrup, if desired. Yield: 4 (4-inch) pancakes.

**Start your day with Granola Pancakes, fresh blueberries, and skim milk.**

Per Pancake:

Calories 119
Calories from Fat 19%
Fat 2.5 g
Saturated Fat 0.4 g
Carbohydrate 20.7 g
Protein 4.1 g
Cholesterol 0 mg
Sodium 68 mg

Exchanges:

1 Starch
½ Fat

# OATMEAL PANCAKES

Per Pancake:

Calories 94
Calories from Fat 28%
Fat 2.9 g
Saturated Fat 0.5 g
Carbohydrate 13.9 g
Protein 3.3 g
Cholesterol 1 mg
Sodium 191 mg

Exchanges:

1 Starch
½ Fat

¼ cup quick-cooking oats, uncooked
¼ cup all-purpose flour
½ teaspoon baking powder
¼ teaspoon baking soda
⅛ teaspoon salt
1 tablespoon sugar
¼ cup plus 2 tablespoons nonfat buttermilk
2 teaspoons vegetable oil
1 egg white, lightly beaten
Butter-flavored vegetable cooking spray

Combine first 6 ingredients in a medium bowl; make a well in center of mixture. Combine buttermilk, oil, and egg white; add to dry ingredients, stirring just until dry ingredients are moistened.

Coat a nonstick griddle with cooking spray; preheat to 350°. For each pancake, pour about 3 tablespoons batter onto hot griddle. Cook pancakes until tops are covered with bubbles and edges look cooked; turn pancakes, and cook other side. Yield: 4 (4-inch) pancakes.

# PARMESAN-ONION POPOVERS

Per Popover:

Calories 116
Calories from Fat 10%
Fat 1.3 g
Saturated Fat 0.4 g
Carbohydrate 18.9 g
Protein 6.5 g
Cholesterol 2 mg
Sodium 153 mg

Exchanges:

1 Starch
½ Skim Milk

Vegetable cooking spray
⅓ cup bread flour
Dash of salt
⅓ cup skim milk
2 teaspoons grated Parmesan cheese
2 teaspoons minced green onions
1 egg white

Heavily coat 2 popover pan cups or 2 muffin pan cups with cooking spray, and set aside.

Combine flour and remaining ingredients in a medium bowl; stir with a wire whisk until smooth. Pour batter evenly into prepared pan. Place in a cold oven. Turn oven on 450°, and bake 15 minutes. Reduce heat to 350°, and bake an additional 40 minutes or until popovers are crusty and brown. Serve immediately. Yield: 2 popovers.

Serve these savory popovers with Individual Shrimp Casseroles (page 111) and a fresh melon salad.

# Irish Soda Bread

½ cup all-purpose flour
¼ teaspoon baking powder
¼ teaspoon baking soda
⅛ teaspoon salt
2 teaspoons sugar
1 tablespoon reduced-calorie stick margarine

3 tablespoons nonfat buttermilk
½ teaspoon all-purpose flour
Butter-flavored vegetable cooking spray

Combine first 5 ingredients in a medium bowl; cut in margarine with a pastry blender until mixture resembles coarse meal. Add buttermilk, stirring with a fork just until dry ingredients are moistened.

Sprinkle ½ teaspoon flour evenly over work surface. Turn dough out onto floured surface, and knead 10 to 12 times. Shape dough into a 3-inch round; place round on a baking sheet coated with cooking spray. Cut a ¼-inch-deep cross in the top of round with a sharp knife. Coat top of round with cooking spray. Bake at 425° for 8 to 10 minutes or until golden. Yield: 1 (3-inch) round.

Try Irish Soda Bread with hearty Beef-Vegetable Stew (page 207).

Try Irish Soda Bread with hearty Beef-Vegetable Stew (page 207).

**Per ½ Round:**

Calories 172
Calories from Fat 21%
Fat 4.1 g
Saturated Fat 0.6 g
Carbohydrate 29.8 g
Protein 4.2 g
Cholesterol 1 mg
Sodium 379 mg

**Exchanges:**

2 Starch
1 Fat

# Garlic Spoonbread

Vegetable cooking spray
2 tablespoons minced green onions
1 clove garlic, minced
⅔ cup skim milk

½ cup water
⅓ cup yellow cornmeal
⅛ teaspoon salt
1 egg, separated

Coat a medium saucepan with cooking spray; place over medium-high heat until hot. Add green onions and garlic; sauté until tender. Add milk and next 3 ingredients; cook over medium heat, stirring constantly with a wire whisk, until mixture is thickened and bubbly. Remove from heat.

Beat egg yolk in a medium bowl. Gradually stir about one-fourth of hot cornmeal mixture into egg yolk; add to remaining cornmeal mixture, stirring constantly with a wire whisk.

Beat egg white at high speed of an electric mixer until stiff peaks form. Fold one-third of egg white into cornmeal mixture; fold in remaining egg white. Pour mixture into a 2-cup casserole coated with cooking spray. Bake at 375° for 35 to 40 minutes or until puffed and golden. Serve immediately. Yield: 2 servings.

Enjoy a leisurely breakfast of fresh grapefruit segments, Garlic Spoonbread, and Baked Tomatoes (page 134).

Enjoy a leisurely breakfast of fresh grapefruit segments, Garlic Spoonbread, and Baked Tomatoes (page 134).

**Per Serving:**

Calories 157
Calories from Fat 19%
Fat 3.4 g
Saturated Fat 1.0 g
Carbohydrate 22.9 g
Protein 8.1 g
Cholesterol 112 mg
Sodium 223 mg

**Exchanges:**

1½ Starch
½ Medium-Fat Meat

# Raisin French Toast with Orange Sauce

¼ cup frozen egg substitute, thawed
¼ cup skim milk
¼ teaspoon grated orange rind
Vegetable cooking spray
1 teaspoon reduced-calorie margarine

4 (1-ounce) slices raisin bread
1 teaspoon sifted powdered sugar
Orange Sauce

Combine first 3 ingredients in a shallow dish, stirring well.

Coat a large nonstick skillet with cooking spray. Add margarine; place over medium heat until margarine melts. Dip bread slices, one at a time, into egg substitute mixture, coating well.

Place bread slices in skillet, and cook 3 to 4 minutes on each side or until browned. Cut each bread slice in half diagonally. Sprinkle powdered sugar evenly over toast, and serve with warm Orange Sauce. Yield: 4 slices.

## Orange Sauce

¼ cup fresh orange juice
1½ teaspoons sugar
1 teaspoon cornstarch
¼ teaspoon grated orange rind

⅛ teaspoon vanilla extract
½ large orange, peeled, sectioned, and coarsely chopped

Combine first 3 ingredients in a small saucepan, stirring until smooth. Bring to a boil over medium heat, stirring constantly; boil 1 minute. Stir in orange rind, vanilla, and orange. Yield: ¼ cup plus 1 tablespoon.

Serve Raisin French Toast with Orange Sauce along with broiled lean ham and cups of steaming chocolate-flavored coffee.

# WHOLE WHEAT WAFFLES

¼ cup whole wheat flour
¼ cup all-purpose flour
1 teaspoon baking powder
¼ teaspoon baking soda
2 teaspoons sugar

½ cup nonfat buttermilk
1 teaspoon vegetable oil
1 egg white, lightly beaten
   Vegetable cooking spray
   Fresh strawberries (optional)

Combine first 5 ingredients in a medium bowl; make a well in center of mixture. Combine buttermilk, oil, and egg white, stirring with a wire whisk. Add to dry ingredients, stirring just until dry ingredients are moistened.

Coat an 8-inch square waffle iron with cooking spray; allow waffle iron to preheat. Pour batter onto hot waffle iron, spreading batter to edges. Bake 3 to 4 minutes or until steaming stops. Cut waffle into 4 squares. Serve with fresh strawberries, if desired. Yield: 4 (4-inch) waffles.

**Per Waffle:**

Calories 89
Calories from Fat 16%
Fat 1.6 g
Saturated Fat 0.3 g
Carbohydrate 15.5 g
Protein 3.8 g
Cholesterol 1 mg
Sodium 126 mg

**Exchanges:**

1 Starch

Whole Wheat Waffles

# CORNMEAL WAFFLES

**Per Waffle:**

Calories 108
Calories from Fat 14%
Saturated Fat 0.3 g
Fat 1.7 g
Carbohydrate 18.9 g
Protein 3.9 g
Cholesterol 1 mg
Sodium 103 mg

**Exchanges:**

1   Starch

⅓   cup all-purpose flour
⅓   cup yellow cornmeal
¾   teaspoon baking powder
⅛   teaspoon salt
¼   teaspoon sugar

½   cup skim milk
1   teaspoon vegetable oil
1   egg white
Vegetable cooking spray

Combine first 5 ingredients in a medium bowl; make a well in center of mixture. Combine milk and oil, stirring with a wire whisk. Add to dry ingredients, stirring just until dry ingredients are moistened.

Beat egg white at high speed of an electric mixer until stiff peaks form. Gently fold beaten egg white into batter.

Coat an 8-inch square waffle iron with cooking spray; allow waffle iron to preheat. Pour batter onto hot waffle iron, spreading batter to edges. Bake 3 to 4 minutes or until steaming stops. Cut waffle into 4 squares. Yield: 4 (4-inch) waffles.

*Tender Cornmeal Waffles are wonderful with a bowl of steaming homemade vegetable soup. And they're equally good for breakfast topped with reduced-calorie margarine or honey.*

# BANANA BREAD

**Per 1-Inch Slice:**

Calories 97
Calories from Fat 20%
Fat 2.2 g
Saturated Fat 0.9 g
Carbohydrate 17.4 g
Protein 2.0 g
Cholesterol 4 mg
Sodium 90 mg

**Exchanges:**

1   Starch
½   Fat

½   cup all-purpose flour
¼   teaspoon baking powder
¼   teaspoon baking soda
    Dash of salt
3   tablespoons sugar
¼   cup low-fat sour cream

¼   cup mashed ripe banana
1   teaspoon vegetable oil
¼   teaspoon vanilla extract
1   egg white, lightly beaten
Vegetable cooking spray

Combine first 5 ingredients in a medium bowl; make a well in center of mixture. Combine sour cream and next 4 ingredients; add to dry ingredients, stirring just until dry ingredients are moistened.

Spoon batter into a 6- x 3- x 2-inch loafpan coated with cooking spray. Bake at 350° for 35 to 40 minutes or until a wooden pick inserted in center comes out clean. Let cool in pan 10 minutes; remove from pan, and let cool on a wire rack. Yield: 1 (6-inch) loaf.

# BLUEBERRY LOAF BREAD

⅔ cup all-purpose flour
½ teaspoon baking powder
¼ teaspoon baking soda
　 Dash of salt
¼ cup sugar
¼ cup plus 2 tablespoons plain
　 nonfat yogurt

2 teaspoons vegetable oil
½ teaspoon vanilla extract
1 egg white, lightly beaten
⅓ cup fresh or frozen
　 blueberries, thawed
　 Vegetable cooking spray

Combine first 5 ingredients in a medium bowl; make a well in center of mixture. Combine yogurt and next 3 ingredients; add to dry ingredients, stirring just until dry ingredients are moistened. Fold in blueberries.

Spoon batter into a 6- x 3- x 2-inch loafpan coated with cooking spray. Bake at 350° for 35 to 40 minutes or until a wooden pick inserted in center comes out clean. Remove from pan immediately, and let cool on a wire rack. Yield: 1 (6-inch) loaf.

Blueberry Loaf Bread

Per 1-Inch Slice:

Calories 113
Calories from Fat 14%
Fat 1.8 g
Saturated Fat 0.3 g
Carbohydrate 21.2 g
Protein 2.8 g
Cholesterol 0 mg
Sodium 97 mg

Exchanges:

1 Starch
½ Fruit

# CARROT-PINEAPPLE BREAD

Per 1-Inch Slice:

Calories 114
Calories from Fat 14%
Fat 1.8 g
Saturated Fat 0.3 g
Carbohydrate 22.0 g
Protein 2.4 g
Cholesterol 0 mg
Sodium 169 mg

Exchanges:

1½ Starch

⅔ cup all-purpose flour
½ teaspoon baking soda
⅛ teaspoon salt
¼ cup sugar
¼ teaspoon ground cinnamon
⅛ teaspoon ground nutmeg
2 tablespoons plain nonfat yogurt
2 tablespoons unsweetened applesauce

2 teaspoons vegetable oil
½ teaspoon vanilla extract
1 egg white, lightly beaten
⅓ cup shredded carrot
¼ cup canned crushed pineapple in juice, well drained
Vegetable cooking spray

Combine first 6 ingredients in a medium bowl; make a well in center of mixture. Combine yogurt and next 4 ingredients; add to dry ingredients, stirring just until dry ingredients are moistened. Gently fold in carrot and pineapple.

Spoon batter into a 6- x 3- x 2-inch loafpan coated with cooking spray. Bake at 350° for 35 to 38 minutes or until a wooden pick inserted in center comes out clean. Cool in pan on a wire rack 5 minutes; remove from pan, and let cool on a wire rack. Yield: 1 (6-inch) loaf.

For even more flavor, spread light process cream cheese product on slices of Carrot-Pineapple Bread.

# GLAZED ORANGE BREAD

Per 1-Inch Slice:

Calories 115
Calories from Fat 8%
Fat 1.0 g
Saturated Fat 0.2 g
Carbohydrate 24.0 g
Protein 2.4 g
Cholesterol 0 mg
Sodium 63 mg

Exchanges:

1½ Starch

¾ cups all-purpose flour
½ teaspoon baking powder
⅛ teaspoon baking soda
Dash of salt
¼ cup sugar
3 tablespoons unsweetened orange juice
2 tablespoons skim milk

1 teaspoon vegetable oil
1 egg white, lightly beaten
Vegetable cooking spray
2 tablespoons sifted powdered sugar
½ teaspoon unsweetened orange juice

Combine first 5 ingredients in a medium bowl; make a well in center of mixture. Combine 3 tablespoons orange juice and next 3 ingredients; add to dry ingredients, stirring just until dry ingredients are moistened.

Spoon batter into a 6- x 3- x 2-inch loafpan coated with cooking spray. Bake at 350° for 40 to 45 minutes or until a wooden pick inserted in center comes out clean. Let cool in pan 10 minutes; remove from pan, and place on a wire rack.

Combine powdered sugar and ½ teaspoon orange juice, stirring well. Drizzle glaze over warm bread. Yield: 1 (6-inch) loaf.

# BLUEBERRY COFFEE CAKE

Vegetable cooking spray
1 teaspoon all-purpose flour
¼ cup plus 1 tablespoon
  reduced-calorie margarine,
  softened
½ cup sugar, divided
3 tablespoons skim milk
3 tablespoons frozen egg
  substitute, thawed
¾ cup all-purpose flour
1¼ teaspoons baking powder

Dash of salt
½ teaspoon vanilla extract
1 tablespoon water
2 teaspoons cornstarch
½ cup fresh or frozen
  blueberries
2 tablespoons regular oats,
  uncooked
1 tablespoon brown sugar
½ teaspoon ground cinnamon

Coat a 6-inch square pan with cooking spray; dust pan with 1 teaspoon flour, and set aside.

Beat margarine at medium speed of an electric mixer until creamy; gradually add ¼ cup plus 2 tablespoons sugar, beating well.

Combine milk and egg substitute, stirring well. Combine ¾ cup flour, baking powder, and salt; add to margarine mixture alternately with milk mixture, beginning and ending with flour mixture. Mix after each addition. Stir in vanilla, and set aside.

Combine remaining 2 tablespoons sugar, water, and cornstarch in a small saucepan, stirring well. Add blueberries, and cook over medium heat, stirring constantly, until thickened and bubbly.

Spoon half of batter into prepared pan. Spoon blueberry mixture over batter. Spoon remaining batter over blueberry mixture. Combine oats, brown sugar, and cinnamon; sprinkle over batter. Bake at 350° for 30 to 35 minutes or until a wooden pick inserted in center comes out clean. Yield: 6 servings.

*After your morning workout, enjoy a piece of Blueberry Coffee Cake with a fresh melon cup and skim milk.*

**Per Serving:**

Calories 206
Calories from Fat 28%
Fat 6.5 g
Saturated Fat 0.9 g
Carbohydrate 35.4 g
Protein 3.0 g
Cholesterol 0 mg
Sodium 133 mg

**Exchanges:**

1 Starch
1 Fruit
1 Fat

# Whole Wheat Casserole Bread

**Per Wedge:**

Calories 136
Calories from Fat 13%
Fat 1.9 g
Saturated Fat 0.3 g
Carbohydrate 26.3 g
Protein 4.4 g
Cholesterol 0 mg
Sodium 174 mg

**Exchanges:**

1½ Starch

1 package active dry yeast
¾ cup warm water (105° to 115°)
1 cup all-purpose flour, divided
1 cup whole wheat flour
2 tablespoons sugar
2 tablespoons frozen egg substitute, thawed
1½ tablespoons reduced-calorie margarine, melted
½ teaspoon salt
Vegetable cooking spray

Combine yeast and warm water in a 1-cup liquid measuring cup; let stand 5 minutes. Combine yeast mixture, ½ cup all-purpose flour, and next 5 ingredients in a medium bowl, stirring well. Gradually stir in enough of the remaining ½ cup all-purpose flour to make a soft dough. (Dough will be sticky.) Let dough rest 15 minutes; shape into a ball.

Place dough in a round 1-quart casserole heavily coated with cooking spray. Cover and let rise in a warm place (85°), free from drafts, 30 minutes or until doubled in bulk. Bake at 375° for 25 minutes or until loaf sounds hollow when tapped. (Cover with aluminum foil the last 10 minutes of baking to prevent over-browning, if necessary.) Remove from casserole immediately, and let cool on wire rack. Yield: 8 wedges.

Whole Wheat Casserole Bread

# FRENCH BREAD

1¼ cups plus 2 tablespoons
    all-purpose flour, divided
1½ teaspoons rapid-rise yeast
1 teaspoon sugar
¼ teaspoon salt
⅓ cup hot water (120° to 130°)
¼ cup low-fat sour cream

1 teaspoon white vinegar
1 tablespoon all-purpose flour
    Vegetable cooking spray
1 egg white
1 tablespoon water
½ teaspoon sesame seeds

Combine ½ cup flour, yeast, sugar, and salt in a medium bowl, stirring well. Gradually add water, sour cream, and vinegar to flour mixture, beating well at low speed of an electric mixer until blended. Beat an additional 2 minutes at medium speed. Gradually stir in enough of the remaining ¾ cup plus 2 tablespoons flour to make a soft dough.

Sprinkle 1 tablespoon flour evenly over work surface. Turn dough out onto floured surface, and knead until smooth and elastic (about 8 minutes). Cover and let rest for 10 minutes.

Punch dough down, and knead lightly 4 or 5 times. Divide dough in half. Roll 1 portion of dough into a 4- x 5-inch rectangle. Roll up dough, starting at long side, pressing firmly to eliminate air pockets; pinch ends to seal. Place dough, seam side down, on a baking sheet coated with cooking spray. Repeat procedure with remaining dough. Cover and let rise in a warm place (85°), free from drafts, 20 minutes or until doubled in bulk.

Gently make 3 or 4 slits, about ¼-inch deep, diagonally across each loaf, using a sharp knife coated with cooking spray. Combine egg white and 1 tablespoon water; brush loaves with egg white mixture, and sprinkle with sesame seeds. Bake at 375° for 15 minutes or until loaves are golden and sound hollow when tapped. Remove from baking sheet, and let cool on a wire rack. Yield: 2 (4-inch) loaves.

**This recipe yields two mini-loaves. Serve one tonight, and store the second loaf in a zip-top plastic bag for later use.**

Per 1-Inch Slice:

Calories 100
Calories from Fat 12%
Fat 1.3 g
Saturated Fat 0.6 g
Carbohydrate 18.4 g
Protein 3.3 g
Cholesterol 3 mg
Sodium 84 mg

Exchanges:

1 Starch

Radicchio Salad (page 59)

# SALAD SENSATIONS

It's a toss-up—should you serve these salads as a meal or with a meal? You decide. The recipes are winners either way.

# CONGEALED BERRY SALADS

**Per Serving:**

Calories 186
Calories from Fat 11%
Fat 2.2 g
Saturated Fat 0.2 g
Carbohydrate 39.4 g
Protein 3.2 g
Cholesterol 0 mg
Sodium 15 mg

**Exchanges:**

1   Starch
1½ Fruit
½   Fat

1¼ teaspoons unflavored gelatin
1   cup cranberry-raspberry-strawberry juice beverage
2   tablespoons sugar
1   tablespoon fresh or frozen unsweetened blueberries, thawed
1   tablespoon fresh or frozen unsweetened raspberries, thawed
2   teaspoons finely chopped pecans
2   large strawberries, sliced
    Vegetable cooking spray
2   tablespoons nonfat sour cream alternative
1   teaspoon powdered sugar
¼   teaspoon poppy seeds
    Green leaf lettuce (optional)
    Grated orange rind (optional)

Sprinkle gelatin over juice in a small saucepan; let stand 2 minutes. Add 2 tablespoons sugar; cook over low heat, stirring until gelatin and sugar dissolve (about 2 minutes). Chill gelatin mixture until the consistency of unbeaten egg white.

Gently fold blueberries and next 3 ingredients into gelatin mixture. Spoon mixture evenly into 2 (½-cup) molds coated with cooking spray. Cover and chill until firm.

Combine sour cream, powdered sugar, and poppy seeds, stirring well. Line 2 salad plates with lettuce, if desired. Unmold salads onto plates; top each serving evenly with sour cream mixture. Sprinkle with grated orange rind, if desired. Yield: 2 servings.

Offer these fruited congealed salads with roasted turkey
at your next holiday meal.

# CITRUS SALAD WITH CREAMY ORANGE DRESSING

**Per Serving:**

Calories 89
Calories from Fat 9%
Fat 0.9 g
Saturated Fat 0.6 g
Carbohydrate 19.3 g
Protein 1.4 g
Cholesterol 0 mg
Sodium 19 mg

**Exchanges:**

1   Fruit

½   cup canned mandarin oranges in light syrup, drained
⅓   cup canned pineapple tidbits in juice, drained
1   medium tangerine, peeled and coarsely chopped
2   tablespoons nonfat sour cream alternative
1½ teaspoons powdered sugar
1   teaspoon frozen orange juice concentrate, undiluted
2   teaspoons flaked coconut, toasted

Combine first 3 ingredients; spoon mixture evenly into 2 serving dishes. Combine sour cream, sugar, and orange juice concentrate; spoon mixture evenly over fruit. Sprinkle with coconut. Yield: 2 servings.

# Honeyed Fruit Salad

2 tablespoons vanilla low-fat
  yogurt
1 tablespoon reduced-calorie
  mayonnaise
1½ teaspoons honey
  Dash of ground ginger
  Dash of ground cinnamon
¾ cup cubed Red Delicious
  apple
¾ cup cubed ripe pear
½ cup fresh orange sections
2 tablespoons golden raisins
2 lettuce leaves

Combine first 5 ingredients in a small bowl, stirring well. Combine apple and next 3 ingredients; toss gently.

To serve, spoon fruit mixture evenly onto 2 lettuce-lined salad plates. Drizzle yogurt mixture evenly over fruit. Yield: 2 servings.

Try Honeyed Fruit Salad with Marinated Pork Tenderloins (page 229).

Try Honeyed Fruit Salad with Marinated Pork Tenderloins (page 229).

**Per Serving:**

Calories 152
Calories from Fat 16%
Fat 2.7 g
Saturated Fat 0.5 g
Carbohydrate 33.3 g
Protein 1.9 g
Cholesterol 3 mg
Sodium 68 mg

**Exchanges:**

2 Fruit
½ Fat

# Fruit Salad in Orange Cups

1 large orange
¼ cup sliced fresh strawberries
¼ cup fresh or frozen
  blueberries, thawed
3 tablespoons vanilla nonfat
  frozen yogurt, slightly
  softened
2 teaspoons frozen orange juice
  concentrate, undiluted
½ teaspoon minced fresh mint
  Fresh mint sprigs (optional)

Cut orange in half crosswise; remove and discard seeds. Carefully remove pulp (do not puncture bottoms of orange halves). Reserve orange cups. Coarsely chop pulp, and place in a small bowl. Add strawberries and blueberries; toss gently. Spoon fruit mixture evenly into orange cups.

Combine yogurt, orange juice concentrate, and minced mint, stirring well. Spoon yogurt mixture evenly over fruit. Garnish with mint sprigs, if desired. Yield: 2 servings.

Children will love eating Fruit Salad in Orange Cups
with a turkey sandwich.

**Per Serving:**

Calories 67
Calories from Fat 3%
Fat 0.2 g
Saturated Fat 0 g
Carbohydrate 16.1 g
Protein 1.5 g
Cholesterol 0 mg
Sodium 13 mg

**Exchanges:**

1 Fruit

# Fruit and Cheese Salad with Raspberry Dressing

**Per Serving:**

Calories 307
Calories from Fat 19%
Fat 6.5 g
Saturated Fat 3.3 g
Carbohydrate 56.4 g
Protein 10.4 g
Cholesterol 19 mg
Sodium 207 mg

**Exchanges:**

1½  Medium-Fat Meat
4    Fruit

1⅓  cups frozen unsweetened
     raspberries, thawed
1   teaspoon cornstarch
2   tablespoons sugar
2   tablespoons plain nonfat
     yogurt
1   small Red Delicious apple,
     cored and sliced
1   small pear, cored and sliced
1   tablespoon lemon juice
½   cup seedless green grapes
1   ounce reduced-fat Monterey
     Jack cheese, cubed
1   ounce reduced-fat Cheddar
     cheese, cubed
4   Bibb lettuce leaves

Place raspberries in a wire-mesh strainer; press with back of spoon against the sides of the strainer to squeeze out ⅓ cup juice. Discard pulp and seeds remaining in strainer.

Combine raspberry juice and cornstarch in a small saucepan; cook over medium heat, stirring constantly, until thickened and bubbly. Let mixture cool slightly. Add sugar and yogurt to raspberry mixture, stirring until blended; set aside.

Place apple and pear slices in a bowl; sprinkle with lemon juice, and toss gently. Arrange apple, pear, grapes, and cheeses on 2 lettuce-lined salad plates. Serve with dressing mixture. Yield: 2 servings.

Fruit and Cheese Salad with Raspberry Dressing

# RADICCHIO SALAD

1 tablespoon chopped fresh
   chives
3 tablespoons white wine
   vinegar
2½ tablespoons water
½ teaspoon minced fresh
   oregano
½ teaspoon minced fresh thyme
1½ teaspoons Dijon mustard

½ teaspoon olive oil
⅛ teaspoon sugar
1 cup torn Bibb lettuce
1 cup torn radicchio
1 cup seeded, chopped tomato
1 tablespoon crumbled feta
   cheese
2 (¼-inch-thick) slices purple
   onion, separated into rings

Combine first 8 ingredients in a jar; cover tightly, and shake vigorously.
   Combine Bibb lettuce and remaining ingredients in a medium bowl.
Pour vinegar mixture over salad; toss gently. Yield: 2 servings.

*You may want to serve this salad in the Italian fashion,
as an interlude between the entrée and dessert.*

Per Serving:

Calories 82
Calories from Fat 31%
Fat 2.8 g
Saturated Fat 0.8 g
Carbohydrate 11.9 g
Protein 3.3 g
Cholesterol 3 mg
Sodium 178 mg

Exchanges:

2 Vegetable
½ Fat

# ORIENTAL GREEN SALAD

1½ teaspoons sesame seeds
½ teaspoon sesame oil
2 tablespoons cider vinegar
2 teaspoons lemon juice
2 teaspoons low-sodium soy
   sauce

2 cups torn fresh spinach
½ cup shredded bok choy
½ cup coarsely shredded carrot
1 tablespoon shredded radish

Combine sesame seeds and sesame oil in a small saucepan. Cook, stirring
constantly, over medium-low heat 1 minute or until sesame seeds are
golden. Let cool completely. Stir in vinegar, lemon juice, and soy sauce;
set aside.
   Combine spinach and remaining ingredients. Add sesame seed mixture,
and toss well. Yield: 2 servings.

*Toss this fresh vegetable salad to go with any stir-fry dish.*

Per Serving:

Calories 45
Calories from Fat 48%
Fat 2.4 g
Saturated Fat 0.3 g
Carbohydrate 5.5 g
Protein 1.4 g
Cholesterol 0 mg
Sodium 157 mg

Exchanges:

1 Vegetable
½ Fat

# SPINACH-ORANGE SALAD

1 tablespoon white balsamic vinegar
1½ teaspoons water
1½ teaspoons honey
1 teaspoon olive oil
¼ teaspoon Dijon mustard
2 cups loosely packed torn fresh spinach
½ cup sliced fresh mushrooms
2 tablespoons chopped purple onion
1 medium-size orange, peeled and sectioned

Combine first 5 ingredients in a jar; cover tightly, and shake vigorously. Chill thoroughly.

Combine spinach and remaining ingredients in a medium bowl; toss gently. Arrange spinach mixture evenly on 2 salad plates. Drizzle vinegar mixture evenly over salads. Yield: 2 servings.

Complement creamy Seafood Casserole (page 233) with this touch-of-citrus spinach salad.

# SPINACH-PEAR SALAD WITH HOT AND SOUR DRESSING

1 tablespoon finely chopped green onions
2 tablespoons white wine vinegar
1 teaspoon minced jalapeño pepper
½ teaspoon sesame oil
1 teaspoon lime juice
½ teaspoon sugar
⅛ teaspoon salt
⅛ teaspoon pepper
2 cups torn fresh spinach
1 small ripe pear, cored and sliced lengthwise
1 small tomato, cut into wedges
2 teaspoons chopped walnuts, toasted

Combine first 8 ingredients in a jar; cover tightly, and shake vigorously. Chill thoroughly.

Place 1 cup spinach on each of 2 salad plates. Arrange pear and tomato evenly over spinach. Sprinkle walnuts evenly over each salad.

Shake vinegar mixture, and pour into a small saucepan. Cook over medium heat until thoroughly heated; spoon warm vinegar mixture over salads. Serve immediately. Yield: 2 servings.

Romaine and Strawberry Salad

# ROMAINE AND STRAWBERRY SALAD

2 cups torn romaine lettuce
½ cup halved fresh strawberries
1 tablespoon coarsely chopped
   purple onion

1 tablespoon slivered almonds,
   toasted
1 tablespoon honey
1 tablespoon balsamic vinegar

Combine romaine lettuce, strawberry halves, chopped onion, and toasted almonds; toss gently.

   Combine honey and vinegar, stirring well. Pour vinegar mixture over salad, and toss gently. Yield: 2 servings.

**Per Serving:**

Calories 81
Calories from Fat 31%
Fat 2.8 g
Saturated Fat 0.3 g
Carbohydrate 14.0 g
Protein 1.8 g
Cholesterol 0 mg
Sodium 4 mg

**Exchanges:**

1    Vegetable
½   Fruit
½   Fat

# Vegetable Medley on Spinach

Per Serving:

Calories 37
Calories from Fat 15%
Fat 0.6 g
Saturated Fat 0 g
Carbohydrate 7.0 g
Protein 1.2 g
Cholesterol 0 mg
Sodium 408 mg

Exchanges:

1   Vegetable

3   tablespoons commercial
    oil-free Italian dressing
1   tablespoon water
2   teaspoons Dijon mustard
1   cup torn fresh spinach
½   cup torn romaine lettuce
½   small sweet red pepper, cut
    into very thin strips

¼   cup sliced cucumber
¼   cup coarsely shredded carrot
¼   cup sliced yellow squash
    Dash of freshly ground
    pepper

Combine first 3 ingredients, stirring well with a wire whisk. Set aside.
   Combine spinach and lettuce, tossing gently. Place salad greens evenly on 2 salad plates; arrange red pepper strips and next 3 ingredients over greens. Drizzle dressing mixture over vegetables. Sprinkle with pepper. Yield: 2 servings.

Make a meal in minutes with this colorful vegetable medley and Peppercorn Tuna (page 108).

# Santa Fe Green Salad

Per Serving:

Calories 158
Calories from Fat 28%
Fat 4.9 g
Saturated Fat 1.2 g
Carbohydrate 24.5 g
Protein 6.0 g
Cholesterol 5 mg
Sodium 91 mg

Exchanges:

1   Starch
2   Vegetable
1   Fat

3   tablespoons chopped fresh
    cilantro
1   tablespoon lime juice
1   tablespoon unsweetened
    apple juice
1   tablespoon plain nonfat
    yogurt
1   teaspoon olive oil
1   teaspoon honey
½   teaspoon garlic powder
½   teaspoon ground cumin
½   teaspoon chili powder

1   cup torn fresh spinach
1   cup torn romaine lettuce
1   cup seeded, chopped tomato
½   cup julienne-sliced jicama
¼   cup thinly sliced zucchini
1   (8½-ounce) can no-salt-
    added whole-kernel corn,
    drained
2   tablespoons (½ ounce)
    shredded reduced-fat
    sharp Cheddar cheese

Position knife blade in a miniature food processor bowl; add first 9 ingredients. Process until smooth, and set aside.
   Combine spinach and lettuce in a bowl; toss well. Place 1 cup salad greens on each of 2 salad plates. Combine tomato and next 3 ingredients in a small bowl. Spoon tomato mixture evenly over salad greens. Sprinkle each serving with 1 tablespoon cheese. Drizzle cilantro dressing mixture evenly over salads. Yield: 2 servings.

Serve Santa Fe Green Salad with low-fat enchiladas or burritos.

# Caesar Salad

| | |
|---|---|
| 2 (¾-inch-thick) slices French bread | ¾ teaspoon anchovy paste |
| Butter-flavored vegetable cooking spray | 3 cups torn romaine lettuce |
| 1 clove garlic, cut in half | 4 fresh mushrooms, sliced |
| 1½ tablespoons red wine vinegar | 2 teaspoons freshly grated Parmesan cheese |
| 1½ tablespoons water | ¼ teaspoon freshly ground pepper |
| 1 teaspoon olive oil | |

Coat both sides of each bread slice with cooking spray; rub both sides of each slice with cut side of garlic clove. Set garlic aside. Cut bread into cubes. Place cubes on a baking sheet; bake at 375° for 8 to 10 minutes or until crisp and browned.

Combine vinegar and next 3 ingredients in a jar; cover tightly, and shake vigorously. Rub inside of a wooden bowl with cut side of garlic clove. Add lettuce and mushrooms; add vinegar mixture to salad, and toss gently to coat. Sprinkle with cheese and pepper. Yield: 2 servings.

*Make Caesar Salad the first course of a low-fat Italian meal.*

**Per Serving:**

Calories 154
Calories from Fat 29%
Fat 4.9 g
Saturated Fat 1.4 g
Carbohydrate 20.7 g
Protein 6.9 g
Cholesterol 4 mg
Sodium 505 mg

**Exchanges:**

1 Starch
1 Vegetable
1 Fat

# Romaine and Peach Salad

| | |
|---|---|
| 1 (8¼-ounce) can sliced peaches in juice | 2 tablespoons chopped purple onion |
| 2 tablespoons white wine vinegar | 1 tablespoon crumbled blue cheese |
| ½ teaspoon olive oil | Freshly ground pepper (optional) |
| ½ teaspoon sugar | |
| 2 cups torn romaine lettuce | |

Drain peaches, reserving 2 tablespoons juice. Set peaches aside. Combine peach juice, vinegar, olive oil, and sugar, stirring well with a wire whisk.

Combine peaches, lettuce, and onion in a medium bowl; toss gently. Arrange lettuce mixture evenly on 2 salad plates; top evenly with blue cheese. Drizzle vinegar mixture evenly over salads. Sprinkle with pepper, if desired. Yield: 2 servings.

*Combine fresh romaine lettuce with peaches and blue cheese for a high-flavor salad to serve with grilled fish.*

**Per Serving:**

Calories 60
Calories from Fat 35%
Fat 2.3 g
Saturated Fat 0.8 g
Carbohydrate 8.5 g
Protein 1.7 g
Cholesterol 3 mg
Sodium 57 mg

**Exchanges:**

½ Vegetable
½ Fruit
½ Fat

# Asparagus Salad

Per Serving:

Calories 106
Calories from Fat 26%
Fat 3.1 g
Saturated Fat 0.9 g
Carbohydrate 18.8 g
Protein 4.5 g
Cholesterol 3 mg
Sodium 216 mg

Exchanges:

3  Vegetable
½  Fat

¼  cup white balsamic vinegar
1  teaspoon garlic powder
2  teaspoons paprika
2  teaspoons prepared horseradish
2  teaspoons honey
2  teaspoons Dijon mustard
½  teaspoon olive oil
½  teaspoon pepper

½  pound fresh asparagus spears (about 9 spears)
1  small yellow squash, sliced
1  plum tomato, cut into wedges
2  cups torn watercress
1  tablespoon crumbled blue cheese

Combine first 8 ingredients in a jar; cover tightly, and shake vigorously. Chill thoroughly.

Snap off tough ends of asparagus. Remove scales from stalks with a knife or vegetable peeler, if desired. Arrange asparagus in a vegetable steamer over boiling water. Cover and steam 4 to 5 minutes or until crisp-tender. Drain; let cool to room temperature.

Arrange asparagus, squash, and tomato on 2 watercress-lined salad plates. Sprinkle evenly with cheese. Drizzle vinegar mixture evenly over salads. Yield: 2 servings.

# Mexican Corn Salad

Per Serving:

Calories 73
Calories from Fat 23%
Fat 1.9 g
Saturated Fat 0.2 g
Carbohydrate 12.6 g
Protein 1.8 g
Cholesterol 0 mg
Sodium 77 mg

Exchanges:

1  Starch
½  Fat

1  (8¾-ounce) can no-salt–added whole-kernel corn, drained
¼  cup chopped cucumber
¼  cup seeded, chopped tomato
1  tablespoon chopped green onions

¾  teaspoon seeded, minced jalapeño pepper
2  teaspoons fresh lime juice
½  teaspoon vegetable oil
⅛  teaspoon ground cumin
   Dash of salt
   Dash of pepper

Combine first 5 ingredients in a medium bowl; toss gently. Combine lime juice and remaining ingredients, stirring with a wire whisk. Pour lime juice mixture over vegetable mixture, and toss gently. Cover and chill thoroughly. Stir just before serving. Yield: 2 servings.

Any hearty Tex-Mex entrée calls for a pepper-flavored side dish like Mexican Corn Salad.

# GREEK COLESLAW

2 tablespoons nonfat sour
   cream alternative
2 tablespoons red wine
   vinegar
½ teaspoon sugar
¼ teaspoon garlic powder
⅛ teaspoon salt
⅛ teaspoon pepper
1 cup shredded cabbage
¼ cup coarsely shredded carrot

1 tablespoon chopped
   cucumber
1 tablespoon crumbled feta
   cheese
1½ teaspoons chopped green
   onions
1½ teaspoons chopped salad
   olives
1½ teaspoons sliced almonds,
   toasted

Combine first 6 ingredients in a small bowl, stirring with a wire whisk until blended.

Combine cabbage and remaining ingredients in a medium bowl. Spoon vinegar mixture over vegetables; toss gently to blend. Yield: 2 servings.

Greek Coleslaw is a perfect side dish for pita bread sandwiches.

**Per Serving:**

Calories 64
Calories from Fat 28%
Fat 2.0 g
Saturated Fat 0.7 g
Carbohydrate 9.1 g
Protein 2.9 g
Cholesterol 3 mg
Sodium 246 mg

**Exchanges:**

2 Vegetable

# VINAIGRETTE COLESLAW

1½ cups finely shredded cabbage
2 tablespoons chopped sweet
   red pepper
1 tablespoon thinly sliced
   green onions
1 tablespoon chopped fresh
   parsley
3 tablespoons water

3 tablespoons white wine
   vinegar
1½ teaspoons sugar
1 teaspoon olive oil
⅛ teaspoon freshly ground
   pepper
⅛ teaspoon dried basil
   Dash of garlic powder

Combine first 4 ingredients in a small bowl; toss well. Combine water and remaining ingredients in a jar; cover tightly, and shake vigorously. Pour vinegar mixture over cabbage mixture. Cover and chill thoroughly. Toss gently before serving. Serve with a slotted spoon. Yield: 2 servings.

Try this zesty coleslaw with grilled or baked chicken breasts.

**Per Serving:**

Calories 52
Calories from Fat 42%
Fat 2.4 g
Saturated Fat 0.3 g
Carbohydrate 7.0 g
Protein 0.9 g
Cholesterol 0 mg
Sodium 14 mg

**Exchanges:**

1 Vegetable
½ Fat

# SNOW PEA SALAD

**Per Serving:**

Calories 72
Calories from Fat 3%
Fat 0.2 g
Saturated Fat 0.1 g
Carbohydrate 14.2 g
Protein 3.0 g
Cholesterol 0 mg
Sodium 209 mg

**Exchanges:**

1   Starch

2   tablespoons rice wine vinegar
1   tablespoon low-sodium soy
    sauce
¼   teaspoon ground ginger
¼   teaspoon garlic powder
1   cup fresh snow pea pods

1   (8-ounce) can water
    chestnuts, drained
1   tablespoon chopped fresh
    parsley
    Green onion fans (optional)

Combine vinegar, soy sauce, ginger, and garlic powder in a jar; cover tightly, and shake vigorously.

Wash snow peas; remove ends. Arrange snow peas in a vegetable steamer over boiling water. Cover and steam 3 minutes; drain and rinse with cold water.

Combine snow peas, water chestnuts, and parsley in a small bowl. Pour vinegar mixture over snow pea mixture; toss gently. Garnish with green onion fans, if desired. Yield: 2 servings.

Snow Pea Salad

# Mexican Marinated Squash

1 cup julienne-sliced yellow
  squash
1 cup julienne-sliced zucchini
2 tablespoons chopped green
  onions
¼ cup white wine vinegar
2 tablespoons chopped fresh
  cilantro

1 teaspoon olive oil
½ teaspoon garlic powder
½ teaspoon onion powder
½ teaspoon ground cumin
¼ teaspoon pepper
⅛ teaspoon salt

Combine first 3 ingredients in a small shallow dish.

Combine vinegar and remaining ingredients in a jar; cover tightly, and shake vigorously. Pour vinegar mixture over vegetable mixture; toss gently. Cover and marinate in refrigerator at least 8 hours. Toss gently before serving. Yield: 2 servings.

Spicy chilled squash salad tastes great alongside Chicken Kabobs with Southwest Salsa (page 94).

**Per Serving:**

Calories 50
Calories from Fat 47%
Fat 2.6 g
Saturated Fat 0.4 g
Carbohydrate 5.4 g
Protein 1.6 g
Cholesterol 0 mg
Sodium 157 mg

**Exchanges:**

1 Vegetable
½ Fat

# Sliced Tomato with Balsamic Vinaigrette

1 tablespoon balsamic vinegar
2 teaspoons chopped fresh basil
1 teaspoon olive oil
½ teaspoon Dijon mustard
1 small clove garlic, crushed

1 large tomato, sliced
2 red leaf lettuce leaves
1 (¼-inch-thick) slice sweet
  onion, separated into rings

Combine first 5 ingredients in a jar; cover tightly, and shake vigorously. Set aside.

Arrange tomato slices evenly on 2 lettuce-lined plates. Arrange onion over tomato. Drizzle vinegar mixture evenly over salads. Yield: 2 servings.

This quick-fix salad complements most chicken, turkey, beef, or pork entrées.

**Per Serving:**

Calories 61
Calories from Fat 43%
Fat 2.9 g
Saturated Fat 0.4 g
Carbohydrate 8.8 g
Protein 1.6 g
Cholesterol 0 mg
Sodium 52 mg

**Exchanges:**

1 Vegetable
½ Fat

# BULGUR SALAD

**Per Serving:**

Calories 216
Calories from Fat 18%
Fat 4.2 g
Saturated Fat 0.6 g
Carbohydrate 41.9 g
Protein 7.7 g
Cholesterol 0 mg
Sodium 306 mg

**Exchanges:**

2½ Starch
1   Vegetable
1   Fat

½ cup boiling water
½ cup bulgur (cracked wheat), uncooked
½ cup chopped cucumber
¼ cup chopped yellow squash
¼ cup chopped sweet red pepper
2 tablespoons chopped purple onion
2 tablespoons chopped fresh parsley
2 tablespoons lemon juice
1 tablespoon water
2 teaspoons chopped fresh mint
½ teaspoon olive oil
¼ teaspoon salt
2 teaspoons pine nuts, toasted

Pour boiling water over bulgur; let stand 20 minutes or until liquid is absorbed. Stir in cucumber and next 9 ingredients; toss well. Cover and chill at least 1 hour. Sprinkle with pine nuts. Yield: 2 servings.

Serve Bulgur Salad with broiled lamb chops.

# ITALIAN PASTA SALAD

**Per Serving:**

Calories 336
Calories from Fat 23%
Fat 8.4 g
Saturated Fat 4.5 g
Carbohydrate 46.4 g
Protein 18.2 g
Cholesterol 25 mg
Sodium 595 mg

**Exchanges:**

3 Starch
1 High-Fat Meat
1 Vegetable

¼ cup sun-dried tomato
¼ cup hot water
4 ounces tricolor rotini (corkscrew) pasta, uncooked
¾ cup (3 ounces) cubed part-skim mozzarella cheese
½ cup sliced zucchini
2 tablespoons white wine vinegar
2 tablespoons commercial oil-free Italian dressing
¾ teaspoon minced garlic
½ teaspoon sugar
½ teaspoon Dijon mustard
¼ teaspoon pepper

Combine tomato and water in a small bowl; cover and let stand 15 minutes. Drain well. Chop tomato, and set aside.

Cook pasta according to package directions, omitting salt and fat. Drain; rinse with cold water, and drain. Combine tomato, pasta, cheese, and zucchini, tossing gently.

Combine vinegar and remaining ingredients, stirring well with a wire whisk. Add vinegar mixture to pasta mixture, and toss gently. Cover and chill 1 hour. Toss gently before serving. Yield: 2 servings.

This main-dish pasta salad is the start of an easy menu. Just add a cup of melon and commercial Italian bread.

# THREE-BEAN PASTA SALAD

2 ounces bow tie pasta,
   uncooked
1 (8-ounce) can no-salt-added
   cut green beans, drained
¼ cup canned garbanzo beans
   (chickpeas), drained
¼ cup canned no-salt-added
   kidney beans, drained
¼ cup chopped green pepper

¼ cup chopped sweet red
   pepper
¼ cup cider vinegar
1 tablespoon sugar
½ teaspoon minced garlic
½ teaspoon olive oil
¼ teaspoon salt
¼ teaspoon pepper

Cook pasta according to package directions, omitting salt and fat. Drain; rinse with cold water, and drain. Combine cooked pasta, green beans, and next 4 ingredients in a bowl; toss well.

Combine vinegar and remaining ingredients in a small bowl, stirring well. Pour vinegar mixture over pasta mixture, and toss well. Cover and chill at least 2 hours. Toss gently before serving. Yield: 2 servings.

Three-Bean Pasta Salad is a natural side dish for a
Roast Beef Poor Boy (page 159).

Per Serving:

Calories 225
Calories from Fat 10%
Fat 2.4 g
Saturated Fat 0.3 g
Carbohydrate 44.3 g
Protein 8.3 g
Cholesterol 0 mg
Sodium 341 mg

Exchanges:

3 Starch
½ Fat

# PASTA PRIMAVERA SALAD

3 tablespoons white wine
   vinegar
1 teaspoon olive oil
¼ teaspoon dried basil
⅛ teaspoon salt
   Dash of garlic powder
   Dash of freshly ground
   pepper
3 ounces fresh asparagus
   spears (about 3 spears)

4 ounces spaghetti, uncooked
½ cup frozen English peas,
   thawed
¼ cup julienne-sliced sweet
   red pepper
1 tablespoon freshly grated
   Parmesan cheese
2 cherry tomatoes, quartered

Combine first 6 ingredients in a small bowl, stirring well. Set aside.

Snap off tough ends of asparagus. Remove scales from spears with a knife or vegetable peeler, if desired. Cut asparagus into 1-inch pieces. Arrange asparagus in a vegetable steamer over boiling water. Cover and steam 4 to 5 minutes or until crisp-tender. Rinse with cold water.

Break spaghetti in half; cook according to package directions, omitting salt and fat. Drain; rinse with cold water, and drain. Place spaghetti in a bowl. Add vinegar mixture, asparagus, peas, and sweet red pepper; toss well. Sprinkle with cheese, and top with cherry tomato quarters. Cover and chill thoroughly. Yield: 2 servings.

Per Serving:

Calories 300
Calories from Fat 14%
Fat 4.5 g
Saturated Fat 1.1 g
Carbohydrate 52.4 g
Protein 12.1 g
Cholesterol 2 mg
Sodium 260 mg

Exchanges:

3 Starch
1 Vegetable
1 Fat

# Italian Rice Salad

½ cup cooked brown rice (cooked without salt or fat)
½ cup seeded, chopped tomato
¼ cup chopped zucchini
1 tablespoon chopped fresh parsley
1½ teaspoons chopped green onions
2 tablespoons white wine vinegar
1 tablespoon chopped ripe olives
½ teaspoon sugar
½ teaspoon ground oregano
½ teaspoon olive oil
½ teaspoon hot sauce

Combine first 5 ingredients in a medium bowl.

Combine vinegar and remaining ingredients in a jar; cover tightly, and shake vigorously. Pour vinegar mixture over rice mixture, and toss gently. Cover and chill at least 1 hour. Toss gently before serving. Yield: 2 servings.

Serve this tangy rice salad with lemon-broiled snapper fillets and steamed green beans.

## Per Serving:

Calories 93
Calories from Fat 25%
Fat 2.6 g
Saturated Fat 0.4 g
Carbohydrate 15.9 g
Protein 2.0 g
Cholesterol 0 mg
Sodium 79 mg

## Exchanges:

1 Starch

# Jalapeño Potato Salad

2 medium-size round red potatoes (about 6 ounces)
1 tablespoon finely chopped radish
1 tablespoon finely chopped green onions
1 tablespoon minced fresh cilantro
2 tablespoons low-fat sour cream
1 tablespoon reduced-calorie mayonnaise
2 teaspoons finely chopped green pepper
1 teaspoon Dijon mustard
1 teaspoon minced jalapeño pepper
¼ teaspoon pepper
⅛ teaspoon salt
⅛ teaspoon dried dillweed

Wash potatoes. Cook in boiling water to cover 20 to 25 minutes or until tender; drain and cool slightly. Dice potatoes, and place in a medium bowl.

Combine radish and remaining ingredients in a small bowl, stirring well.

Spoon sour cream mixture over potato, and toss gently. Cover and chill thoroughly. Yield: 2 servings.

Round out a picnic meal of oven-fried chicken and coleslaw with this piquant potato salad.

## Per Serving:

Calories 150
Calories from Fat 25%
Fat 4.2 g
Saturated Fat 1.5 g
Carbohydrate 25.2 g
Protein 3.8 g
Cholesterol 8 mg
Sodium 296 mg

## Exchanges:

1½ Starch
1 Fat

Potato Salad with Asparagus

# POTATO SALAD WITH ASPARAGUS

2  medium-size round red
    potatoes (about 6 ounces)
¼  pound fresh asparagus spears
    (about 5 spears)
1  tablespoon sliced green
    onions
2  tablespoons white wine
    vinegar

1  teaspoon olive oil
½  teaspoon Dijon mustard
    Dash of salt
    Dash of ground white pepper
2  Bibb lettuce leaves

**Per Serving:**

Calories 98
Calories from Fat 23%
Fat 2.5 g
Saturated Fat 0.4 g
Carbohydrate 16.5 g
Protein 2.9 g
Cholesterol 0 mg
Sodium 117 mg

**Exchanges:**

1  Starch
½  Fat

Wash potatoes. Cook in boiling water to cover 20 to 25 minutes or until tender; drain and cool slightly. Cut each potato into 6 wedges. Set aside.

Snap off tough ends of asparagus. Remove scales from spears with a knife or vegetable peeler, if desired. Cut asparagus into 1-inch pieces. Arrange asparagus in a vegetable steamer over boiling water. Cover and steam 4 to 5 minutes or until crisp-tender. Rinse with cold water.

Combine potato wedges, asparagus, and green onions in a shallow dish. Combine vinegar and next 4 ingredients; pour over potato mixture, and toss gently. Cover and chill at least 1 hour, stirring occasionally. Spoon potato mixture evenly onto 2 lettuce-lined salad plates. Yield: 2 servings.

# STEAK SALAD WITH CREAMY MUSTARD DRESSING

**Per Serving:**

Calories 258
Calories from Fat 35%
Fat 10.0 g
Saturated Fat 2.8 g
Carbohydrate 19.2 g
Protein 24.1 g
Cholesterol 58 mg
Sodium 327 mg

**Exchanges:**

3  Lean Meat
2  Vegetable
½  Fruit

2  tablespoons plain nonfat yogurt
2  teaspoons reduced-calorie mayonnaise
2  teaspoons Dijon mustard
1  teaspoon white wine vinegar
1  teaspoon honey
1  small cucumber
   Vegetable cooking spray
6  ounces lean boneless sirloin steak, cut into thin strips
2  green onions, coarsely chopped
1  tablespoon chopped walnuts
½  teaspoon dried basil
¼  teaspoon garlic powder
2  cups torn red leaf lettuce
1  cup torn fresh spinach
1  medium-size ripe nectarine, cut into wedges
2  tablespoons (½ ounce) shredded reduced-fat Edam cheese

Combine first 5 ingredients in a small bowl, stirring well. Set aside.

Slice cucumber lengthwise into thin strips, using a vegetable peeler and applying firm pressure. (Reserve center core of cucumber for another use.) Set cucumber strips aside.

Coat a small nonstick skillet with cooking spray; place over medium heat until hot. Add steak and next 4 ingredients; sauté 3 to 4 minutes or until steak is done. Set aside.

Combine lettuce and spinach; place evenly on 2 salad plates. Arrange cucumber strips, steak mixture, and nectarine wedges over salad greens. Drizzle vinegar mixture evenly over salads, and sprinkle with cheese. Yield: 2 servings.

**Steak Salad with Creamy Mustard Dressing**

# Cajun Beef and Pasta Salad

6 ounces lean flank steak
2 tablespoons dry red wine
¾ teaspoon Cajun seasoning, divided
2 ounces fusilli (corkscrew) pasta, uncooked
1 cup sliced fresh mushrooms
½ cup julienne-sliced green pepper
2 tablespoons sliced pimiento
¼ teaspoon dried oregano
¼ teaspoon dried thyme
3 tablespoons nonfat mayonnaise
2 tablespoons white wine vinegar
Vegetable cooking spray

Trim fat from steak; place steak in a shallow dish. Pour wine over steak, and sprinkle with ¼ teaspoon Cajun seasoning. Cover and marinate steak in refrigerator 1 hour.

Cook pasta according to package directions, omitting salt and fat. Drain; rinse with cold water, and drain. Place in a medium bowl. Stir in mushrooms and next 4 ingredients. Combine mayonnaise, vinegar, and remaining ½ teaspoon Cajun seasoning; spoon over pasta mixture, and toss gently. Cover and chill.

Remove steak from marinade, and discard marinade. Place steak on rack of a broiler pan coated with cooking spray. Broil 5½ inches from heat (with electric oven door partially opened) 5 minutes on each side or to desired degree of doneness. Cut steak diagonally across grain into ¼-inch slices; cut slices into 1-inch pieces. Add steak to pasta mixture, and toss gently. Yield: 2 servings.

Per Serving:

Calories 310
Calories from Fat 31%
Fat 10.8 g
Saturated Fat 4.2 g
Carbohydrate 31.1 g
Protein 21.3 g
Cholesterol 45 mg
Sodium 641 mg

Exchanges:

2 Starch
2 Medium-Fat Meat

# Chicken-Vegetable Slaw

¼ cup nonfat mayonnaise
¼ cup rice wine vinegar
1 teaspoon sugar
⅛ teaspoon salt
⅛ teaspoon freshly ground pepper
2 cups finely shredded cabbage
1 cup chopped cooked chicken breast (skinned before cooking and cooked without salt)
¼ cup seeded, chopped tomato
¼ cup coarsely shredded carrot
2 tablespoons chopped cucumber
1 tablespoon chopped green onions
2 teaspoons chopped unsalted cashews

Combine first 5 ingredients in a small bowl, stirring well with a wire whisk.

Combine cabbage and next 5 ingredients; add mayonnaise mixture, and toss gently. Sprinkle with cashews just before serving. Yield: 2 servings.

Per Serving:

Calories 279
Calories from Fat 45%
Fat 14.0 g
Saturated Fat 2.6 g
Carbohydrate 13.0 g
Protein 24.6 g
Cholesterol 70 mg
Sodium 446 mg

Exchanges:

1 Starch
3 Lean Meat

# CURRIED CHICKEN AND RICE SALAD

Per Serving:

Calories 355
Calories from Fat 12%
Fat 4.8 g
Saturated Fat 1.1 g
Carbohydrate 48.3 g
Protein 29.8 g
Cholesterol 72 mg
Sodium 578 mg

Exchanges:

3   Starch
3   Lean Meat

¼  cup plus 1 tablespoon
     nonfat mayonnaise salad
     dressing
2  tablespoons white wine
     vinegar
½  teaspoon curry powder
⅛  teaspoon salt
⅛  teaspoon pepper
1  cup chopped cooked chicken
     breast (skinned before
     cooking and cooked
     without salt)
1  cup cooked long-grain rice
     (cooked without salt or fat)
1  cup seedless red grape halves
¼  cup chopped celery
1  tablespoon chopped green
     onions
2  red leaf lettuce leaves
2  teaspoons sliced almonds,
     toasted

Combine first 5 ingredients, stirring well. Combine chicken and next 4 ingredients. Add mayonnaise mixture to chicken mixture; toss gently.

Spoon chicken mixture evenly onto 2 lettuce-lined salad plates. Sprinkle evenly with almonds. Yield: 2 servings.

Make a meal with Curried Chicken and Rice Salad, Herb-Sour Cream Biscuits (page 37), and Strawberry Soup (page 169).

# CHICKEN FAJITA SALAD

Per Serving:

Calories 225
Calories from Fat 26%
Fat 6.5 g
Saturated Fat 2.5 g
Carbohydrate 8.0 g
Protein 32.7 g
Cholesterol 80 mg
Sodium 325 mg

Exchanges:

4   Lean Meat
1½ Vegetable

½  pound chicken breast tenders
1  tablespoon plus 1 teaspoon
     lime juice
½  teaspoon chili powder
¼  teaspoon ground cumin
⅛  teaspoon salt
⅛  teaspoon pepper
     Vegetable cooking spray
2  cups shredded romaine
     lettuce
½  cup seeded, chopped tomato
2  tablespoons sliced green
     onions
¼  cup (1 ounce) shredded
     reduced-fat Monterey Jack
     cheese
2  tablespoons nonfat sour
     cream alternative
¼  cup chunky salsa

Place chicken in a shallow dish. Combine lime juice and next 4 ingredients; pour over chicken, turning to coat. Cover and marinate in refrigerator 45 minutes.

Place chicken on rack of a broiler pan coated with cooking spray. Broil 5½ inches from heat (with electric oven door partially opened) 7 to 8 minutes or until done, turning after 4 minutes. Remove from oven; slice chicken into ½-inch strips, and set aside.

Place 1 cup lettuce on each of 2 salad plates, and top evenly with chicken, tomato, and remaining ingredients. Yield: 2 servings.

# SALMON PASTA SALAD

2  ounces tricolor fusilli
   (corkscrew) pasta,
   uncooked
¼  cup nonfat sour cream
   alternative
2  teaspoons capers
¼  teaspoon dried tarragon
⅛  teaspoon pepper
   Dash of salt
   Vegetable cooking spray

1  (8-ounce) salmon fillet
2  tablespoons dry white wine
2  tablespoons water
2  tablespoons chopped purple
   onion
1  tablespoon chopped fresh
   parsley
1  small tomato, cut into
   wedges
2  romaine lettuce leaves

Cook pasta according to package directions, omitting salt and fat. Drain; rinse with cold water, and drain. Place in a medium bowl. Combine sour cream and next 4 ingredients, stirring well. Cover and set aside.

Coat a small nonstick skillet with cooking spray. Place fillet in skillet; pour wine and water over fillet. Bring to a boil; cover, reduce heat, and simmer 8 minutes or until fish flakes easily when tested with a fork. Remove from liquid, discarding liquid. Let cool slightly. Remove and discard skin from fillet; cut fillet into bite-size pieces, and place in a medium bowl.

Add cooked pasta, onion, parsley, and tomato, tossing gently. Spoon sour cream mixture over salmon mixture; stir gently. To serve, spoon salmon mixture evenly onto 2 lettuce-lined salad plates. Yield: 2 servings.

**Per Serving:**

Calories 340
Calories from Fat 28%
Fat 10.6 g
Saturated Fat 1.8 g
Carbohydrate 27.8 g
Protein 30.8 g
Cholesterol 77 mg
Sodium 454 mg

**Exchanges:**

2  Starch
3  Lean Meat

# CITRUS SEAFOOD SALAD

½  pound unpeeled medium-
   size fresh shrimp
4  cups water
¼  pound fresh lump crabmeat,
   drained
⅓  cup chopped celery
2  tablespoons chopped green
   pepper
1  tablespoon chopped onion
2  tablespoons reduced-calorie
   mayonnaise

2  tablespoons frozen orange
   juice concentrate, undiluted
1  tablespoon plus 1 teaspoon
   lime juice
2  teaspoons chopped fresh
   parsley
¼  teaspoon grated lime rind
4  green leaf lettuce leaves

Peel and devein shrimp. Bring water to a boil; add shrimp, and cook 3 to 5 minutes or until shrimp turns pink. Drain well; rinse with cold water.

Combine shrimp, crabmeat, and next 3 ingredients in a medium bowl. Combine mayonnaise and next 4 ingredients, stirring well. Add mayonnaise mixture to shrimp mixture, and toss well. Cover and chill thoroughly. To serve, spoon shrimp mixture evenly onto 2 lettuce-lined salad plates. Yield: 2 servings.

**Per Serving:**

Calories 201
Calories from Fat 26%
Fat 5.8 g
Saturated Fat 0.9 g
Carbohydrate 12.0 g
Protein 24.8 g
Cholesterol 176 mg
Sodium 425 mg

**Exchanges:**

3  Lean Meat
2  Vegetable

Salad Niçoise

# SALAD NIÇOISE

**Per Serving:**

Calories 234
Calories from Fat 29%
Fat 7.5 g
Saturated Fat 1.5 g
Carbohydrate 17.9 g
Protein 23.4 g
Cholesterol 33 mg
Sodium 211 mg

**Exchanges:**

1   Starch
3   Lean Meat

3   tablespoons white wine
      vinegar
2   tablespoons water
1½  teaspoons Dijon mustard
½   teaspoon olive oil
⅛   teaspoon freshly ground
      pepper
¼   pound fresh green beans
2   small round red potatoes
      (about ¼ pound)
2   tablespoons julienne-sliced
      sweet red pepper

1   tablespoon chopped purple
      onion
1   (6-ounce) tuna steak
      (¾ inch thick)
½   teaspoon olive oil
      Vegetable cooking spray
2   cups torn fresh spinach
4   cherry tomatoes, quartered
1   tablespoon sliced ripe olives

Combine first 5 ingredients in a small jar; cover tightly, and shake vigorously. Set aside.

Wash beans; remove ends. Arrange beans in a vegetable steamer over boiling water. Cover and steam 5 minutes or until crisp-tender. Drain.

Wash potatoes. Cook in boiling water to cover 20 minutes or just until tender. Drain and cool slightly. Cut potatoes into ¼-inch-thick slices.

Combine green beans, potato, sweet red pepper, and onion; toss gently. Add half of vinegar mixture; toss gently. Cover and chill 2 hours.

Brush tuna steak with ½ teaspoon olive oil. Place on rack of a broiler pan coated with cooking spray. Broil 5½ inches from heat (with electric oven door partially opened) 3 to 4 minutes on each side or until fish flakes easily when tested with a fork. Flake fish into pieces.

Place spinach on a serving plate. Arrange green bean mixture, tuna, tomato, and olives evenly over spinach. Drizzle remaining vinegar mixture evenly over salad. Yield: 2 servings.

# Shrimp Salad in Melon Cups

| | |
|---|---|
| 1 pound unpeeled medium-size fresh shrimp | 1 tablespoon finely chopped onion |
| 3 cups water | 2 teaspoons lemon juice |
| 1/3 cup nonfat sour cream alternative | 1/8 teaspoon salt |
| 2 tablespoons finely chopped celery | 1/8 teaspoon curry powder |
| | 1 small cantaloupe |
| | 2 green leaf lettuce leaves |

Peel and devein shrimp. Bring water to a boil; add shrimp, and cook 3 to 5 minutes or until shrimp turns pink. Drain well; rinse with cold water. Cut each shrimp in half crosswise, and place in a small bowl.

Combine sour cream and next 5 ingredients, stirring well. Add sour cream mixture to shrimp, and toss gently. Cover and chill thoroughly.

Cut cantaloupe in half crosswise with a sharp knife to form 2 large cups; remove and discard seeds. If needed, slice about 1/8 inch from bottom of each melon half so that it will sit flat. Spoon shrimp mixture evenly into lettuce-lined cantaloupe halves. Yield: 2 servings.

Serve this main-dish salad with slices of
Carrot-Pineapple Bread (page 50).

Per Serving:

Calories 215
Calories from Fat 8%
Fat 1.9 g
Saturated Fat 0.6 g
Carbohydrate 20.8 g
Protein 28.4 g
Cholesterol 221 mg
Sodium 453 mg

Exchanges:

4   Lean Meat
1   Fruit

# Shrimp and Orzo Salad

| | |
|---|---|
| 12 ounces unpeeled medium-size fresh shrimp | 2 tablespoons chopped sweet red pepper |
| 3 cups water | 2 tablespoons reduced-calorie mayonnaise |
| 1 lemon half | 1 tablespoon lemon juice |
| 1 bay leaf | 1/8 teaspoon salt |
| 1/3 cup uncooked orzo | 1/8 teaspoon ground white pepper |
| 1/3 cup peeled, seeded, and diced cucumber | 2 cups shredded romaine lettuce |
| 1/4 cup thinly sliced celery | |
| 2 tablespoons thinly sliced green onions | |

Peel and devein shrimp. Combine water, lemon half, and bay leaf in a Dutch oven; bring to a boil. Add shrimp, and cook 3 to 5 minutes or until shrimp turns pink. Drain well; rinse with cold water. Chill. Discard lemon half and bay leaf.

Cook orzo according to package instructions, omitting salt and fat. Drain; rinse with cold water, and drain.

Combine shrimp, orzo, cucumber, and next 7 ingredients in a bowl; toss gently. Cover and chill thoroughly.

Place 1 cup shredded lettuce on each of 2 salad plates. Spoon chilled shrimp mixture evenly over lettuce. Yield: 2 servings.

Per Serving:

Calories 277
Calories from Fat 19%
Fat 5.7 g
Saturated Fat 1.0 g
Carbohydrate 31.8 g
Protein 23.9 g
Cholesterol 171 mg
Sodium 470 mg

Exchanges:

2   Starch
2½ Lean Meat

Chicken Stir-Fry (page 92)

# THE MAIN EVENT

Start with smaller cuts of meat, poultry, and fish, and put the spotlight on couple-sized entrées presented with flair.

# Hearty Spaghetti

Per Serving:

Calories 413
Calories from Fat 17%
Fat 7.8 g
Saturated Fat 2.5 g
Carbohydrate 55.5 g
Protein 28.2 g
Cholesterol 55 mg
Sodium 501 mg

Exchanges:

3   Starch
2   Lean Meat
2   Vegetable

6   ounces ground round
    Vegetable cooking spray
½   cup sliced fresh mushrooms
¼   cup chopped carrot
¼   cup chopped green pepper
¼   cup chopped celery
1   teaspoon minced garlic
1   (14.5-ounce) can no-salt-added whole tomatoes, drained and chopped
1   (8-ounce) can no-salt-added tomato sauce
3   tablespoons dry red wine
2   tablespoons no-salt-added tomato paste
1   tablespoon chopped fresh parsley
2   teaspoons chopped ripe olives
1¼  teaspoons minced fresh basil
1¼  teaspoons minced fresh oregano
1   teaspoon sugar
¼   teaspoon salt
⅛   teaspoon crushed red pepper
1   bay leaf
1½  cups cooked spaghetti (cooked without salt or fat)
2   teaspoons grated Parmesan cheese

Cook ground round in a medium saucepan over medium-high heat until browned, stirring until it crumbles. Drain and pat dry with paper towels. Wipe drippings from pan with a paper towel. Set meat aside.

Coat saucepan with cooking spray; place over medium heat until hot. Add mushrooms, carrot, green pepper, celery, and garlic; sauté 3 minutes. Return meat to pan. Add tomato and next 11 ingredients; bring to a boil. Cover, reduce heat, and simmer 20 minutes. Uncover and simmer 20 minutes or until thickened, stirring occasionally. Remove and discard bay leaf. Spoon sauce over spaghetti. Sprinkle with Parmesan cheese. Yield: 2 servings.

# Individual Meat Loaves

Per Serving:

Calories 244
Calories from Fat 29%
Fat 7.8 g
Saturated Fat 2.4 g
Carbohydrate 8.4 g
Protein 33.3 g
Cholesterol 96 mg
Sodium 423 mg

Exchanges:

½   Starch
4   Lean Meat

5   ounces ground round
4   ounces ground veal
¼   cup frozen egg substitute, thawed
2   tablespoons chopped onion
1   tablespoon soft breadcrumbs
1   tablespoon chopped fresh parsley
1½  teaspoons ketchup
¼   teaspoon garlic powder
¼   teaspoon low-sodium Worcestershire sauce
    Dash of salt
    Vegetable cooking spray
2   tablespoons ketchup

Combine first 10 ingredients in a medium bowl, stirring well. Shape mixture into 2 (5½-inch) loaves. Place loaves on a rack in a roasting pan coated with cooking spray. Spread 1 tablespoon ketchup over each loaf. Bake at 350° for 1 hour. Remove from oven; let stand 5 minutes. Yield: 2 servings.

# BEEF STROGANOFF

6 ounces lean, boneless beef
   sirloin steak
   Vegetable cooking spray
1½ cups sliced fresh mushrooms
¼ cup sliced onion
½ teaspoon minced garlic
¼ cup canned no-salt-added
   beef broth, undiluted
2 tablespoons no-salt-added
   tomato sauce

½ teaspoon low-sodium
   Worcestershire sauce
¼ teaspoon salt
⅛ teaspoon pepper
3 tablespoons low-fat sour cream
1½ cups cooked medium egg
   noodles (cooked without
   salt or fat)
2 teaspoons chopped fresh
   parsley

Partially freeze steak; trim fat from steak. Slice steak diagonally across grain into ¼-inch-wide strips. Coat a nonstick skillet with cooking spray; place over medium-high heat until hot. Add steak; cook 3 minutes or until steak strips are browned on both sides. Remove from skillet. Drain and pat dry with paper towels. Wipe drippings from skillet with a paper towel.

   Coat skillet with cooking spray; place over medium-high heat until hot. Return steak to skillet. Add mushrooms, onion, and garlic; sauté 3 minutes. Add beef broth and next 4 ingredients; bring to a boil. Cover, reduce heat, and simmer 45 minutes or until meat is tender. Remove from heat; stir in sour cream. Spoon over noodles; sprinkle with parsley. Yield: 2 servings.

Per Serving:

Calories 357
Calories from Fat 25%
Fat 10.0 g
Saturated Fat 4.0 g
Carbohydrate 37.0 g
Protein 28.5 g
Cholesterol 108 mg
Sodium 368 mg

Exchanges:

2½ Starch
3   Lean Meat

# BEEF SUKIYAKI

¼ pound lean, boneless beef
   sirloin steak
   Vegetable cooking spray
1 teaspoon peanut oil
½ cup thinly sliced onion,
   separated into rings
½ cup sliced carrot
½ cup sliced fresh mushrooms
¼ cup sliced celery
½ cup canned no-salt-added
   beef broth, undiluted

2 teaspoons dry sherry
1½ teaspoons low-sodium soy
   sauce
½ teaspoon sugar
¼ teaspoon salt
½ cup sliced green onions
2 cups cooked long-grain rice
   (cooked without salt or fat)

Partially freeze steak; trim fat from steak. Slice steak diagonally across grain into ¼-inch-wide strips. Coat a nonstick skillet with cooking spray; add oil. Place over medium-high heat until hot. Add onion rings and carrot; sauté 3 minutes or until vegetables are crisp-tender. Add steak, mushrooms, and celery; sauté 3 minutes.

   Combine beef broth and next 4 ingredients, stirring well. Add broth mixture and green onions to skillet; cook, uncovered, 5 minutes or until liquid is absorbed. Spoon over rice. Yield: 2 servings.

Per Serving:

Calories 372
Calories from Fat 14%
Fat 5.9 g
Saturated Fat 1.5 g
Carbohydrate 59.8 g
Protein 17.9 g
Cholesterol 35 mg
Sodium 455 mg

Exchanges:

3   Starch
1   Medium-Fat Meat
2   Vegetable

# BEEF AND VEGETABLE KABOBS

½ pound lean, boneless beef
    sirloin steak
2 tablespoons dry red wine
2 tablespoons reduced-calorie
    maple syrup
1 tablespoon red wine vinegar
1 teaspoon olive oil
½ teaspoon minced garlic
½ teaspoon curry powder
¼ teaspoon pepper

2 small onions, quartered
1 small sweet red pepper, cut
    into 1-inch pieces
1 medium zucchini, cut into
    4 (1-inch) pieces
1 medium-size yellow squash,
    cut into 4 (1-inch) pieces
4 medium-size fresh
    mushrooms
    Vegetable cooking spray

Trim fat from steak; cut steak into 1-inch pieces. Place steak in a heavy-duty, zip-top plastic bag. Combine wine and next 6 ingredients in a small bowl, stirring well. Pour wine mixture over steak. Seal bag, and shake until steak is well coated. Marinate in refrigerator at least 8 hours, turning bag occasionally.

Remove steak from marinade, reserving marinade. Thread steak, onion, sweet red pepper, zucchini, yellow squash, and mushrooms alternately onto 4 (10-inch) skewers.

Coat grill rack with cooking spray; place on grill over medium-hot coals (350° to 400°). Place kabobs on rack; grill, covered, 12 to 14 minutes or to desired degree of doneness, turning and basting frequently with reserved marinade. Yield: 2 servings.

Beef and Vegetable Kabobs

# Italian Beef Rolls

2 (4-ounce) lean, boneless beef
   sirloin steaks
2 tablespoons shredded lean
   cooked ham
1 tablespoon chopped fresh
   flat-leaf parsley
2 teaspoons freshly grated
   Romano cheese
2 teaspoons shredded fresh
   basil
1 teaspoon minced garlic
¼ teaspoon freshly ground
   pepper

Olive oil-flavored vegetable
   cooking spray
2 tablespoons finely chopped
   onion
⅓ cup peeled, seeded, and
   chopped tomato
3 tablespoons dry red wine
3 tablespoons canned no-salt-
   added beef broth, undiluted
Fresh basil sprigs (optional)

Per Serving:

Calories 196
Calories from Fat 33%
Fat 7.2 g
Saturated Fat 2.8 g
Carbohydrate 4.1 g
Protein 27.2 g
Cholesterol 76 mg
Sodium 192 mg

Exchanges:

3½ Lean Meat
1 Vegetable

Trim fat from steaks. Place steaks between 2 sheets of heavy-duty plastic wrap, and flatten to ½-inch thickness, using a meat mallet or rolling pin.

Combine ham and next 5 ingredients in a small bowl, stirring well. Spread ham mixture evenly over steaks, leaving a ½-inch border on each. Roll up each steak, jellyroll fashion, starting at short side; secure with heavy string.

Coat a small nonstick skillet with cooking spray. Place over medium heat until hot; add onion, and sauté 3 minutes. Add beef rolls; cook until browned on all sides. Add tomato, wine, and beef broth. Bring to a boil; cover, reduce heat, and simmer 40 to 45 minutes or until meat is tender. Remove rolls to warm plates; spoon tomato sauce mixture over rolls. Garnish with basil sprigs, if desired. Yield: 2 servings.

For a rustic Italian dinner, serve Italian Beef Rolls, Fettuccine
with Pesto (page 139), commercial Italian bread, and
Blackberry Granita (page 170).

# Fillet of Beef with Peppercorns

2 teaspoons green
   peppercorns, drained and
   divided
Butter-flavored vegetable
   cooking spray
2 tablespoons Cognac

½ cup canned no-salt-added
   beef broth, undiluted
1 (8-ounce) beef tenderloin
   steak (1½ inches thick)
1 tablespoon water

Crush 1½ teaspoons peppercorns, using a meat mallet or rolling pin. Coat a small heavy saucepan with cooking spray; place over medium heat until hot. Add crushed peppercorns, and cook 1 minute. Add Cognac; heat just until warm. Ignite with a long match; let flames die down. Add beef broth; cook over high heat 5 minutes or until reduced by half. Set aside.

Wrap handle of a small nonstick skillet with aluminum foil. Coat skillet with cooking spray; place over medium-high heat until hot. Add steak, and cook 2 minutes on each side. Immediately place skillet in oven. Bake at 400° for 5 minutes. Turn steak, and cook an additional 5 minutes or to desired degree of doneness. Remove skillet from oven. Place steak on a serving plate, and keep warm, reserving drippings in skillet.

Add reduced broth mixture, water, and remaining ½ teaspoon peppercorns to drippings in skillet. Place over medium-high heat; bring to a boil, stirring constantly. Slice meat into ¼-inch-thick slices. Spoon broth mixture over meat, and serve immediately. Yield: 2 servings.

Tender and flavorful, this steak recipe will become a favorite.
We suggest serving it with a mixed green salad, Dilled Carrots
(page 123), and commercial whole wheat rolls.

Per Serving:

Calories 205
Calories from Fat 36%
Fat 8.2 g
Saturated Fat 3.0 g
Carbohydrate 7.0 g
Protein 23.7 g
Cholesterol 70 mg
Sodium 168 mg

Exchanges:

½ Starch
3 Lean Meat

# Individual Beef Wellingtons

Olive oil-flavored vegetable cooking spray
1 cup sliced fresh mushrooms, minced
1½ teaspoons minced green onions
⅛ teaspoon salt
2 (4-ounce) beef tenderloin steaks
½ teaspoon coarsely ground pepper
4 sheets frozen phyllo pastry, thawed

Coat a small nonstick skillet with cooking spray. Place over medium-high heat until hot. Add mushrooms, green onions, and salt; sauté 8 minutes. Remove mushroom mixture from skillet, and set aside.

Sprinkle both sides of each steak with pepper. Coat skillet with cooking spray; place over high heat until hot. Add steaks, and cook 1½ to 2 minutes on each side or until lightly browned. Remove steaks from skillet; drain and pat dry with paper towels. Set aside.

Place 1 sheet of phyllo on a damp towel (keeping remaining phyllo covered). Lightly coat phyllo with cooking spray. Top with another sheet of phyllo, and coat with cooking spray; fold in half crosswise, bringing short ends together. Place 1 steak 3 inches from one end of phyllo. Spoon half of mushroom mixture over steak. Fold short end of phyllo over mushroom mixture; fold lengthwise edges of phyllo over steak, and roll up, jellyroll fashion. Repeat procedure with remaining 2 sheets of phyllo, mushroom mixture, and steak.

Lightly coat phyllo packets with cooking spray; place, seam side down, on a baking sheet coated with cooking spray. Bake at 425° for 15 to 17 minutes or until golden. Serve immediately. Yield: 2 servings.

**Feature Individual Beef Wellingtons for a special meal.
Round out the menu with wild rice, steamed asparagus,
and Irish Coffee-Caramel Dessert (page 179).**

**Per Serving:**

Calories 306
Calories from Fat 33%
Fat 11.2 g
Saturated Fat 3.5 g
Carbohydrate 22.4 g
Protein 27.2 g
Cholesterol 70 mg
Sodium 388 mg

**Exchanges:**

1½ Starch
3½ Lean Meat

# RAGOÛT OF VEAL

Per Serving:

Calories 282
Calories from Fat 29%
Fat 9.1 g
Saturated Fat 2.2 g
Carbohydrate 21.9 g
Protein 27.7 g
Cholesterol 88 mg
Sodium 434 mg

Exchanges:

1½ Starch
3   Lean Meat

½ pound lean, boneless veal
1 tablespoon all-purpose flour
½ teaspoon freshly ground pepper
  Olive oil-flavored vegetable cooking spray
1 teaspoon olive oil, divided
1 cup canned no-salt-added beef broth, undiluted
¼ cup plus 2 tablespoons dry vermouth
¾ cup sliced leeks
¾ cup peeled, seeded, and chopped tomato
1½ teaspoons chopped garlic
¼ teaspoon dried rosemary
3 bay leaves
1½ cups sliced fresh mushrooms
3 tablespoons chopped fresh parsley
3 tablespoons coarsely chopped pitted ripe olives
⅛ teaspoon salt

Trim fat from veal; cut veal into 1-inch cubes. Combine flour and pepper in a shallow dish; dredge veal in flour mixture. Coat a medium nonstick skillet with cooking spray; add ½ teaspoon olive oil. Place over medium-high heat until hot. Add veal; cook until browned on all sides, stirring frequently. Drain and pat dry with paper towels. Wipe drippings from skillet with a paper towel.

Add beef broth and vermouth to skillet; bring to a boil. Add veal, leeks, and next 4 ingredients. Cover, reduce heat, and simmer 1 hour.

Coat a small nonstick skillet with cooking spray; add remaining ½ teaspoon oil. Place over medium-high heat until hot. Add mushrooms; sauté 4 minutes or until tender. Add parsley, olives, and salt; stir well. Add mushroom mixture to veal; cook, covered, 15 minutes or until veal is tender. Remove and discard bay leaves. Yield: 2 servings.

# VEAL PICCATA

Per Serving:

Calories 170
Calories from Fat 30%
Fat 5.7 g
Saturated Fat 1.3 g
Carbohydrate 4.9 g
Protein 23.9 g
Cholesterol 94 mg
Sodium 193 mg

Exchanges:

3   Lean Meat

½ pound veal cutlets (¼ inch thick)
1 tablespoon all-purpose flour
⅛ teaspoon pepper
  Dash of salt
  Vegetable cooking spray
½ teaspoon vegetable oil
½ teaspoon reduced-calorie margarine
¼ cup plus 2 tablespoons canned low-sodium chicken broth, undiluted
1 tablespoon chopped fresh parsley
1 tablespoon lemon juice
2 (⅛-inch-thick) lemon slices, cut into quarters

Trim fat from veal; cut veal into 3-inch pieces. Place veal between 2 sheets of heavy-duty plastic wrap, and flatten to ⅛-inch thickness, using a meat mallet or rolling pin. Combine flour, pepper, and salt in a shallow dish; dredge veal in flour mixture.

Coat a nonstick skillet with cooking spray; add oil and margarine. Place over medium-high heat until margarine melts. Add veal; cook 3 minutes on each side or until browned. Remove veal from skillet. Drain and pat dry with paper towels.

Add chicken broth, parsley, and lemon juice to skillet; stir, scraping up any loose bits. Return veal to skillet. Bring to a boil; reduce heat, and simmer, uncovered, 5 minutes. Add lemon; simmer 1 minute. Yield: 2 servings.

# Veal with Sour Cream Sauce

| | |
|---|---|
| ½ pound lean ground veal | ¼ teaspoon paprika |
| ⅛ teaspoon salt | ⅛ teaspoon freshly ground |
| ⅛ teaspoon pepper | pepper |
| Vegetable cooking spray | 3 tablespoons nonfat sour |
| 2 tablespoons chopped shallots | cream alternative |
| ⅓ cup canned low-sodium | 2 teaspoons chopped fresh |
| chicken broth, undiluted | parsley |
| 1 tablespoon sherry | |

Combine first 3 ingredients in a small bowl, stirring well. Shape mixture into 2 (½-inch-thick) patties.

Coat a medium nonstick skillet with cooking spray; place over medium-high heat until hot. Add veal patties; cook 2 to 3 minutes on each side or until browned. Remove patties from skillet, and keep warm. Add shallots to skillet; sauté 1 minute. Add chicken broth and next 3 ingredients; cook 2 minutes, stirring occasionally. Return veal patties to skillet; cook, covered, over low heat 10 minutes or until meat is no longer pink. Transfer veal to a serving platter, and keep warm.

Pour broth mixture in skillet through a wire-mesh strainer into a small bowl, reserving 2 tablespoons. Discard remaining broth mixture and solids. Add sour cream to reserved broth mixture; stir to blend. Spoon sauce over patties, and sprinkle with parsley. Yield: 2 servings.

Make a meal of Veal with Sour Cream Sauce,
hot noodles, and Sautéed Spinach (page 131).

**Per Serving:**

Calories 163
Calories from Fat 22%
Fat 4.0 g
Saturated Fat 2.8 g
Carbohydrate 3.9 g
Protein 25.8 g
Cholesterol 88 mg
Sodium 235 mg

**Exchanges:**

3 Lean Meat

# GRILLED LAMB CHOPS DIJON

Per Serving:

Calories 168
Calories from Fat 39%
Fat 7.2 g
Saturated Fat 2.3 g
Carbohydrate 2.4 g
Protein 20.9 g
Cholesterol 63 mg
Sodium 256 mg

Exchanges:

3   Lean Meat

2   (5-ounce) lean lamb loin
    chops (¾ inch thick)
2   tablespoons dry red wine
2   tablespoons water
1   tablespoon chopped garlic
2   teaspoons dried rosemary,
    crushed

Vegetable cooking spray
2   tablespoons plain nonfat
    yogurt
1   teaspoon Dijon mustard
1   teaspoon capers
½   teaspoon lemon juice
⅛   teaspoon hot sauce

Trim fat from lamb chops; place chops in a small heavy-duty, zip-top plastic bag. Combine wine and next 3 ingredients; pour over chops. Seal bag, and shake until chops are well coated. Marinate in refrigerator 8 hours, turning bag occasionally.

Remove chops from bag, discarding marinade. Coat grill rack with cooking spray, and place on grill over medium-hot coals (350° to 400°). Place chops on rack; grill, covered, 10 minutes on each side or to desired degree of doneness. Transfer to serving plates, and keep warm.

Combine yogurt and remaining ingredients, stirring well. Spoon yogurt mixture over chops. Yield: 2 servings.

# SKILLET-BARBECUED PORK CHOPS

Per Serving:

Calories 274
Calories from Fat 37%
Fat 11.4 g
Saturated Fat 4.0 g
Carbohydrate 16.7 g
Protein 24.6 g
Cholesterol 74 mg
Sodium 437 mg

Exchanges:

1   Starch
3   Medium-Fat Meat

Vegetable cooking spray
2   (4-ounce) lean boneless
    center-cut loin pork chops
    (¾ inch thick)
2   tablespoons minced onion
2   teaspoons minced garlic
½   cup water

¼   cup no-salt-added tomato
    paste
2   tablespoons brown sugar
1½  tablespoons low-sodium soy
    sauce
2   teaspoons lemon juice
    Dash of salt

Coat a small nonstick skillet with cooking spray; place over medium-high heat until hot. Add pork chops, and cook 2 minutes on each side or until browned. Remove chops from skillet. Drain and pat dry with paper towels. Wipe drippings from skillet with a paper towel.

Coat skillet with cooking spray; place over medium-high heat until hot. Add onion and garlic; sauté 1 minute. Add water and remaining ingredients to skillet; stir well. Return chops to skillet; bring to a boil. Reduce heat, and simmer, uncovered, 20 minutes or until tender. Yield: 2 servings.

For a meal that reminds you of your childhood, prepare Skillet-Barbecued Pork Chops, Parmesan Potato Wedges (page 129), steamed green beans, and Chocolate-Banana Bread Pudding (page 183).

# FETTUCCINE FLORENTINE

2 teaspoons reduced-calorie margarine
1 small clove garlic, minced
½ cup plus 2 tablespoons skim milk
1½ teaspoons all-purpose flour
1 tablespoon light process cream cheese product
¼ cup plus 2 teaspoons freshly grated Parmesan cheese, divided

2 ounces fettuccine, uncooked
2 ounces spinach fettuccine, uncooked
⅓ cup diced cooked reduced-fat, low-salt ham
¼ cup frozen English peas, thawed
Freshly ground pepper

Melt margarine in a small saucepan over medium-high heat. Add garlic; sauté until tender. Combine milk and flour, stirring until smooth. Add to garlic mixture; cook over medium heat, stirring constantly, 6 to 8 minutes or until slightly thickened. Stir in cream cheese and ¼ cup Parmesan cheese; cook, stirring constantly, 2 minutes or until cheeses melt.

Cook pastas according to package directions, omitting salt and fat; drain. Place pasta in a serving bowl. Add cheese mixture, ham, and peas; toss gently. Sprinkle with remaining 2 teaspoons Parmesan cheese and pepper. Serve immediately. Yield: 2 servings.

Per Serving:

Calories 394
Calories from Fat 25%
Fat 11.1 g
Saturated Fat 4.7 g
Carbohydrate 50.2 g
Protein 23.2 g
Cholesterol 31 mg
Sodium 632 mg

Exchanges:

3 Starch
2 Medium-Fat Meat
1 Vegetable

Fettuccine Florentine

# PORK MEDAILLONS WITH SUN-DRIED CHERRIES

Per Serving:

Calories 188
Calories from Fat 27%
Fat 5.6 g
Saturated Fat 1.5 g
Carbohydrate 7.6 g
Protein 25.3 g
Cholesterol 79 mg
Sodium 80 mg

Exchanges:

½ Starch
3 Lean Meat

1 tablespoon sun-dried cherries
2 tablespoons hot water
  Butter-flavored vegetable cooking spray
½ pound pork tenderloin, trimmed and cut into ¾-inch-thick slices
½ teaspoon reduced-calorie margarine
1 cup sliced crimini mushrooms

1 tablespoon chopped green onions
¼ cup canned no-salt-added beef broth, undiluted
1 tablespoon dry red wine
1 teaspoon low-sodium Worcestershire sauce
⅛ teaspoon pepper
2 teaspoons chopped fresh parsley

Combine cherries and water in a small bowl; cover and let stand 15 minutes. Drain and set aside.

Coat a large nonstick skillet with cooking spray; place over medium-high heat until hot. Add pork medaillons; cook 2 to 3 minutes on each side or until done. Remove pork from skillet. Drain and pat dry with paper towels; set aside, and keep warm. Wipe drippings from skillet with a paper towel.

Coat skillet with vegetable cooking spray; add margarine. Place over medium-high heat until margarine melts. Add mushrooms and green onions; sauté 1 minute.

Combine cherry mixture, beef broth, and next 3 ingredients, stirring well; add to mushroom mixture in skillet. Cook 2 to 3 minutes, stirring frequently.

Arrange pork medaillons on a serving plate. Spoon mushroom mixture over pork, and sprinkle with parsley. Yield: 2 servings.

Impress a dinner guest by serving Pork Medaillons with Sun-Dried Cherries, Creamy Herbed Pasta (page 141), and Roasted Green Beans (page 122). Commercial sorbet makes an easy dessert.

# Venison with Sautéed Beet Greens

½ pound venison tenderloin,
    cut into 1¼-inch cubes
2 tablespoons dry red wine
2 tablespoons canned no-salt-
    added beef broth, undiluted
1 teaspoon chopped fresh
    rosemary
1 teaspoon chopped fresh
    thyme
1 teaspoon coarsely ground
    pepper

1 teaspoon minced garlic
1 teaspoon olive oil
¾ pound fresh beets (including
    greens)
    Vegetable cooking spray
2 teaspoons reduced-calorie
    margarine
½ teaspoon salt-free lemon-
    pepper seasoning
2 teaspoons lemon juice

**Per Serving:**

Calories 249
Calories from Fat 29%
Fat 8.1 g
Saturated Fat 1.8 g
Carbohydrate 16.0 g
Protein 28.7 g
Cholesterol 96 mg
Sodium 267 mg

**Exchanges:**

1 Starch
4 Lean Meat

Place venison in a small heavy-duty, zip-top plastic bag. Combine wine and next 6 ingredients; pour over venison. Seal bag, and shake until meat is well coated. Marinate in refrigerator 2 hours, turning bag occasionally.

Trim stems and roots from beets; discard stems and roots, and reserve greens. Peel beets; cut into ½-inch-thick slices. Cook beets in boiling water to cover 8 to 10 minutes or until crisp-tender; drain. Remove and discard stems from beet greens. Wash greens thoroughly, and pat dry with paper towels. Shred greens, and set aside.

Coat a large piece of heavy-duty aluminum foil with cooking spray. Place beets on one end of foil; top beets with margarine, and sprinkle evenly with lemon-pepper seasoning. Fold end of foil over beets; bring edges together. Fold edges over to seal; pleat and crimp edges of foil to make an airtight seal.

Drain venison, reserving marinade. Thread venison onto 2 (10-inch) skewers. Coat grill rack with cooking spray; place on grill over medium-hot coals (350° to 400°). Place beet packet on rack; grill, uncovered, 10 minutes or until packets are puffed and beets are tender. Place kabobs on rack; grill, covered, 4 to 5 minutes on each side or to desired degree of doneness, basting frequently with reserved marinade. Remove beets and kabobs from grill; set aside, and keep warm.

Coat a large nonstick skillet with cooking spray; place over medium-high heat until hot. Add beet greens; sauté 6 minutes or until greens are wilted. Stir in lemon juice.

Place greens evenly on serving plates; top each with a venison kabob. Serve with grilled beets. Yield: 2 servings.

For beef kabobs, use eight ounces boneless beef sirloin steak cut into ¼-inch cubes. Grill, covered, over medium-hot coals (350° to 400°) 5 to 6 minutes on each side or to desired degree of doneness, basting frequently.

# Chicken Stir-Fry

2   (4-ounce) skinned, boned chicken breast halves
    Vegetable cooking spray
1   teaspoon sesame oil
1   cup fresh broccoli flowerets
1   cup sliced fresh mushrooms
¼   cup chopped green onions
2   teaspoons minced garlic
¾   cup fresh bean sprouts
¾   cup fresh snow pea pods
¼   cup canned, sliced water chestnuts, drained

½   cup canned low-sodium chicken broth, undiluted
1   tablespoon dry sherry
1   tablespoon low-sodium soy sauce
1   teaspoon cornstarch
⅛   teapoon salt
2   cups cooked long-grain rice (cooked without salt or fat)

Cut chicken into ¼-inch-thick strips.

Coat a medium nonstick skillet or stir-fry pan with cooking spray; add oil. Place over medium-high heat until hot; add chicken, and stir-fry 2 minutes. Add broccoli and next 3 ingredients; stir-fry 2 minutes. Add bean sprouts, snow peas, and water chestnuts; stir-fry 1 minute.

Combine chicken broth and next 4 ingredients, stirring until smooth; add to chicken mixture. Cook, stirring constantly, until mixture is slightly thickened and thoroughly heated. Spoon chicken mixture over cooked rice. Yield: 2 servings.

Chicken Stir-Fry

# Chicken Curry

Butter-flavored vegetable
    cooking spray
1 teaspoon reduced-calorie
    margarine
¼ cup chopped onion
½ cup canned low-sodium
    chicken broth, undiluted
¼ cup skim milk
1 tablespoon all-purpose flour
1 teaspoon curry powder
1 cup chopped cooked chicken
    breast (skinned before
    cooking and cooked
    without salt)
2 teaspoons dry sherry
1 tablespoon lemon juice
¼ teaspoon salt
1½ cups cooked long-grain rice
    (cooked without salt or fat)
¼ cup peeled, chopped banana
1 tablespoon chutney
1 tablespoon chopped unsalted
    dry-roasted peanuts
2 tablespoons chopped green
    onions

Coat a medium nonstick skillet with cooking spray; add margarine. Place over medium-high heat until margarine melts. Add onion; sauté until tender.

Combine chicken broth, milk, flour, and curry powder, stirring until smooth. Add to onion mixture. Cook over medium heat, stirring constantly, until mixture is thickened. Stir in chicken and next 3 ingredients. Cook over medium heat 6 to 7 minutes or until thoroughly heated, stirring occasionally.

Spoon chicken mixture over rice. Top evenly with banana, chutney, peanuts, and green onions. Yield: 2 servings.

**Per Serving:**

Calories 436
Calories from Fat 17%
Fat 8.0 g
Saturated Fat 1.6 g
Carbohydrate 56.6 g
Protein 33.6 g
Cholesterol 73 mg
Sodium 430 mg

**Exchanges:**

2½ Starch
3 Lean Meat
1½ Fruit

# Jerk Chicken

½ cup chopped onion
1 tablespoon brown sugar
2 tablespoons low-sodium soy
    sauce
2 tablespoons red wine vinegar
1 teaspoon chopped fresh
    thyme
1 teaspoon chopped garlic
½ teaspoon sesame oil
¼ teaspoon ground allspice
1 Scotch Bonnet or habanero
    chili pepper
2 (4-ounce) skinned, boned
    chicken breast halves
Vegetable cooking spray
Fresh thyme sprigs (optional)

Position knife blade in food processor bowl; add first 9 ingredients. Pulse 12 times, scraping sides of processor bowl once. Place ⅓ cup onion mixture in a heavy-duty, zip-top plastic bag; reserve remaining onion mixture. Add chicken to bag; seal bag, and marinate chicken in refrigerator 1 hour, turning bag occasionally.

Remove chicken from marinade, discarding marinade. Coat grill rack with cooking spray; place rack on grill over medium-hot coals (350° to 400°). Place chicken and thyme sprigs, if desired, on rack; grill, covered, 4 minutes on each side or until chicken is done. Discard thyme sprigs. Serve chicken with reserved onion mixture. Yield: 2 servings.

**Per Serving:**

Calories 176
Calories from Fat 21%
Fat 4.1 g
Saturated Fat 1.0 g
Carbohydrate 6.3 g
Protein 26.1 g
Cholesterol 70 mg
Sodium 324 mg

**Exchanges:**

3 Lean Meat
1 Vegetable

# CHICKEN ENCHILADAS

Per Serving:

Calories 453
Calories from Fat 24%
Fat 11.9 g
Saturated Fat 4.5 g
Carbohydrate 45.8 g
Protein 40.9 g
Cholesterol 89 mg
Sodium 420 mg

Exchanges:

3  Starch
4  Lean Meat

Vegetable cooking spray
½  teaspoon vegetable oil
¼  cup chopped green onions
1  teaspoon minced garlic
½  cup water
1½  teaspoons chili powder
1  teaspoon ground cumin
2  (8-ounce) cans no-salt-added tomato sauce
4  (6-inch) corn tortillas
2  (4-ounce) skinned, boned chicken breast halves, cooked without salt and thinly sliced
¼  cup (1 ounce) shredded reduced-fat Monterey Jack cheese, divided
¼  cup (1 ounce) shredded reduced-fat Cheddar cheese, divided
2  tablespoons nonfat sour cream alternative

Coat a nonstick skillet with cooking spray; add oil. Place over medium-high heat until hot. Add green onions and garlic; sauté 2 minutes. Add water and next 3 ingredients; bring to a boil. Reduce heat; simmer, uncovered, 10 minutes.

Wrap tortillas in aluminum foil; bake at 325° for 12 minutes. Combine ¼ cup tomato sauce mixture, chicken, and 1 tablespoon of each cheese. Spoon chicken mixture evenly down center of tortillas; roll up tortillas.

Spread ¼ cup tomato sauce mixture in an 11- x 7- x 1½-inch baking dish coated with cooking spray. Arrange tortillas, seam side down, over sauce. Top tortillas with remaining tomato sauce mixture. Cover and bake at 350° for 20 minutes. Sprinkle with remaining cheese. Bake, uncovered, an additional 5 minutes. Top with sour cream. Yield: 2 servings.

# CHICKEN KABOBS WITH SOUTHWEST SALSA

Per Serving:

Calories 218
Calories from Fat 33%
Fat 8.0 g
Saturated Fat 1.6 g
Carbohydrate 9.5 g
Protein 27.3 g
Cholesterol 70 mg
Sodium 204 mg

Exchanges:

3  Lean Meat
2  Vegetable

¾  cup seeded, chopped tomato
¼  cup chopped avocado
2  tablespoons fresh lime juice
1  tablespoon chopped green onions
1  tablespoon chopped fresh cilantro
1  teaspoon finely chopped jalapeño pepper
¼  teaspoon minced garlic
2  (4-ounce) skinned, boned chicken breast halves, cut into 1-inch pieces
2  tablespoons fresh lime juice
2  teaspoons low-sodium soy sauce
1  teaspoon garlic
Mesquite chips
Vegetable cooking spray

Combine first 7 ingredients. Cover and chill. Place chicken in a shallow dish. Combine 2 tablespoons lime juice, soy sauce, and garlic. Pour over chicken. Cover and marinate in refrigerator 1 hour.

Soak mesquite chips in water 30 minutes; drain.

Remove chicken from marinade, reserving marinade. Thread chicken onto 2 (10-inch) skewers. Place chips directly on medium-hot coals (350° to 400°). Coat grill rack with cooking spray; place rack on grill. Place chicken on rack; grill, covered, 6 to 8 minutes or until chicken is done, turning occasionally and basting with reserved marinade.

To serve, spoon tomato mixture onto a serving plate; place chicken kabobs over tomato mixture. Yield: 2 servings.

# CHICKEN AND BROCCOLI IN PHYLLO

¾ cup chopped fresh broccoli
⅔ cup diced cooked chicken breast (skinned before cooking and cooked without salt)
¼ cup (1 ounce) shredded reduced-fat Cheddar cheese
1½ tablespoons light process cream cheese product, softened

2 tablespoons canned no-salt-added chicken broth, undiluted
2 teaspoons lemon juice
¼ teaspoon pepper
⅛ teaspoon salt
2 sheets frozen phyllo pastry, thawed
Vegetable cooking spray

Arrange broccoli in a vegetable steamer over boiling water. Cover and steam 3 minutes or until crisp-tender. Set aside.

Combine chicken, Cheddar cheese, and cream cheese in a small bowl, stirring well. Add broccoli, chicken broth, and next 3 ingredients; stir well. Place 1 sheet of phyllo on a damp towel (keeping remaining phyllo covered). Lightly coat phyllo with cooking spray; fold phyllo in half crosswise, bringing short ends together. Lightly coat with cooking spray. Spoon half of chicken mixture onto narrow end of phyllo; fold over lengthwise edges of phyllo to partially enclose filling. Fold narrow end of phyllo over mixture, and roll up, jellyroll fashion. Repeat procedure with remaining phyllo and chicken mixture.

Place phyllo packets, seam side down, on a baking sheet coated with cooking spray. Lightly coat tops of packets with cooking spray. Bake at 350° for 20 to 25 minutes or until golden. Yield: 2 servings.

Serve Chicken and Broccoli in Phyllo with Sliced Tomato with Balsamic Vinaigrette (page 67) and Mediterranean Orzo (page 142).

**Per Serving:**

Calories 249
Calories from Fat 33%
Fat 9.2 g
Saturated Fat 3.9 g
Carbohydrate 14.7 g
Protein 26.3 g
Cholesterol 65 mg
Sodium 474 mg

**Exchanges:**

1   Starch
3   Lean Meat

# HAM AND CHEESE CHICKEN

2   (4-ounce) skinned, boned
    chicken breast halves
⅛   teaspoon pepper
2   teaspoons light process
    cream cheese product
1   teaspoon minced fresh
    parsley
⅛   teaspoon minced garlic
½   ounce very thinly sliced lean
    cooked ham
1½  tablespoons fine, dry
    breadcrumbs

½   teaspoon dried Italian
    seasoning
½   teaspoon grated Parmesan
    cheese
¼   cup skim milk
    Vegetable cooking spray
2   teaspoons reduced-calorie
    margarine, melted
1   teaspoon lemon juice
    Dash of paprika
    Fresh oregano (optional)
    Lemon slices (optional)

Place chicken between 2 sheets of heavy-duty plastic wrap, and flatten to
¼-inch thickness, using a meat mallet or rolling pin. Sprinkle with pepper.

Combine cream cheese, parsley, and garlic, stirring well. Place half of ham
on each chicken breast half. Spread cheese mixture evenly over ham. Roll
up chicken, jellyroll fashion, starting with short end and tucking ends
under. Secure chicken rolls with wooden picks, if necessary.

Combine breadcrumbs, Italian seasoning, and Parmesan cheese. Dip
chicken rolls in milk, and dredge in breadcrumb mixture. Place, seam side
down, in a small shallow baking dish coated with cooking spray.

Combine margarine and lemon juice; drizzle over chicken. Sprinkle with
paprika. Bake, uncovered, at 350° for 30 minutes or until tender. Remove
wooden picks before serving. If desired, garnish with fresh oregano and
lemon slices. Yield: 2 servings.

Ham and Cheese Chicken

# MARIACHI CHICKEN

2 tablespoons Neufchâtel
  cheese, softened
1 tablespoon chopped green
  onions
1 tablespoon chopped fresh
  parsley
1 tablespoon grated carrot
⅛ teaspoon garlic powder
2 (4-ounce) skinned, boned
  chicken breast halves

2 teaspoons reduced-calorie
  margarine, melted
2 tablespoons fat-free whole
  wheat cracker crumbs
  Butter-flavored vegetable
  cooking spray
2 tablespoons commercial salsa
  verde
1 tablespoon low-fat sour
  cream, divided

Combine first 5 ingredients in a small bowl, stirring well; set aside.

Place chicken between 2 sheets of heavy-duty plastic wrap, and flatten to ¼-inch thickness, using a meat mallet or rolling pin. Spread cheese mixture evenly over chicken. Roll up chicken, jellyroll fashion, starting with short end. Secure chicken with wooden picks. Brush chicken with margarine; dredge in cracker crumbs.

Place chicken rolls, seam side down, in a small shallow baking dish coated with cooking spray. Bake at 350° for 30 to 35 minutes or until chicken is tender. Remove wooden picks, and top each chicken roll with 1 tablespoon salsa verde and 1½ teaspoons sour cream. Yield: 2 servings.

**Per Serving:**

Calories 315
Calories from Fat 24%
Fat 8.4 g
Saturated Fat 3.4 g
Carbohydrate 24.1 g
Protein 33.0 g
Cholesterol 79 mg
Sodium 465 mg

**Exchanges:**

1 Starch
4 Lean Meat
1 Vegetable

# SAFFRON CHICKEN WITH MATCHSTICK VEGETABLES

  Vegetable cooking spray
½ teaspoon olive oil
2 (4-ounce) skinned, boned
  chicken breast halves
½ cup julienne-sliced carrot
½ cup julienne-sliced onion
¼ cup julienne-sliced celery
1 tablespoon minced garlic
⅓ cup peeled, seeded, and
  chopped tomato

¼ cup dry white wine
¼ cup canned low-sodium
  chicken broth, undiluted
2 teaspoons no-salt-added
  tomato paste
¼ teaspoon salt
¼ teaspoon dried thyme
⅛ teaspoon ground saffron
⅛ teaspoon hot sauce
  Dash of pepper

Coat a small nonstick skillet with cooking spray; add oil. Place over medium-high heat until hot. Add chicken, and cook 2 minutes on each side or until browned. Transfer chicken to a 7- x 5¼- x 1½-inch baking dish; set aside.

Coat skillet with cooking spray; place over medium-high heat until hot. Add carrot and next 3 ingredients; sauté 3 minutes or until vegetables are tender. Add tomato and remaining ingredients to skillet; bring to a boil. Pour vegetable mixture over chicken. Cover; bake at 350° for 20 minutes or until chicken is tender. Spoon vegetables evenly onto 2 serving plates, using a slotted spoon. Place chicken over vegetables. Yield: 2 servings.

**Per Serving:**

Calories 192
Calories from Fat 17%
Fat 3.7 g
Saturated Fat 0.8 g
Carbohydrate 11.1 g
Protein 28.0 g
Cholesterol 66 mg
Sodium 417 mg

**Exchanges:**

3 Lean Meat
2 Vegetable

# Sesame Chicken with Summer Vegetables

Vegetable cooking spray
1   teaspoon sesame oil
2   (4-ounce) skinned, boned chicken breast halves, cut into thin strips
1   cup chopped yellow squash
1   cup sliced zucchini
1   small onion, cut into wedges
½   cup sliced sweet red pepper
3   tablespoons canned low-sodium chicken broth, undiluted
2   teaspoons low-sodium soy sauce
2   teaspoons sesame seeds, toasted

Coat a medium nonstick skillet with cooking spray; add oil. Place over medium-high heat until hot. Add chicken, and cook 5 minutes, stirring frequently. Remove from skillet, and keep warm. Wipe drippings from skillet with a paper towel.

Coat skillet with cooking spray. Add yellow squash and zucchini; sauté 7 minutes. Stir in onion and red pepper; sauté 1 minute. Add chicken, chicken broth, and soy sauce. Cook 3 minutes, stirring frequently. Sprinkle with sesame seeds. Yield: 2 servings.

# Chipper Chicken Drumsticks

½   teaspoon chili powder
⅛   teaspoon garlic powder
⅛   teaspoon ground thyme
⅛   teaspoon ground oregano
    Dash of pepper
4   chicken drumsticks, skinned (about ¾ pound)
    Olive oil-flavored vegetable cooking spray
½   cup crushed nonfat barbecue potato chips

Combine first 5 ingredients in a small bowl, stirring well. Coat drumsticks with cooking spray; sprinkle evenly with chili powder mixture. Cover and chill 30 minutes.

Dredge drumsticks in crushed potato chips. Place drumsticks on a rack in a roasting pan. Bake at 400° for 20 minutes. Turn drumsticks, and bake an additional 15 minutes or until done. Yield: 2 servings.

Children will love a meal with Congealed Berry Salads (page 56), Chipper Chicken Drumsticks, rice, and steamed broccoli.

Honey-Roasted Cornish Hen

# Honey-Roasted Cornish Hen

1 tablespoon honey
1 teaspoon chopped fresh
  oregano
1 teaspoon lemon juice
⅛ teaspoon salt
⅛ teaspoon pepper
1 (1-pound) Cornish hen,
  skinned

4 sprigs fresh oregano
1 lemon wedge
  Vegetable cooking spray
½ teaspoon vegetable oil
  Honey (optional)
  Lemon slices (optional)
  Fresh oregano sprigs
  (optional)

Combine first 5 ingredients in a small bowl, stirring well; set aside.

Remove giblets from hen; reserve for another use. Rinse hen under cold water, and pat dry.

Place 4 oregano sprigs and lemon wedge in cavity of hen; close cavity with skewers. Tie ends of legs together with string or cord. Lift wingtips up and over back of hen, tucking wingtips under hen. Place hen, breast side up, on a rack in a roasting pan coated with cooking spray. Brush with oil.

Place hen in a 450° oven. Reduce heat to 350°, and bake 35 minutes. Brush hen with half of honey mixture; bake 10 minutes. Brush with remaining honey mixture, and bake an additional 10 minutes or until hen is done. Transfer hen to a serving plate. If desired, drizzle additional honey on serving plate, and garnish with additional lemon slices and oregano sprigs. To serve, split hen in half lengthwise, using an electric knife. Remove and discard oregano sprigs and lemon wedge inside hen. Yield: 2 servings.

Per Serving:

Calories 203
Calories from Fat 34%
Fat 7.6 g
Saturated Fat 1.9 g
Carbohydrate 9.2 g
Protein 23.8 g
Cholesterol 73 mg
Sodium 212 mg

Exchanges:

½ Starch
3 Lean Meat

# Turkey Fajitas

Per Serving:

Calories 343
Calories from Fat 24%
Fat 9.3 g
Saturated Fat 2.1 g
Carbohydrate 31.3 g
Protein 31.8 g
Cholesterol 71 mg
Sodium 498 mg

Exchanges:

2   Starch
3   Lean Meat
1   Vegetable

½   pound turkey breast cutlets
2   tablespoons low-sodium soy
    sauce
1   tablespoon fresh lime juice
1   tablespoon water
2   teaspoons minced garlic
1   teaspoon olive oil
½   teaspoon cracked pepper
¼   teaspoon ground cumin
2   tablespoons chopped avocado
1   tablespoon commercial
    tomatillo salsa
1   tablespoon low-fat sour
    cream

1   teaspoon minced onion
¾   teaspoon minced fresh
    cilantro
½   teaspoon minced jalapeño
    pepper
    Olive oil-flavored vegetable
    cooking spray
1   cup thinly sliced sweet red
    pepper
½   cup thinly sliced onion
2   (8-inch) flour tortillas

Cut turkey into strips; place in a small shallow dish. Combine soy sauce and next 6 ingredients; pour over turkey. Cover and marinate in refrigerator 2 hours.

Place avocado in a small bowl and mash; stir in salsa and next 4 ingredients. Set aside.

Remove turkey from marinade, discarding marinade. Coat a nonstick skillet with cooking spray; place over medium-high heat until hot. Add turkey; sauté 2 minutes. Add red pepper and onion; sauté 6 minutes or until turkey is done and vegetables are tender. Spoon mixture evenly down centers of tortillas. Roll up tortillas, folding in sides. Serve with avocado sauce. Yield: 2 servings.

To round out a meal of Turkey Fajitas, serve Mexican Corn Salad (page 64) and Watermelon Sorbet (page 171).

# Grilled Turkey Breast with Roasted Red Pepper

½ pound turkey breast cutlets
3 tablespoons unsweetened orange juice
1 teaspoon minced garlic
¼ teaspoon pepper
⅛ teaspoon dried thyme
1 medium-size sweet red pepper
Vegetable cooking spray
1 tablespoon chopped fresh cilantro
1 tablespoon sliced ripe olives
1 teaspoon lime juice
½ teaspoon vegetable oil
⅛ teaspoon salt
1½ tablespoons crumbled goat cheese

Place turkey in a heavy-duty, zip-top plastic bag. Combine orange juice, garlic, pepper, and thyme; pour over turkey. Seal bag, and shake until turkey is well coated. Marinate in refrigerator 30 minutes, turning bag once.

Cut pepper in half lengthwise; remove and discard seeds and membrane. Flatten pepper with palm of hand. Coat grill rack with cooking spray; place on grill over medium-hot coals (350° to 400°). Place pepper, skin side down, on rack; grill, covered, 15 to 20 minutes or until charred. Place pepper in ice water until cool. Remove from water; peel and discard skin. Slice pepper into thin strips.

Combine pepper strips, cilantro, and next 4 ingredients in a small bowl, stirring well. Set aside.

Remove turkey from marinade; discard marinade. Place turkey on grill rack; grill, covered, 1 minute on each side or until turkey is tender. Transfer turkey to a serving plate. Spoon red pepper mixture evenly over turkey. Sprinkle with cheese. Yield: 2 servings.

Creamy Herbed Pasta (page 141) and Whole Wheat Casserole Bread (page 52) complement the robust flavors of the roasted pepper and goat cheese that top the turkey.

**Per Serving:**

Calories 210
Calories from Fat 33%
Fat 7.6 g
Saturated Fat 3.0 g
Carbohydrate 7.3 g
Protein 27.4 g
Cholesterol 67 mg
Sodium 379 mg

**Exchanges:**

3½ Lean Meat
1 Vegetable

# Italian Turkey-Stuffed Zucchini

Per Serving:

Calories 254
Calories from Fat 23%
Fat 6.6 g
Saturated Fat 2.2 g
Carbohydrate 26.9 g
Protein 24.0 g
Cholesterol 49 mg
Sodium 488 mg

Exchanges:

2    Starch
2½   Lean Meat

2    medium zucchini
     Olive oil-flavored vegetable
       cooking spray
¼    cup chopped onion
½    teaspoon minced garlic
¼    pound freshly ground raw
       turkey
1    ounce lean cooked ham,
       chopped
¼    cup fine, dry breadcrumbs
¼    teaspoon dried basil
⅛    teaspoon pepper
⅛    teaspoon dried crushed red
       pepper
2    tablespoons grated Asiago
       cheese, divided
1    cup commercial low-sodium
       spaghetti sauce

Cut zucchini in half lengthwise, leaving stems intact. Carefully remove pulp, leaving ¼-inch-thick shells. Dice pulp, and set aside; reserve shells.

Coat a nonstick skillet with cooking spray; place over medium-high heat until hot. Add zucchini pulp, onion, and garlic; sauté 5 minutes. Transfer zucchini mixture to a medium bowl, and set aside.

Combine turkey and ham in skillet; cook over medium heat until turkey is browned, stirring until it crumbles. Combine turkey mixture, zucchini mixture, breadcrumbs, basil, peppers, and 1 teaspoon cheese, stirring well. Spoon turkey mixture evenly into reserved zucchini shells. Spoon spaghetti sauce into bottom of an 8-inch square baking dish; place stuffed zucchini shells over sauce. Sprinkle remaining cheese evenly over zucchini shells. Cover and bake at 350° for 30 minutes. Uncover and bake an additional 20 minutes. Yield: 2 servings.

# Cod en Papillote

Per Serving:

Calories 122
Calories from Fat 8%
Fat 1.1 g
Saturated Fat 0.2 g
Carbohydrate 6.2 g
Protein 21.8 g
Cholesterol 49 mg
Sodium 363 mg

Exchanges:

3    Lean Meat
1    Vegetable

     Vegetable cooking spray
¼    cup chopped green onions
2    teaspoons minced garlic
2    tablespoons dry white wine
2    (4-ounce) cod fillets
¾    cup sliced crimini mushrooms
½    cup chopped plum tomatoes
2    teaspoons chopped fresh
       oregano
2    teaspoons chopped fresh
       basil
¼    teaspoon salt
¼    teaspoon pepper
¼    teaspoon chopped serrano
       chili pepper
2    bay leaves

Coat a medium nonstick skillet with cooking spray; place over medium-high heat until hot. Add green onions and garlic; sauté until tender. Remove from heat; stir in wine.

Cut 2 (12-inch) squares of parchment paper; fold each square in half, and trim each into a heart shape. Place parchment hearts on a baking sheet, and open out flat. Coat open side of parchment paper with vegetable cooking spray.

Place 1 fillet on half of each parchment heart near the crease. Spoon mushrooms evenly over fillets; top evenly with tomato. Combine oregano and next 4 ingredients, and sprinkle evenly over fillets; top each fillet with 1 bay leaf. Spoon onion mixture evenly over fillets.

Fold paper edges over to seal securely. Starting with rounded edges of hearts, pleat and crimp edges of parchment to make an airtight seal. Bake at 425° for 15 minutes or until packets are puffed and lightly browned.

To serve, place packets on serving plates; cut an opening in the top of each packet, and fold paper back. Remove and discard bay leaves. Yield: 2 servings.

# CRABMEAT-STUFFED FLOUNDER

Butter-flavored vegetable
  cooking spray
1 teaspoon reduced-calorie
  margarine
2 tablespoons chopped fresh
  mushrooms
1 tablespoon chopped green
  onions
1 tablespoon Neufchâtel cheese
½ teaspoon minced fresh
  marjoram
⅛ teaspoon pepper

2 ounces fresh lump crabmeat,
  drained
2 tablespoons soft breadcrumbs
1 teaspoon lemon juice
2 (3-ounce) flounder fillets
  (¼ inch thick)
2 tablespoons (½ ounce)
  shredded reduced-fat Swiss
  cheese
Lemon wedges (optional)
Fresh marjoram sprigs
  (optional)

Coat a small nonstick skillet with cooking spray; add margarine. Place over medium-high heat until margarine melts. Add mushrooms and green onions; sauté 2 minutes. Add cheese, minced marjoram, and pepper; cook, stirring constantly, until cheese melts. Remove from heat; add crabmeat, breadcrumbs, and lemon juice, and stir well.

Spoon crabmeat mixture evenly onto fillets; roll up each fillet, jellyroll fashion, beginning at narrow end. Secure with wooden picks. Place rolls, seam side down, in a small baking dish coated with cooking spray. Bake, uncovered, at 350° for 10 minutes. Sprinkle Swiss cheese over rolls; bake an additional 10 minutes or until fish flakes easily when tested with a fork. Remove wooden picks, and, if desired, garnish with lemon wedges and marjoram sprigs. Yield: 2 servings.

**Per Serving:**

Calories 192
Calories from Fat 33%
Fat 7.1 g
Saturated Fat 2.9 g
Carbohydrate 3.2 g
Protein 27.8 g
Cholesterol 83 mg
Sodium 241 mg

**Exchanges:**

4 Lean Meat

Oriental Grilled Salmon

# ORIENTAL GRILLED SALMON

**Per Serving:**

Calories 243
Calories from Fat 37%
Fat 10.0 g
Saturated Fat 1.7 g
Carbohydrate 11.9 g
Protein 24.5 g
Cholesterol 77 mg
Sodium 449 mg

**Exchanges:**

1  Starch
3  Lean Meat

1½  tablespoons brown sugar
 3  tablespoons water
 1  tablespoon low-sodium soy
    sauce
 2  teaspoons peeled, minced
    gingerroot
 2  teaspoons minced green
    onions
 2  teaspoons lemon juice
½  teaspoon minced garlic
    Dash of dried crushed red
    pepper

 2  (4-ounce) salmon steaks
    (½ inch thick)
    Vegetable cooking spray
 2  tablespoons nonfat
    mayonnaise
 1  tablespoon finely chopped
    cilantro
½  teaspoon peeled, grated
    gingerroot
¼  teaspoon crushed garlic
    Fresh cilantro (optional)

Combine first 8 ingredients in a large heavy-duty, zip-top plastic bag; add salmon steaks. Seal bag, and marinate steaks in refrigerator 2 hours, turning bag occasionally. Remove salmon steaks from marinade, reserving marinade.

Coat grill rack with cooking spray; place on grill over medium-hot coals (350° to 400°). Place steaks on rack; grill, uncovered, 5 to 6 minutes on each side or until fish flakes easily when tested with a fork, basting frequently with reserved marinade.

Combine mayonnaise and next 3 ingredients, stirring well. Top each salmon steak with 1 tablespoon mayonnaise mixture. Garnish with fresh cilantro, if desired. Yield: 2 servings.

# SOLE WITH WINE SAUCE

2   (4-ounce) sole fillets
    Vegetable cooking spray
⅛   teaspoon salt
⅛   teaspoon ground white
    pepper
½   cup dry white wine
1   teaspoon lemon juice
1   teaspoon reduced-calorie
    margarine
2   teaspoons minced shallots

¼   teaspoon minced garlic
1½  cups sliced fresh mushrooms
⅓   cup skim milk, divided
1   tablespoon all-purpose flour
2   tablespoons (½ ounce)
    shredded reduced-fat Swiss
    cheese
1   tablespoon freshly grated
    Parmesan cheese

Arrange fillets in an 11- x 7- x 1½-inch baking dish coated with cooking spray. Sprinkle with salt and pepper. Pour wine and lemon juice over fillets. Cover and bake at 400° for 10 minutes. Drain fillets, reserving liquid.

Melt margarine in a nonstick skillet over medium-high heat. Add shallots and garlic; sauté until tender. Add mushrooms; sauté until liquid evaporates.

Combine 2 tablespoons milk and flour, stirring with a wire whisk until smooth. Place reserved liquid in a small saucepan over medium-high heat; cook until reduced by half. Add remaining milk to reduced liquid, stirring constantly. Add flour mixture to milk mixture, and bring to a boil; cook, stirring constantly, 1 minute or until wine sauce is thickened and bubbly.

Spoon mushroom mixture over fillets; top with wine sauce, and sprinkle with cheeses. Bake, uncovered, at 375° for 10 minutes. Broil 5½ inches from heat (with electric oven door partially opened) 2 minutes or until lightly browned. Serve immediately. Yield: 2 servings.

**Per Serving:**

Calories 200
Calories from Fat 24%
Fat 5.3 g
Saturated Fat 1.8 g
Carbohydrate 9.4 g
Protein 28.2 g
Cholesterol 68 mg
Sodium 354 mg

**Exchanges:**

4   Lean Meat
1   Vegetable

# SWORDFISH IN BASIL SAUCE

2   teaspoons lime juice
¼   teaspoon prepared mustard
¼   teaspoon olive oil
    Dash of ground red pepper
2   (4-ounce) swordfish fillets
    Vegetable cooking spray
2   tablespoons Neufchâtel
    cheese, softened

1½  tablespoons canned low-
    sodium chicken broth,
    undiluted
1   teaspoon chopped fresh basil
⅛   teaspoon minced garlic
    Fresh basil leaves (optional)

Combine first 4 ingredients; add fillets, turning to coat both sides with marinade. Cover and marinate in refrigerator 30 minutes, turning once.

Remove fillets from marinade; discard marinade. Place fillets in a 7- x 5- x 1½-inch baking dish coated with cooking spray. Bake, uncovered, at 350° for 20 to 25 minutes or until fish flakes easily when tested with a fork. Transfer fillets to a serving plate, and keep warm.

Coat a saucepan with cooking spray; add cheese and next 3 ingredients. Cook over medium heat until thoroughly heated, stirring frequently. Spoon over fillets. Garnish with basil leaves, if desired. Yield: 2 servings.

**Per Serving:**

Calories 183
Calories from Fat 43%
Fat 8.7 g
Saturated Fat 3.5 g
Carbohydrate 0.7 g
Protein 24.0 g
Cholesterol 55 mg
Sodium 164 mg

**Exchanges:**

3   Lean Meat

# SWORDFISH KABOBS WITH RED PEPPER PESTO

2 tablespoons dry white wine
2½ teaspoons minced garlic, divided
1 teaspoon dried oregano
1 (8-ounce) swordfish steak
1 large sweet red pepper
2 tablespoons chopped fresh basil
1 teaspoon balsamic vinegar
½ teaspoon olive oil
⅛ teaspoon salt
Vegetable cooking spray

Combine wine, 2 teaspoons garlic, and oregano in a small bowl, stirring well. Cut swordfish steak into 1¼-inch cubes; add to wine mixture. Cover and marinate in refrigerator 1 hour.

Cut pepper in half lengthwise; remove and discard seeds and membrane. Place pepper, skin side up, on a baking sheet; flatten with palm of hand. Broil 5½ inches from heat (with electric oven door partially opened) 15 to 20 minutes or until charred. Place pepper in ice water until cool. Remove from water; peel and discard skin.

Position knife blade in food processor bowl; add roasted red pepper, remaining ½ teaspoon garlic, basil, and next 3 ingredients. Process until smooth. Transfer mixture to a small saucepan. Cook over medium heat until thoroughly heated. Remove from heat; set aside, and keep warm.

Remove swordfish from marinade, reserving marinade. Thread fish onto 2 (10-inch) skewers. Coat grill rack with cooking spray; place on grill over medium-hot coals (350° to 400°). Place kabobs on rack; grill, uncovered, 4 to 5 minutes on each side or until fish flakes easily when tested with a fork, basting frequently with marinade. Serve kabobs with red pepper mixture. Yield: 2 servings.

**Vary your usual grill menu by serving these seafood kabobs along with Italian Rice Salad (page 70) and grilled zucchini.**

# VEGETABLE-TOPPED TILAPIA

Butter-flavored vegetable
  cooking spray
¼ cup julienne-sliced carrot
¼ cup julienne-sliced zucchini
⅛ teaspoon minced garlic
¼ cup julienne-sliced leeks
1 tablespoon canned low-
  sodium chicken broth,
  undiluted

2 teaspoons chopped fresh
  parsley
2 teaspoons lemon juice
⅛ teaspoon salt
⅛ teaspoon ground white
  pepper
1 teaspoon reduced-calorie
  margarine
½ pound tilapia fillets

Per Serving:

Calories 143
Calories from Fat 30%
Fat 4.8 g
Saturated Fat 0.8 g
Carbohydrate 3.5 g
Protein 21.6 g
Cholesterol 80 mg
Sodium 234 mg

Exchanges:

3 Lean Meat

Coat a small nonstick skillet with cooking spray. Place over medium-high heat until hot. Add carrot, zucchini, and garlic; sauté 2 minutes. Add leeks, and sauté 1 minute or until vegetables are crisp-tender. Add chicken broth and next 4 ingredients; cook 30 seconds or until liquid is absorbed. Remove vegetable mixture from skillet, and set aside. Wipe skillet dry with a paper towel.

Coat skillet with cooking spray; add margarine. Place over medium-high heat until margarine melts. Add fillets, and cook 2 minutes on each side or until fish flakes easily when tested with a fork. Transfer fillets to 2 serving plates. Spoon vegetable mixture evenly over each serving. Yield: 2 servings.

For a colorful menu, present Romaine and Strawberry Salad (page 61), Vegetable-Topped Tilapia, Saffron Rice (page 144), and commercial whole wheat rolls.

# BROILED RAINBOW TROUT

Per Serving:

Calories 115
Calories from Fat 29%
Fat 3.7 g
Saturated Fat 0.6 g
Carbohydrate 0.8 g
Protein 18.6 g
Cholesterol 51 mg
Sodium 29 mg

Exchanges:

2½ Lean Meat

2   (10-ounce) whole rainbow
      trout, dressed
½   cup canned low-sodium
      chicken broth, undiluted
2   teaspoons minced garlic
2   teaspoons dried basil
2   teaspoons dried oregano
2   teaspoons balsamic vinegar
½   teaspoon sesame oil
      Vegetable cooking spray
6   thin slices lemon
      Lemon wedges (optional)
      Fresh parsley sprigs (optional)

Rinse trout thoroughly with cold water. Pat dry with paper towels. Place trout in a large heavy-duty, zip-top plastic bag. Combine chicken broth and next 5 ingredients; pour over fish. Seal bag, and marinate in refrigerator 3 hours, turning bag occasionally.

Remove fish from marinade, and discard marinade. Place fish on rack of a broiler pan coated with cooking spray. Place 3 lemon slices in each fish cavity. Broil 5½ inches from heat (with electric oven door partially opened) 4 minutes on each side or until fish flakes easily when tested with a fork. If desired, garnish with lemon wedges and parsley sprigs. Yield: 2 servings.

Team Broiled Rainbow Trout with Asparagus Salad
(page 64) and steamed new potatoes.

# PEPPERCORN TUNA

Per Serving:

Calories 179
Calories from Fat 34%
Fat 6.8 g
Saturated Fat 1.6 g
Carbohydrate 1.4 g
Protein 26.7 g
Cholesterol 43 mg
Sodium 338 mg

Exchanges:

3½ Lean Meat

2   (4-ounce) tuna steaks
      (¾ inch thick)
½   teaspoon olive oil
¼   teaspoon salt
1   teaspoon whole black
      peppercorns, crushed
½   teaspoon whole pink
      peppercorns, crushed
½   teaspoon whole green
      peppercorns, crushed
      Lemon wedges (optional)
      Fresh sage sprigs (optional)

Brush both sides of each tuna steak evenly with oil; sprinkle with salt. Combine crushed peppercorns; press into both sides of each steak.

Place a medium cast-iron skillet over high heat until almost smoking. Add steaks; cook 4 to 5 minutes on each side or until fish flakes easily when tested with a fork. If desired, garnish with lemon wedges and sage sprigs. Yield: 2 servings.

Serve Peppercorn Tuna with a fresh spinach salad, Golden Raisin Couscous (page 137), and Gingered Pear Pie (page 176).

# ANGEL HAIR PASTA WITH FRESH CLAMS

1 dozen littleneck clams
2 teaspoons cornmeal
  Olive oil-flavored vegetable cooking spray
1½ teaspoons minced garlic
2 cups peeled, seeded, and chopped tomato
¼ cup clam juice
¼ cup dry white wine
⅛ teaspoon crushed red pepper
4 ounces capellini (angel hair pasta), uncooked
1½ teaspoons chopped flat-leaf parsley

Scrub clams thoroughly, discarding any that are cracked or open. Place remaining clams in a large bowl; cover with cold water, and sprinkle with cornmeal. Let stand 30 minutes. Drain and rinse clams, discarding cornmeal. Set clams aside.

Coat a medium nonstick skillet with cooking spray. Place over medium-high heat until hot. Add garlic, and sauté 30 seconds. Add tomato and next 3 ingredients. Bring to a boil; reduce heat, and simmer, uncovered, 15 minutes, stirring occasionally.

Place clams on top of tomato mixture. Cover and cook 8 to 10 minutes or until clams open. Remove and discard any unopened clams.

Cook pasta according to package directions, omitting salt and fat. Drain. Remove clams from tomato mixture; set aside. Toss pasta with tomato mixture, and transfer to serving plates. Arrange clams evenly over pasta. Sprinkle with parsley. Yield: 2 servings.

**Per Serving:**

Calories 282
Calories from Fat 7%
Fat 2.2 g
Saturated Fat 0.3 g
Carbohydrate 53.4 g
Protein 12.9 g
Cholesterol 9 mg
Sodium 106 mg

**Exchanges:**

3 Starch
½ Lean Meat
1 Vegetable

Angel Hair Pasta with Fresh Clams

# CRABMEAT CRÊPES

**Per Serving:**

Calories 254
Calories from Fat 18%
Fat 5.2 g
Saturated Fat 1.3 g
Carbohydrate 29.0 g
Protein 22.8 g
Cholesterol 62 mg
Sodium 443 mg

**Exchanges:**

2  Starch
2  Lean Meat

| | |
|---|---|
| 12 | very thin asparagus spears |
| 1 | tablespoon plus 1½ teaspoons all-purpose flour |
| ½ | cup 1% low-fat milk, divided |
| 2 | tablespoons instant nonfat dry milk powder |
| 1½ | teaspoons reduced-calorie margarine |
| ¼ | pound fresh lump crabmeat, drained |
| 1 | tablespoon chopped green onions |
| 2½ | teaspoons chopped fresh thyme |
| 1½ | teaspoons chopped fresh parsley |
| 2 | teaspoons dry sherry |
| ½ | teaspoon lemon juice |
| ⅛ | teaspoon salt |
| ⅛ | teaspoon ground red pepper |
| 4 | Crêpes |

Snap off tough ends of asparagus. Remove scales from stalks with a knife or vegetable peeler, if desired. Arrange asparagus in a vegetable steamer over boiling water. Cover and steam 4 to 5 minutes or until crisp-tender.

Combine flour and 1 tablespoon milk, stirring until smooth. Combine flour mixture, remaining ¼ cup plus 3 tablespoons milk, milk powder, and margarine in a small saucepan, stirring well. Cook over medium heat, stirring constantly, until mixture is thickened and bubbly. Remove from heat; stir in crabmeat and next 7 ingredients. Reserve ¼ cup crabmeat mixture.

Arrange 3 asparagus spears in center of each Crêpe. Spoon remaining crabmeat mixture evenly over asparagus. Roll up Crêpes, and place, seam side down, in an 11- x 7- x 1½-inch baking dish. Top with reserved crabmeat mixture. Cover and bake at 350° for 15 minutes. Yield: 2 servings.

## Crêpes

**Per Crêpe:**

Calories 45
Calories from Fat 14%
Fat 0.7 g
Saturated Fat 0.2 g
Carbohydrate 7.1 g
Protein 2.2 g
Cholesterol 1 mg
Sodium 22 mg

**Exchanges:**

½  Starch

| | |
|---|---|
| ¼ | cup all-purpose flour |
| ⅓ | cup 1% low-fat milk |
| 2 | tablespoons frozen egg substitute, thawed |
| ¼ | teaspoon vegetable oil |
| | Vegetable cooking spray |

Combine first 4 ingredients in a small bowl, stirring with a wire whisk just until smooth. Refrigerate batter at least 1 hour.

Coat a 6-inch crêpe pan or nonstick skillet with cooking spray; place over medium heat until hot. Pour 2 tablespoons batter into pan; quickly tilt pan in all directions so batter covers pan in a thin film. Cook 1 minute or until crêpe can be shaken loose from pan. Flip crêpe, and cook about 30 seconds.

Place crêpe on a towel to cool. Repeat until all batter is used. Stack crêpes between layers of wax paper to prevent sticking. Yield: 4 (6-inch) crêpes.

Invite a friend for brunch and serve Crabmeat Crêpes, Fruit Salad in Orange Cups (page 57), and Herb-Sour Cream Biscuits (page 37).

# Sautéed Soft-Shell Crabs

| | |
|---|---|
| 4 soft-shell crabs, cleaned | Vegetable cooking spray |
| 2 tablespoons all-purpose flour | 1 teaspoon vegetable oil |
| 2 tablespoons yellow cornmeal | 2 tablespoons lemon juice |
| ½ teaspoon ground red pepper | 2 teaspoons chopped fresh |
| ¼ cup skim milk | parsley |

Rinse crabs thoroughly with cold water. Pat dry with paper towels.

Combine flour, cornmeal, and pepper in a shallow dish. Dip crabs in milk, and dredge in flour mixture. Coat a nonstick skillet with cooking spray; add oil. Place over medium-high heat until hot. Add crabs; cook 2 to 3 minutes on each side or until browned. Transfer to a serving plate. Sprinkle evenly with lemon juice and parsley. Yield: 2 servings.

**Per Serving:**

Calories 196
Calories from Fat 19%
Fat 4.2 g
Saturated Fat 0.7 g
Carbohydrate 14.6 g
Protein 23.6 g
Cholesterol 94 mg
Sodium 357 mg

**Exchanges:**

1 Starch
3 Lean Meat

# Individual Shrimp Casseroles

| | |
|---|---|
| 5 ounces orzo, uncooked | 1 tablespoon dry white wine |
| ½ pound unpeeled medium-size fresh shrimp | ½ cup shredded fresh basil |
| Olive oil-flavored vegetable cooking spray | 1½ teaspoons chopped fresh oregano |
| ¼ teaspoon olive oil | Dash of freshly ground pepper |
| 2 teaspoons minced garlic | ¼ cup crumbled feta cheese |
| ¾ cup peeled, seeded, and chopped tomato | |

Cook orzo according to package directions, omitting salt and fat; drain. Set aside, and keep warm.

Peel and devein shrimp; set aside.

Coat a small nonstick skillet with cooking spray; add oil. Place over medium-high heat until hot. Add garlic, and sauté 30 seconds. Add tomato, and sauté 2 minutes. Reduce heat to medium. Add shrimp and wine; sauté 2 minutes. Add basil, oregano, and pepper; sauté 2 minutes or until shrimp turns pink.

Combine shrimp mixture and orzo, stirring well. Spoon mixture evenly into 2 (2-cup) casseroles coated with cooking spray. Sprinkle evenly with feta cheese. Bake, uncovered, at 500° for 5 minutes or until cheese melts. Yield: 2 servings.

**Per Serving:**

Calories 394
Calories from Fat 15%
Fat 6.4 g
Saturated Fat 2.6 g
Carbohydrate 59.5 g
Protein 23.7 g
Cholesterol 99 mg
Sodium 256 mg

**Exchanges:**

4 Starch
1½ Lean Meat

# GRILLED SHRIMP AND SCALLOPS

¼ pound unpeeled large fresh shrimp
¼ pound sea scallops
1 tablespoon minced shallots
2 tablespoons dry white wine
1 tablespoon lemon juice
2 teaspoons chopped fresh basil
2 teaspoons chopped fresh oregano
1 teaspoon minced garlic
2 teaspoons white wine Worcestershire sauce
1 teaspoon olive oil
⅛ teaspoon pepper
Vegetable cooking spray
2 teaspoons chopped fresh parsley
Lemon wedges (optional)

Peel and devein shrimp. Place shrimp and scallops in a small heavy-duty, zip-top plastic bag. Combine shallots and next 8 ingredients; pour over shrimp and scallops. Seal bag, and shake until shrimp and scallops are well coated. Marinate in refrigerator 1 hour, turning bag occasionally.

Remove shrimp and scallops from marinade, reserving marinade. Thread shrimp and scallops onto 2 (12-inch) skewers. Coat grill rack with cooking spray; place on grill over medium-hot coals (350° to 400°). Place kabobs on rack; grill, uncovered, 3 minutes on each side or until scallops are opaque, basting frequently with marinade. Sprinkle with parsley; garnish with lemon wedges, if desired. Serve immediately. Yield: 2 servings.

Enjoy a dinner on the patio with Grilled Shrimp and Scallops, Italian Pasta Salad (page 68), sliced fresh tomatoes, and commercial hard rolls.

# LOBSTER-ARTICHOKE LASAGNA

1 (8-ounce) fresh or frozen
   lobster tail, thawed
½ cup 1% low-fat cottage
   cheese
1 tablespoon chopped fresh
   parsley
¼ teaspoon dried basil
¼ teaspoon minced garlic
¼ teaspoon pepper
½ cup coarsely chopped
   canned artichoke hearts,
   drained

1 teaspoon reduced-calorie
   margarine
1 tablespoon all-purpose flour
⅔ cup 1% low-fat milk
1 tablespoon dry white wine
3 lasagna noodles, uncooked
   Vegetable cooking spray
3 tablespoons shredded part-
   skim mozzarella cheese,
   divided
2 tablespoons freshly grated
   Romano cheese

Cook lobster tail in boiling water 6 to 8 minutes or until done; drain. Rinse with cold water. Split and clean tail. Coarsely chop lobster meat; set aside.

Combine cottage cheese and next 4 ingredients in a small bowl, stirring well. Stir in chopped lobster and artichoke hearts; set aside.

Melt margarine in a small heavy saucepan over medium heat; add flour. Cook, stirring constantly with a wire whisk, 1 minute. Gradually add milk, stirring constantly. Cook, stirring constantly, 5 minutes or until white sauce is thickened and bubbly. Stir in wine. Remove from heat, and keep warm.

Cook lasagna noodles according to package directions, omitting salt and fat; drain. Cut each noodle in half crosswise.

Spoon one-third of white sauce onto bottom of a 7- x 5¼- x 1½-inch baking dish coated with cooking spray. Place 2 noodle halves lengthwise in a single layer over white sauce, and top with half of lobster mixture and 1½ tablespoons mozzarella cheese. Repeat procedure with half of remaining white sauce, 2 noodle halves, remaining lobster mixture, and remaining mozzarella cheese. Top with remaining 2 noodle halves and remaining white sauce. Sprinkle with Romano cheese. Cover and bake at 350° for 15 minutes; uncover and bake an additional 30 to 35 minutes or until lightly browned. Let stand 10 minutes before serving. Yield: 2 servings.

Per Serving:

Calories 391
Calories from Fat 17%
Fat 7.6 g
Saturated Fat 3.5 g
Carbohydrate 46.5 g
Protein 33.0 g
Cholesterol 60 mg
Sodium 672 mg

Exchanges:

3 Starch
3½ Lean Meat
1 Vegetable

# West Coast Breakfast Burritos

Per Serving:

Calories 242
Calories from Fat 30%
Fat 8.0 g
Saturated Fat 2.4 g
Carbohydrate 26.1 g
Protein 15.9 g
Cholesterol 9 mg
Sodium 418 mg

Exchanges:

1   Starch
1½ Medium-Fat Meat
2   Vegetable

½ cup seeded, chopped tomato
1 tablespoon chopped green onions
1 tablespoon cold water
1 teaspoon chopped jalapeño pepper
2 teaspoons lime juice
⅛ teaspoon dried oregano
  Vegetable cooking spray
½ cup frozen egg substitute, thawed
¼ cup diced ripe avocado
¼ cup nonfat sour cream alternative
2 tablespoons canned chopped green chiles, drained
¼ cup (1 ounce) shredded reduced-fat Monterey Jack cheese
2 (10-inch) flour tortillas, heated

Combine first 6 ingredients in a small bowl; set aside.

Coat a small nonstick skillet with cooking spray; place over medium heat until hot. Pour egg substitute into skillet. As mixture begins to cook, gently lift edges of omelet with a spatula, and tilt pan to allow uncooked portion to flow underneath. When set, add avocado, sour cream, chiles, and cheese; stir gently until cheese melts.

Spoon egg substitute mixture evenly down center of each tortilla. Roll up tortillas, folding in sides. Place, seam side down, on a serving plate. Top evenly with tomato mixture. Yield: 2 servings.

# Spinach and Mushroom Omelet

Per Serving:

Calories 145
Calories from Fat 43%
Fat 7.0 g
Saturated Fat 3.1 g
Carbohydrate 6.2 g
Protein 15.0 g
Cholesterol 123 mg
Sodium 440 mg

Exchanges:

2   Lean Meat
1   Vegetable

  Butter-flavored vegetable cooking spray
1 cup sliced fresh mushrooms
1 tablespoon chopped green onions
3 cups loosely packed fresh spinach, coarsely chopped
2 tablespoons light process cream cheese product, softened
½ cup frozen egg substitute, thawed
⅛ teaspoon salt
⅛ teaspoon pepper
1 egg
2 tablespoons (½ ounce) shredded reduced-fat sharp Cheddar cheese
2 teaspoons chopped fresh flat-leaf parsley

Coat a 10-inch nonstick skillet with cooking spray; place over medium-high heat until hot. Add mushrooms and green onions; sauté until tender. Remove from skillet. Set aside, and keep warm.

Add spinach to skillet, and sauté until spinach wilts. Remove from heat; stir in cream cheese. Remove from skillet. Set aside, and keep warm.

Wipe skillet with a paper towel. Combine egg substitute and next 3 ingredients in a small bowl, stirring well.

Coat skillet with cooking spray; place over medium heat until hot. Pour egg substitute mixture into skillet. As mixture begins to cook, gently lift edges of omelet with a spatula, and tilt pan to allow uncooked portion to flow underneath. When set, spoon mushroom mixture, spinach mixture, and Cheddar cheese over half of omelet. Loosen omelet with a spatula, and carefully fold in half. Cook an additional 1 to 2 minutes or until cheese begins to melt. Slide omelet onto a serving plate, and cut in half. Sprinkle with parsley. Yield: 2 servings.

# Gourmet Pizzas

3   tablespoons no-salt-added
    tomato paste
1   teaspoon dried oregano
1   teaspoon chopped fresh
    garlic
¼   teaspoon dried basil
¼   teaspoon dried crushed red
    pepper
2   (4-ounce) Italian cheese-
    flavored pizza crusts (such
    as Boboli)

1½  tablespoons coarsely
    chopped kalamata olives,
    pitted
½   cup canned artichoke hearts,
    drained and cut into
    eighths
2   tablespoons crumbled goat
    cheese

Per Serving:

Calories 387
Calories from Fat 19%
Fat 8.2 g
Saturated Fat 3.2 g
Carbohydrate 60.4 g
Protein 17.1 g
Cholesterol 17 mg
Sodium 761 mg

Exchanges:

4   Starch
1   High-Fat Meat

Combine first 5 ingredients in a small bowl, stirring well.

Spread mixture evenly over pizza crusts, leaving a ½-inch border around sides. Sprinkle evenly with olives; arrange artichoke on top. Bake at 450° for 5 minutes. Sprinkle evenly with cheese; bake an additional 5 minutes or until cheese melts. Yield: 2 servings.

Gourmet Pizzas

# ROASTED VEGETABLE LASAGNA

Per Serving:

Calories 368
Calories from Fat 26%
Fat 10.7 g
Saturated Fat 5.9 g
Carbohydrate 49.4 g
Protein 21.0 g
Cholesterol 32 mg
Sodium 431 mg

Exchanges:

3  Starch
2  Medium-Fat Meat
1  Vegetable

½  medium-size sweet red
   pepper
   Olive oil-flavored vegetable
   cooking spray
½  medium eggplant
1  small zucchini, cut in half
   lengthwise
1  clove garlic
2  tablespoons chopped fresh
   basil
2  teaspoons chopped fresh
   oregano
1  tablespoon plus 1 teaspoon
   red wine vinegar
¼  teaspoon pepper
⅛  teaspoon salt
1  cup peeled, seeded, and
   finely chopped tomato
⅓  cup no-salt-added tomato
   sauce
½  cup part-skim ricotta cheese
2  tablespoons freshly grated
   Parmesan cheese
2  lasagna noodles, uncooked
¼  cup (1 ounce) shredded part-
   skim mozzarella cheese

Cut pepper in half lengthwise; remove and discard seeds and membrane. Place pepper, skin side up, on rack of a broiler pan coated with cooking spray; flatten with palm of hand. Coat pepper with cooking spray. Broil 5½ inches from heat (with electric oven door partially opened) 5 minutes. Coat eggplant and zucchini with cooking spray, and place, skin side up, on rack of broiler pan; add garlic. Broil 12 minutes or until skins of red pepper and eggplant are charred and zucchini and garlic are tender.

Place pepper in ice water until cool. Remove from water; peel and discard skin. Cut pepper into strips. Peel and discard skin from eggplant; cut eggplant into small pieces. Slice zucchini; peel garlic, and mince. Combine roasted vegetables in a medium bowl; set aside.

Combine basil and next 4 ingredients; add half of basil mixture to roasted vegetable mixture. Set aside.

Coat a small nonstick skillet with cooking spray; place over medium heat until hot. Add chopped tomato and remaining half of basil mixture. Cook 10 minutes or until tomato is tender; stir in tomato sauce. Remove from heat, and set aside.

Combine ricotta cheese and Parmesan cheese in a small bowl, stirring well. Set aside.

Cook lasagana noodles according to package directions, omitting salt and fat. Drain; cut each noodle in half crosswise.

Place 2 noodle halves lengthwise in a single layer on bottom of a 7- x 5¼- x 1½-inch baking dish coated with cooking spray; spoon ricotta mixture over noodles. Top with roasted vegetable mixture. Place remaining 2 noodle halves over vegetable mixture; spoon tomato mixture over noodles with a slotted spoon. Cover and bake at 350° for 25 minutes. Uncover and sprinkle with mozzarella cheese; bake an additional 10 minutes or until cheese melts. Let stand 10 minutes before serving. Yield: 2 servings.

**For a hearty meatless meal, serve Roasted Vegetable Lasagna, mixed green salad, and commercial breadsticks.**

# VEGETABLE STRATA

¾ cup chopped fresh broccoli
2 (1-ounce) slices white bread, cubed
  Butter-flavored vegetable cooking spray
½ cup (2 ounces) shredded reduced-fat Jarlsberg cheese
2 tablespoons coarsely shredded carrot
1 tablespoon chopped sweet red pepper
1 tablespoon chopped green onions
¾ cup 1% low-fat milk
½ cup frozen egg substitute, thawed
¼ teaspoon dry mustard
¼ teaspoon hot sauce
¼ teaspoon low-sodium Worcestershire sauce
⅛ teaspoon pepper
  Dash of salt

Arrange broccoli in a vegetable steamer over boiling water. Cover and steam 3 minutes or until crisp-tender. Set aside.

Place bread cubes in a 1-quart casserole coated with cooking spray; sprinkle with cheese. Top with broccoli, carrot, red pepper, and green onions. Combine milk and remaining ingredients in a small bowl, stirring well; pour over broccoli mixture. Cover and chill 8 hours.

Remove from refrigerator, and let stand, covered, at room temperature 30 minutes. Bake, uncovered, at 350° for 40 minutes or until set. Let stand 10 minutes before serving. Yield: 2 servings.

It's breakfast or brunch with fresh fruit salad, Vegetable Strata, and Mushroom Grits (page 137).

**Per Serving:**

Calories 262
Calories from Fat 26%
Fat 7.5 g
Saturated Fat 3.6 g
Carbohydrate 26.0 g
Protein 23.1 g
Cholesterol 22 mg
Sodium 428 mg

**Exchanges:**

1 Starch
2 Medium-Fat Meat
2 Vegetable

Roasted Green Beans (page 122), Rutabaga Puree (page 131),
Wild Rice with Mushrooms and Almonds (page 145)

# ON THE SIDE

Turn your attention to the side of the plate with vegetable, pasta,
and rice recipes that can become major attractions.

# BAKED BABY ARTICHOKES

**Per Serving:**

Calories 50
Calories from Fat 38%
Fat 2.1 g
Saturated Fat 0.6 g
Carbohydrate 6.9 g
Protein 2.3 g
Cholesterol 2 mg
Sodium 77 mg

**Exchanges:**

1 Vegetable

6 baby artichokes (about ½ pound)
Olive oil-flavored vegetable cooking spray
3 teaspoons canned low-sodium chicken broth, undiluted
1 teaspoon minced garlic

½ teaspoon olive oil
¼ teaspoon dried basil
⅛ teaspoon freshly ground pepper
1 tablespoon lemon juice
2 teaspoons freshly grated Parmesan cheese

Wash artichokes by plunging them up and down in cold water. Cut off stem ends, and trim ½ inch from top of each artichoke. Remove and discard any loose bottom leaves. Cook artichokes in boiling water to cover 10 minutes. Drain and cut each artichoke in half lengthwise.

Place artichokes, cut side up, in a 7- x 5¼- x 1½-inch baking dish coated with cooking spray. Combine chicken broth and next 4 ingredients, stirring well. Drizzle broth mixture evenly over artichokes. Cover and bake at 400° for 15 minutes. Uncover and sprinkle with lemon juice and Parmesan cheese. Bake an additional 8 to 10 minutes or until lower leaves pull out easily. Yield: 2 servings.

Baked artichokes are delicious with Honey-Roasted Cornish Hen (page 99) and steamed carrots.

# ASPARAGUS WITH MUSTARD SAUCE

**Per Serving:**

Calories 44
Calories from Fat 33%
Fat 1.6 g
Saturated Fat 0.9 g
Carbohydrate 6.4 g
Protein 2.5 g
Cholesterol 4 mg
Sodium 120 mg

**Exchanges:**

1 Vegetable

½ pound fresh asparagus (about 9 spears)
1½ tablespoons low-fat sour cream
1 tablespoon nonfat mayonnaise

½ teaspoon prepared mustard
½ teaspoon lemon juice
⅛ teaspoon hot sauce
Dash of paprika

Snap off tough ends of asparagus. Remove scales from stalks with a knife or vegetable peeler, if desired. Arrange asparagus in a vegetable steamer over boiling water. Cover and steam 6 to 8 minutes or until crisp-tender. Transfer asparagus to a serving dish. Set aside, and keep warm.

Combine sour cream and next 4 ingredients in a small saucepan. Place over medium heat; cook, stirring constantly, 1 minute or until thoroughly heated. Spoon sauce over asparagus, and sprinkle with paprika. Yield: 2 servings.

For a hearty weeknight meal, serve this saucy asparagus with grilled lamb chops and Garlic-Roasted New Potatoes (page 128).

Green Beans Parmesan

# GREEN BEANS PARMESAN

1 teaspoon reduced-calorie
   margarine
1 large shallot, sliced and
   separated into rings
½ pound fresh green beans

½ cup canned low-sodium
   chicken broth, undiluted
   Dash of salt
2 tablespoons shaved fresh
   Parmesan cheese

Melt margarine in a small nonstick skillet over medium-high heat. Add shallot; cook 20 minutes or until golden, stirring occasionally. Remove from heat, and set aside.

   Wash beans; remove ends. Place beans, chicken broth, and salt in a medium saucepan; bring mixture to a boil. Cover, reduce heat, and simmer 12 to 14 minutes or until beans are tender. Drain beans, and stir in shallot. Transfer to a serving dish, and sprinkle with cheese. Yield: 2 servings.

To shave Parmesan cheese into thin slivers, pull a vegetable peeler across
the top of a wedge of fresh Parmesan.

**Per Serving:**

Calories 67
Calories from Fat 35%
Fat 2.6 g
Saturated Fat 0.9 g
Carbohydrate 8.8 g
Protein 3.9 g
Cholesterol 2 mg
Sodium 171 mg

**Exchanges:**

2 Vegetable
½ Fat

# ROASTED GREEN BEANS

½ pound fresh green beans
1 clove garlic, sliced
  Olive oil-flavored vegetable
  cooking spray
1 teaspoon lemon juice
½ teaspoon olive oil
1 teaspoon salt-free lemon-
  pepper seasoning

Wash beans; remove ends. Place beans in a 13- x 9- x 2-inch pan; add garlic. Coat beans and garlic with cooking spray; toss well. Drizzle lemon juice and olive oil over beans and garlic; sprinkle with lemon-pepper seasoning.

Bake at 450° for 8 minutes or until beans are crisp-tender, stirring once. Yield: 2 servings.

Pair these robust beans with Veal Piccata (page 86).

# BROCCOLI CASSEROLE

1½ cups coarsely chopped fresh
  broccoli
3 tablespoons canned 99% fat-
  free cream of mushroom
  soup, undiluted
2 tablespoons (½ ounce)
  shredded reduced-fat sharp
  Cheddar cheese
2 tablespoons chopped onion
2 tablespoons nonfat
  mayonnaise
½ teaspoon lemon juice
⅛ teaspoon ground thyme
⅛ teaspoon pepper
  Vegetable cooking spray
2 tablespoons crumbled low-
  fat cheese crackers (about
  10 crackers)

Arrange broccoli in a vegetable steamer over boiling water. Cover and steam 5 to 6 minutes or until crisp-tender.

Combine soup and next 6 ingredients, stirring well. Stir in broccoli. Spoon mixture into a 10-ounce custard cup coated with cooking spray. Sprinkle with cracker crumbs. Bake, uncovered, at 350° for 30 minutes. Yield: 2 servings.

For an informal supper in the kitchen, try pan-broiled turkey cutlets, Broccoli Casserole, and Honeyed Fruit Salad (page 57).

## Per Serving:

Calories 52
Calories from Fat 28%
Fat 1.6 g
Saturated Fat 0.2 g
Carbohydrate 9.0 g
Protein 2.2 g
Cholesterol 0 mg
Sodium 7 mg

## Exchanges:

1 Vegetable

## Per Serving:

Calories 85
Calories from Fat 26%
Fat 2.5 g
Saturated Fat 1.1 g
Carbohydrate 11.9 g
Protein 4.9 g
Cholesterol 7 mg
Sodium 389 mg

## Exchanges:

½ Starch
1 Vegetable
½ Fat

# Brussels Sprouts with Cheese Sauce

18  small fresh brussels sprouts
     (about ¾ pound)
¾   cup water
1½  teaspoons reduced-calorie
     margarine
2   teaspoons all-purpose flour

¼   cup skim milk
1   (¾-ounce) slice low-fat
     process Swiss cheese, cut
     into strips
Dash of dry mustard

Wash brussels sprouts thoroughly, and remove discolored leaves. Using a sharp knife, cut off stem ends, and cut a shallow X in bottom of each sprout. Bring water to a boil in a medium saucepan; add brussels sprouts. Cover, reduce heat, and simmer 12 minutes or until brussels sprouts are tender. Drain and keep warm.

Melt margarine in a small heavy saucepan over low heat; add flour, stirring until smooth. Cook, stirring constantly, 1 minute. Gradually add milk; cook over medium heat, stirring constantly, until mixture is thickened and bubbly. Add cheese and mustard, stirring until cheese melts. Spoon sauce over warm brussels sprouts. Yield: 2 servings.

Per Serving:

Calories 102
Calories from Fat 23%
Fat 2.6 g
Saturated Fat 0.7 g
Carbohydrate 14.4 g
Protein 7.9 g
Cholesterol 1 mg
Sodium 203 mg

Exchanges:

1   Starch
½   Lean Meat

# Dilled Carrots

⅓   cup canned low-sodium
     chicken broth, undiluted
¼   teaspoon sugar
⅛   teaspoon salt
3   medium carrots (about ½
     pound), scraped and cut
     into very thin strips

1   teaspoon chopped fresh
     dillweed
½   teaspoon reduced-calorie
     margarine

Combine first 3 ingredients in a small saucepan; bring to a boil. Add carrot; cover and cook over medium heat 8 minutes or until tender. Drain.

Combine carrot, dillweed, and margarine; toss until margarine melts. Yield: 2 servings.

Serve this quick carrot dish with Crabmeat-Stuffed Flounder (page 103).

Per Serving:

Calories 51
Calories from Fat 18%
Fat 1.0 g
Saturated Fat 0.2 g
Carbohydrate 10.0 g
Protein 1.3 g
Cholesterol 0 mg
Sodium 200 mg

Exchanges:

2   Vegetable

# Carrots in Horseradish Sauce

Per Serving:

Calories 135
Calories from Fat 16%
Fat 2.5 g
Saturated Fat 0.3 g
Carbohydrate 22.7 g
Protein 6.7 g
Cholesterol 3 mg
Sodium 273 mg

Exchanges:

1½ Starch
½ Fat

| | |
|---|---|
| 2 cups scraped and sliced carrot | 2 teaspoons prepared horseradish |
| 2¼ teaspoons all-purpose flour | 1½ teaspoons spicy brown mustard |
| ½ cup skim milk, divided | Dash of salt |
| 2 tablespoons instant nonfat dry milk powder | |
| 1½ teaspoons reduced-calorie margarine | |

Arrange carrot in a vegetable steamer over boiling water. Cover and steam 6 to 7 minutes or until crisp-tender. Set aside, and keep warm.

Combine flour and 2 tablepoons skim milk, stirring until smooth. Combine flour mixture, remaining ¼ cup plus 2 tablespoons milk, milk powder, and margarine in a small saucepan, stirring well. Cook over medium heat, stirring constantly, until mixture is thickened and bubbly. Remove from heat; stir in horseradish, mustard, and salt. Combine carrot and horseradish mixture; toss gently to coat. Yield: 2 servings.

*These zesty carrots are a perfect match for slices of lean roast beef and a tossed green salad.*

# Cauliflower with Herbs

Per Serving:

Calories 40
Calories from Fat 45%
Fat 2.0 g
Saturated Fat 0.3 g
Carbohydrate 5.4 g
Protein 2.3 g
Cholesterol 0 mg
Sodium 443 mg

Exchanges:

1 Vegetable

| | |
|---|---|
| 1 tablespoon chopped fresh parsley | 1 teaspoon reduced-calorie margarine, melted |
| 2 teaspoons chopped fresh chives | 1 cup water |
| 1 teaspoon chopped fresh thyme | 1 teaspoon chicken-flavored bouillon granules |
| 1 teaspoon fresh lemon juice | 2 cups cauliflower flowerets |

Combine first 5 ingredients in a small bowl, stirring well. Set aside.

Combine water and bouillon granules in a small saucepan; bring to a boil. Add cauliflower, and cook, uncovered, 4 minutes or until crisp-tender; drain. Combine cauliflower and herb mixture; toss gently. Yield: 2 servings.

*Serve this herbed cauliflower dish with lean flank steak and Baked Tomatoes (page 134).*

# Fresh Corn Sauté

Butter-flavored vegetable
  cooking spray
1 teaspoon margarine
¼ cup chopped onion
¼ cup chopped green pepper

1 cup fresh corn cut from cob
  (about 2 ears)
3 tablespoons water
1½ teaspoons diced pimiento
⅛ teaspoon salt

Coat a small nonstick skillet with cooking spray; add margarine. Place over medium-high heat until margarine melts. Add onion and pepper; sauté 2 minutes or until tender. Add corn and water to vegetables in skillet, stirring well. Cover, reduce heat, and cook 10 minutes, stirring frequently. Uncover and add pimiento and salt. Cook 1 to 2 minutes or until liquid is absorbed. Yield: 2 servings.

Fresh corn is an ideal side dish for Mariachi Chicken (page 97).

Per Serving:

Calories 97
Calories from Fat 30%
Fat 3.2 g
Saturated Fat 0.5 g
Carbohydrate 17.1 g
Protein 2.9 g
Cholesterol 0 mg
Sodium 176 mg

Exchanges:

1 Starch
½ Fat

# Ratatouille

Olive oil-flavored vegetable
  cooking spray
½ teaspoon olive oil
½ cup chopped onion
½ cup green pepper strips
1½ teaspoons minced garlic
1½ cups peeled, cubed eggplant
1 cup peeled, seeded, and
  chopped tomato

½ cup sliced zucchini
1 teaspoon chopped fresh
  oregano
¼ teaspoon salt
¼ teaspoon pepper
2 teaspoons chopped fresh
  parsley

Coat a medium nonstick skillet with cooking spray; add oil. Place over medium heat until hot. Add onion, green pepper, and garlic; sauté 2 minutes. Stir in eggplant and next 5 ingredients. Cover and cook 5 minutes or until tender, stirring twice. Sprinkle with parsley. Yield: 2 servings.

This zesty eggplant dish is delicious paired with Chicken and Broccoli in Phyllo (page 95).

Per Serving:

Calories 79
Calories from Fat 24%
Fat 2.1 g
Saturated Fat 0.3 g
Carbohydrate 14.9 g
Protein 2.8 g
Cholesterol 0 mg
Sodium 308 mg

Exchanges:

1 Starch

# Mushrooms on Toast Points

**Per Serving:**

Calories 91
Calories from Fat 30%
Fat 3.0 g
Saturated Fat 1.3 g
Carbohydrate 13.6 g
Protein 4.2 g
Cholesterol 6 mg
Sodium 225 mg

**Exchanges:**

1   Starch
½   Fat

Butter-flavored vegetable
   cooking spray
8   ounces fresh mushrooms,
   halved
1   tablespoon chopped green
   onions
1   tablespoon chopped fresh
   parsley
2   teaspoons dry white wine
⅛   teaspoon salt
⅛   teaspoon pepper
2   tablespoons low-fat sour
   cream
2   (1-ounce) slices white bread,
   toasted and cut in half
   diagonally

Coat a medium nonstick skillet with cooking spray; place over medium heat until hot. Add mushrooms and green onions; sauté 3 minutes or until tender. Add parsley, wine, salt, and pepper; sauté 1 minute. Remove from heat; stir in sour cream. Spoon mushroom mixture evenly over toast, and serve immediately. Yield: 2 servings.

# Parmesan-Crusted Mushrooms

**Per Serving:**

Calories 81
Calories from Fat 33%
Fat 3.0 g
Saturated Fat 0.7 g
Carbohydrate 11.6 g
Protein 4.2 g
Cholesterol 1 mg
Sodium 361 mg

**Exchanges:**

½   Starch
1   Vegetable
½   Fat

2   tablespoons chopped
   sun-dried tomato
½   cup hot water
4   fresh jumbo mushrooms
   Olive oil-flavored vegetable
   cooking spray
½   teaspoon olive oil
1   small clove garlic, minced
¼   cup soft whole wheat
   breadcrumbs
2   tablespoons chopped fresh
   basil
1   tablespoon canned low-
   sodium chicken broth,
   undiluted
⅛   teaspoon salt
1   tablespoon freshly grated
   Parmesan cheese

Combine tomato and water in a small bowl; cover and let stand 15 minutes. Drain tomato, and set aside.

Clean mushrooms with damp paper towels. Remove mushroom stems; mince stems, and set aside. Coat a medium nonstick skillet with cooking spray; place over medium-high heat until hot. Add mushroom caps, and sauté 5 minutes. Remove from skillet, and drain on paper towels; place caps on rack of a broiler pan coated with cooking spray.

Coat a nonstick skillet with cooking spray; add oil. Place over medium-high heat until hot. Add mushroom stems and garlic; sauté until tender. Remove from heat; stir in tomato, breadcrumbs, and next 3 ingredients. Spoon tomato mixture into mushroom caps; sprinkle with Parmesan cheese. Broil 5½ inches from heat (with electric oven door partially opened) 2 to 3 minutes or until cheese melts. Serve immediately. Yield: 2 servings.

# HERBED PEPPER MEDLEY

1 medium-size sweet red
    pepper
1 medium-size sweet yellow
    pepper
1 medium-size green pepper
    Olive oil-flavored vegetable
    cooking spray

½ cup onion strips
1 tablespoon canned low-
    sodium chicken broth,
    undiluted
½ teaspoon sugar
⅛ teaspoon salt
⅛ teaspoon dried thyme

Cut peppers in half lengthwise through stems. Remove and discard seeds
and membrane. If desired, set 2 pepper halves with stems aside, and reserve
a third half for another use. Remove and discard stems from remaining 3
pepper halves; slice pepper halves into thin strips.

    Coat a medium nonstick skillet with cooking spray; place over medium-
high heat until hot. Add pepper strips and onion; sauté 4 minutes. Add
chicken broth and remaining ingredients; sauté 2 minutes. If desired, spoon
pepper mixture evenly into reserved pepper halves. Yield: 2 servings.

**Per Serving:**

Calories 45
Calories from Fat 16%
Fat 0.8 g
Saturated Fat 0.1 g
Carbohydrate 9.2 g
Protein 1.3 g
Cholesterol 0 mg
Sodium 153 mg

**Exchanges:**

2 Vegetable

Herbed Pepper Medley

# Endive Potato Casserole

Per Serving:

Calories 220
Calories from Fat 30%
Fat 7.4 g
Saturated Fat 0.9 g
Carbohydrate 31.0 g
Protein 9.1 g
Cholesterol 6 mg
Sodium 300 mg

Exchanges:

2    Starch
1½  Fat

1½  tablespoons reduced-calorie
     margarine
1½  tablespoons all-purpose flour
 ¾  cup skim milk
 ¼  teaspoon salt
     Butter-flavored vegetable
     cooking spray
1¼  cups sliced Belgian endive
     (about ⅓ pound)

1    cup peeled, sliced baking
     potato
1½  tablespoons chopped shallot
2    tablespoons (½ ounce)
     shredded reduced-fat Swiss
     cheese, divided

Melt margarine in a small heavy saucepan over medium heat; add flour, and stir until smooth. Cook, stirring constantly with a wire whisk, 1 minute. Gradually add milk, stirring constantly until white sauce is thickened and bubbly. Remove from heat; stir in salt. Set aside.

Coat a 7- x 5¼- x 1½-inch baking dish with cooking spray. Arrange half of endive slices in bottom of dish. Arrange half of potato slices over endive; sprinkle with half of shallot and 1 tablespoon cheese. Top with half of white sauce. Repeat layers, ending with remaining white sauce and remaining 1 tablespoon cheese. Bake, uncovered, at 350° for 45 minutes or until potato is tender. Yield: 2 servings.

Meat and potato fans will enjoy the combination of creamy, rich-tasting Endive Potato Casserole and Fillet of Beef with Peppercorns (page 84).

# Garlic-Roasted New Potatoes

Per Serving:

Calories 134
Calories from Fat 18%
Fat 2.7 g
Saturated Fat 0.4 g
Carbohydrate 24.9 g
Protein 3.4 g
Cholesterol 0 mg
Sodium 157 mg

Exchanges:

1½  Starch
 ½  Fat

6    new potatoes (about
     1 pound), cut in half
     Olive oil-flavored vegetable
     cooking spray
1    teaspoon olive oil
3    bay leaves

2    cloves garlic, peeled and cut
     in half
2    sprigs fresh rosemary
 ¼  teaspoon coarsely ground
     pepper
 ⅛  teaspoon salt

Coat potato halves with cooking spray. Coat a 9-inch cast-iron skillet with cooking spray; add oil. Place over medium heat until hot; add potato, bay leaves, garlic, and rosemary, stirring gently. Sprinkle with pepper and salt.

Bake at 450° for 40 minutes or until browned, stirring twice. Remove and discard bay leaves and rosemary. Yield: 2 servings.

Roast new potatoes with herbs and garlic to serve with
Beef and Vegetable Kabobs (page 82).

# TWICE-BAKED POTATOES

1 medium baking potato
   (about 8 ounces)
3 tablespoons low-fat sour
   cream
⅛ teaspoon garlic powder
⅛ teaspoon salt

⅛ teaspoon pepper
1 tablespoon chopped fresh
   chives
2 tablespoons (½ ounce)
   shredded reduced-fat sharp
   Cheddar cheese

Scrub potato; bake at 425° for 1 hour or until tender. Let potato cool to touch.

Cut potato in half lengthwise; carefully scoop out pulp, leaving ¼-inch-thick shells. Set shells aside. Place pulp in a small bowl; mash until smooth.

Combine mashed potato, sour cream, and next 3 ingredients, beating until smooth. Stir in chives. Spoon potato mixture evenly into potato shells, and sprinkle evenly with cheese. Place potato shells in a small ungreased baking dish. Bake at 425° for 5 minutes or until cheese melts. Yield: 2 servings.

Serve these stuffed potato shells with Swordfish Kabobs with
Red Pepper Pesto (page 106) and fresh green beans.

**Per Serving:**

Calories 154
Calories from Fat 25%
Fat 4.2 g
Saturated Fat 2.5 g
Carbohydrate 24.8 g
Protein 4.9 g
Cholesterol 13 mg
Sodium 214 mg

**Exchanges:**

1½ Starch
1   Fat

# PARMESAN POTATO WEDGES

1 medium baking potato
   (about 8 ounces)
   Butter-flavored vegetable
   cooking spray
2 teaspoons reduced-calorie
   margarine, melted

¼ teaspoon dried oregano
⅛ teaspoon garlic powder
⅛ teaspoon salt
⅛ teaspoon paprika
2 teaspoons grated Parmesan
   cheese

Scrub potato; cut into 6 wedges. Soak potato wedges in ice water for 30 minutes; drain and pat dry with paper towels.

Coat an 8-inch square pan with cooking spray. Arrange potato wedges in one layer in pan; brush with margarine. Combine oregano and next 3 ingredients; sprinkle mixture evenly over potato wedges. Bake at 350° for 30 minutes, turning twice. Remove from oven; sprinkle with cheese, and serve immediately. Yield: 2 servings.

Try these tasty alternatives to French fries with
Open-Faced Steak Sandwiches (page 159).

**Per Serving:**

Calories 121
Calories from Fat 25%
Fat 3.4 g
Saturated Fat 0.7 g
Carbohydrate 20.4 g
Protein 3.4 g
Cholesterol 1 mg
Sodium 217 mg

**Exchanges:**

1   Starch
½   Fat

# SWEET POTATO BAKE

**Per Serving:**

Calories 205
Calories from Fat 22%
Fat 5.0 g
Saturated Fat 1.1 g
Carbohydrate 35.2 g
Protein 5.5 g
Cholesterol 111 mg
Sodium 126 mg

**Exchanges:**

2   Starch
1   Fat

| | |
|---|---|
| 1   **small sweet potato, peeled and cubed** | **Dash of salt** |
| 1½   **tablespoons 1% low-fat milk** | ⅛   **teaspoon ground allspice** |
| 2   **tablespoons brown sugar, divided** | 1   **egg, separated** |
| 1   **tablespoon unsweetened orange juice** | **Butter-flavored vegetable cooking spray** |
| | 2   **teaspoons chopped pecans** |

Cook sweet potato in a medium saucepan in boiling water to cover 10 minutes or until tender. Drain. Beat sweet potato at high speed of an electric mixer until smooth. Add milk, 1 tablespoon brown sugar, orange juice, salt, allspice, and egg yolk; beat at high speed until smooth.

Beat egg white at high speed of an electric mixer until stiff peaks form; fold egg white into sweet potato mixture. Spoon mixture into 2 (6-ounce) ramekins coated with cooking spray. Sprinkle remaining 1 tablespoon brown sugar and pecans evenly over potato mixture. Bake at 400° for 20 to 25 minutes or until thoroughly heated. Yield: 2 servings.

**Sweet Potato Bake**

# RUTABAGA PUREE

½ small rutabaga
½ cup water
1 tablespoon canned low-
    sodium chicken broth,
    undiluted
1 tablespoon low-fat sour
    cream

½ teaspoon reduced-calorie
    margarine
Dash of salt
Dash of pepper

Peel rutabaga; cut into quarters. Bring water to a boil in a small saucepan; add rutabaga. Cover, reduce heat, and simmer 25 to 30 minutes or until tender. Drain.

Position knife blade in food processor bowl. Add rutabaga, chicken broth, and remaining ingredients; process until smooth. Serve immediately. Yield: 2 servings.

*Instead of mashed potatoes, try creamy Rutabaga Puree
with grilled tuna steaks and roasted vegetables.*

**Per Serving:**

Calories 78
Calories from Fat 22%
Fat 1.9 g
Saturated Fat 0.7 g
Carbohydrate 14.3 g
Protein 2.3 g
Cholesterol 3 mg
Sodium 119 mg

**Exchanges:**

1   Starch

# SAUTÉED SPINACH

Olive oil-flavored vegetable
    cooking spray
½ teaspoon olive oil
2 cloves garlic, peeled and cut
    in half

1 pound torn fresh spinach
1 tablespoon fresh lemon juice
⅛ teaspoon salt

Coat a large nonstick skillet with cooking spray; add oil. Place over medium-high heat until hot. Add garlic; sauté 3 to 4 minutes or until garlic starts to brown. Add spinach; sauté 2 to 3 minutes or just until wilted. Remove and discard garlic. Add lemon juice and salt; cook 2 to 3 minutes, stirring occasionally. Yield: 2 servings.

*Update your favorite "down-home" foods by serving Sautéed Spinach,
grilled lean pork chops, and Hush Puppy Muffins (page 41).*

**Per Serving:**

Calories 67
Calories from Fat 30%
Fat 2.2 g
Saturated Fat 0.3 g
Carbohydrate 9.1 g
Protein 6.6 g
Cholesterol 0 mg
Sodium 326 mg

**Exchanges:**

2   Vegetable
1   Fat

# Summer Squash Sauté

Olive oil-flavored vegetable
   cooking spray
½ teaspoon olive oil
1 small yellow squash, sliced
1 small zucchini, sliced
1 clove garlic, minced
2 tablespoons canned
   no-salt-added beef broth,
   undiluted
⅛ teaspoon salt
⅛ teaspoon pepper
2 teaspoons chopped fresh
   parsley

Coat a small nonstick skillet with cooking spray; add oil. Place over medium heat until hot. Add yellow squash and zucchini; sauté 2 minutes. Add garlic; sauté 1 minute. Stir in beef broth, salt, and pepper. Cover and cook 3 minutes or until squash is tender. Sprinkle with parsley. Yield: 2 servings.

**Per Serving:**

Calories 30
Calories from Fat 42%
Fat 1.4 g
Saturated Fat 0.2 g
Carbohydrate 3.9 g
Protein 1.2 g
Cholesterol 0 mg
Sodium 144 mg

**Exchanges:**

1 Vegetable

# Squash Casserole

Vegetable cooking spray
⅓ cup chopped onion
1 cup coarsely grated zucchini
1 cup coarsely grated yellow
   squash
1 tablespoon chopped fresh
   parsley
¼ teaspoon dried oregano
⅛ teaspoon salt
⅛ teaspoon freshly ground
   pepper
¼ cup frozen egg substitute,
   thawed
1 tablespoon 1% low-fat milk
¼ cup (1 ounce) shredded
   reduced-fat sharp Cheddar
   cheese, divided

Coat a small nonstick skillet with cooking spray; place over medium-high heat until hot. Add onion; sauté 2 minutes. Add zucchini and yellow squash; sauté 3 minutes or until squash and onion are tender. Remove from heat; stir in parsley and next 3 ingredients.

  Combine egg substitute and milk in a small bowl, stirring with a wire whisk until smooth. Add milk mixture and 3 tablespoons cheese to squash mixture; stir well. Spoon mixture into a 2-cup casserole coated with cooking spray. Sprinkle squash mixture with remaining 1 tablespoon cheese. Bake, uncovered, at 350° for 40 minutes or until set. Yield: 2 servings.

Make a meal of vegetables with Squash Casserole, Roasted Green Beans (page 122), and Spinach-Stuffed Tomatoes (page 133).

**Per Serving:**

Calories 95
Calories from Fat 32%
Fat 3.4 g
Saturated Fat 1.7 g
Carbohydrate 8.1 g
Protein 9.2 g
Cholesterol 10 mg
Sodium 297 mg

**Exchanges:**

1 Lean Meat
1 Vegetable

# Baked Acorn Squash

1 medium acorn squash (about
   1 pound)
1½ tablespoons brown sugar
⅛ teaspoon ground cinnamon
⅛ teaspoon ground nutmeg
1 tablespoon unsweetened
   orange juice

1 teaspoon nonfat margarine,
   melted
1 tablespoon finely chopped
   pecans, toasted

Cut squash in half crosswise; remove and discard seeds. Place squash halves, cut side down, in an 11- x 7- x 1½-inch baking dish. Add water to depth of ½ inch. Bake, uncovered, at 350° for 40 minutes. Remove from oven, and invert squash halves.

Combine brown sugar and next 4 ingredients in a small bowl, stirring well. Spoon brown sugar mixture evenly into squash halves. Bake, uncovered, an additional 20 minutes, basting occasionally. Sprinkle with pecans. Yield: 2 servings.

*When fall is in the air, serve Baked Acorn Squash with grilled pork tenderloin and steamed brown rice.*

**Per Serving:**

Calories 127
Calories from Fat 24%
Fat 3.4 g
Saturated Fat 0.3 g
Carbohydrate 25.3 g
Protein 1.7 g
Cholesterol 0 mg
Sodium 23 mg

**Exchanges:**

1½ Starch
½ Fat

# Spinach-Stuffed Tomatoes

2 medium tomatoes
   Olive oil-flavored vegetable
   cooking spray
½ teaspoon olive oil
1 tablespoon finely chopped
   shallot
2 cups shredded fresh spinach
½ cup cooked basmati rice
   (cooked without salt or fat)

2 tablespoons (½ ounce)
   shredded reduced-fat Swiss
   cheese, divided
1½ tablespoons nonfat
   mayonnaise
1 teaspoon fresh lemon juice

Slice ¼ inch from stem end of each tomato; discard stem ends. Carefully scoop out pulp, leaving shells intact. Chop pulp; set aside. Invert tomato shells on paper towels to drain.

Coat a medium nonstick skillet with cooking spray; add oil. Place over medium-high heat until hot. Add shallot; sauté 3 minutes. Add reserved tomato pulp and spinach; cook 3 minutes, stirring frequently.

Transfer vegetable mixture to a bowl. Stir in rice, 1 tablespoon cheese, mayonnaise, and lemon juice. Spoon vegetable mixture evenly into tomato shells. Place tomatoes in a small shallow casserole coated with cooking spray. Bake at 325° for 15 minutes; sprinkle with remaining 1 tablespoon cheese. Bake an additional 3 minutes or until cheese melts. Yield: 2 servings.

**Per Serving:**

Calories 129
Calories from Fat 22%
Fat 3.2 g
Saturated Fat 0.9 g
Carbohydrate 21.1 g
Protein 5.2 g
Cholesterol 4 mg
Sodium 186 mg

**Exchanges:**

1 Starch
1 Vegetable
½ Fat

# Tabbouleh-Filled Tomatoes

2   medium tomatoes
½   cup boiling water
¼   cup bulgur (cracked wheat), uncooked
½   cup chopped fresh flat-leaf parsley
¼   cup chopped green onions
1½  tablespoons lemon juice
2   teaspoons chopped fresh mint
1   teaspoon olive oil
⅛   teaspoon salt
    Dash of pepper
2   lemon twists (optional)
2   mint sprigs (optional)

Slice ¼ inch from stem end of each tomato; discard stem ends. Carefully scoop out pulp, leaving shells intact. Discard pulp and seeds. Invert tomato shells on paper towels to drain.

Pour water over bulgur in a small bowl; cover and let stand 30 minutes. Drain thoroughly. Combine bulgur, parsley, and next 6 ingredients, stirring well. Spoon mixture evenly into tomato shells. If desired, garnish with lemon and mint. Yield: 2 servings.

Grilled Lamb Chops Dijon (page 88) and these grain-filled tomatoes make a perfect weeknight meal.

# Baked Tomatoes

2   small tomatoes, cut into ½-inch-thick slices
    Olive oil-flavored vegetable cooking spray
2   tablespoons chopped green onions
1   teaspoon minced garlic
¼   teaspoon sugar
⅛   teaspoon salt
⅛   teaspoon pepper
1   tablespoon freshly grated Romano cheese
1   tablespoon shredded fresh basil
1   teaspoon chopped fresh oregano

Arrange tomato slices in an 11- x 7- x 1½-inch baking dish coated with cooking spray. Sprinkle tomato with green onions and next 4 ingredients. Bake at 350° for 10 minutes. Remove from oven, and sprinkle with cheese, basil, and oregano. Serve warm. Yield: 2 servings.

Treat yourself to brunch or a light lunch of Vegetable Strata (page 117), Baked Tomatoes, and fresh fruit.

# MIXED VEGETABLE GRILL

2 tablespoons white balsamic
   vinegar
2 tablespoons canned
   no-salt-added chicken
   broth, undiluted
1 teaspoon chopped fresh
   oregano
1 teaspoon olive oil
½ teaspoon minced garlic
⅛ teaspoon pepper
1 medium-size sweet red
   pepper, cut into quarters

½ small eggplant (about
   ¼ pound), sliced
1 small yellow squash, cut into
   quarters
1 small zucchini, cut in half
   lengthwise
2 (½-inch-thick) slices purple
   onion
   Vegetable cooking spray
   Fresh oregano (optional)

**Per Serving:**

Calories 111
Calories from Fat 28%
Fat 3.4 g
Saturated Fat 0.4 g
Carbohydrate 19.4 g
Protein 3.7 g
Cholesterol 0 mg
Sodium 19 mg

**Exchanges:**

3 Vegetable
½ Fat

Combine first 6 ingredients in a small bowl, stirring well with a wire whisk. Place sweet red pepper and next 4 ingredients on a baking sheet; brush vegetables with half of vinegar mixture.

Coat grill rack with cooking spray; place on grill over medium-hot coals (350° to 400°). Place vegetables, cut side down, on rack; grill, covered, 5 minutes. Brush with remaining vinegar mixture; turn vegetables, and grill an additional 5 to 6 minutes or until vegetables are tender. Remove vegetables from grill; cut onion slices into quarters. Garnish with oregano, if desired. Yield: 2 servings.

Mixed Vegetable Grill

# CORNBREAD DRESSING

Per Serving:

Calories 276
Calories from Fat 26%
Fat 8.1 g
Saturated Fat 1.0 g
Carbohydrate 40.7 g
Protein 9.0 g
Cholesterol 2 mg
Sodium 513 mg

Exchanges:

3   Starch
1½ Fat

½ cup yellow cornmeal
½ teaspoon baking powder
⅛ teaspoon baking soda
⅛ teaspoon salt
¼ cup plus 3 tablespoons
    nonfat buttermilk
1 tablespoon frozen egg
    substitute, thawed
1½ teaspoons vegetable oil
    Vegetable cooking spray
2½ teaspoons reduced-calorie
    margarine

¼ cup chopped celery
¼ cup chopped onion
1 (1-ounce) slice white bread,
    torn into small pieces
1 cup canned no-salt-added
    chicken broth, undiluted
2 tablespoons frozen egg
    substitute, thawed
½ teaspoon poultry seasoning
¼ teaspoon rubbed sage
⅛ teaspoon pepper
    Dash of salt

Combine first 4 ingredients in a small bowl; make a well in center of mixture. Combine buttermilk, 1 tablespoon egg substitute, and oil; add to cornmeal mixture, stirring just until dry ingredients are moistened.

Pour batter into a 6-inch cast-iron skillet coated with cooking spray. Bake at 450° for 20 minutes or until golden. Remove from skillet, and cool completely.

Coat a small nonstick skillet with cooking spray; add margarine. Place over medium-high heat until margarine melts. Add celery and onion; sauté 4 to 5 minutes or until tender.

Crumble cornbread into a bowl. Add vegetable mixture, bread, and remaining ingredients; stir well. Spoon mixture into a 7- x 5- x 1½-inch baking dish coated with cooking spray. Bake at 325° for 40 to 45 minutes or until golden. Yield: 2 servings.

If you don't have a 6-inch cast-iron skillet, bake the cornbread
in a 6-inch square pan at 450° for 15 minutes.

# GOLDEN RAISIN COUSCOUS

½  cup canned low-sodium
    chicken broth, undiluted
⅛  teaspoon salt
¼  cup couscous, uncooked
    Vegetable cooking spray
½  teaspoon peanut oil
½  cup sliced fresh mushrooms
2  tablespoons thinly sliced
    celery

1  tablespoon thinly sliced
    green onions
1½ tablespoons golden raisins
1  tablespoon unsalted
    sunflower kernels, toasted
1  teaspoon lemon juice

Combine chicken broth and salt in a small saucepan; bring to a boil. Remove from heat. Add couscous; cover and let stand 5 minutes or until couscous is tender and liquid is absorbed.

Coat a small nonstick skillet with cooking spray; add oil. Place over medium-high heat until hot. Add mushrooms, celery, and green onions; sauté 5 minutes or until celery is tender.

Add vegetable mixture, raisins, sunflower kernels, and lemon juice to couscous; toss gently. Yield: 2 servings.

Serve this raisin-accented grain dish with Peppercorn Tuna (page 108) and Sautéed Spinach (page 131).

**Per Serving:**

Calories 201
Calories from Fat 24%
Fat 5.4 g
Saturated Fat 0.8 g
Carbohydrate 33.8 g
Protein 6.4 g
Cholesterol 0 mg
Sodium 181 mg

**Exchanges:**

2  Starch
1  Fat

# MUSHROOM GRITS

3  tablespoons grits, uncooked
¼  cup (1 ounce) shredded
    reduced-fat Cheddar
    cheese
    Butter-flavored vegetable
    cooking spray
⅓  cup chopped fresh
    mushrooms
1  teaspoon minced garlic

1  tablespoon canned
    no-salt-added beef broth,
    undiluted
1  teaspoon chopped fresh
    parsley
1  teaspoon fresh lemon juice
¼  teaspoon hot sauce
⅛  teaspoon salt

Cook grits in a small saucepan according to package directions, omitting salt and fat. Add cheese, stirring until cheese melts. Cover and keep warm.

Coat a small nonstick skillet with cooking spray; place over medium heat until hot. Add mushrooms; sauté 2 minutes. Add garlic; sauté 1 minute. Remove from heat. Stir in beef broth and remaining ingredients.

Add mushroom mixture to grits, stirring well. Serve immediately. Yield: 2 servings.

Prepare Mushroom Grits to serve with Ham and Swiss Omelets (page 210).

**Per Serving:**

Calories 101
Calories from Fat 28%
Fat 3.1 g
Saturated Fat 1.6 g
Carbohydrate 12.8 g
Protein 5.8 g
Cholesterol 9 mg
Sodium 257 mg

**Exchanges:**

1  Starch
½  Medium-Fat Meat

Indonesian Pasta

# INDONESIAN PASTA

Per Serving:

Calories 191
Calories from Fat 23%
Fat 4.9 g
Saturated Fat 0.8 g
Carbohydrate 30.2 g
Protein 7.8 g
Cholesterol 0 mg
Sodium 256 mg


Exchanges:

2  Starch
1  Fat

¼  cup canned low-sodium
   chicken broth, undiluted
1  tablespoon plus 1 teaspoon
   reduced-fat creamy peanut
   butter
1  tablespoon low-sodium soy
   sauce
2  teaspoons lemon juice
1½  teaspoons minced onion
1  teaspoon seeded, minced
   serrano chile pepper
⅛  teaspoon brown sugar
   Dash of ground cumin

Vegetable cooking spray
¼  pound fresh asparagus spears
   (about 9 spears)
2  tablespoons julienne-sliced
   sweet red pepper
3  tablespoons sliced green
   onions
1  tablespoon chopped fresh
   parsley
2  ounces capellini (angel hair
   pasta), uncooked
   Asparagus spears (optional)

Combine first 8 ingredients in a small saucepan; bring to a boil, stirring constantly. Set aside, and keep warm.

Coat a nonstick skillet with cooking spray; place over medium-high heat until hot. Add asparagus and red pepper; sauté 3 minutes or until tender. Add green onions; sauté 30 seconds. Remove from heat; stir in parsley.

Cook pasta according to package directions, omitting salt and fat; drain. Place pasta in a serving bowl. Add peanut sauce and vegetable mixture; toss gently. Serve warm. Garnish with additional asparagus spears, if desired. Yield: 2 servings.

# FETTUCCINE PRIMAVERA

Olive oil-flavored vegetable
    cooking spray
½ cup broccoli flowerets
½ cup cauliflower flowerets
½ cup fresh snow pea pods,
    trimmed
2 teaspoons minced garlic
½ cup julienne-sliced zucchini
¼ cup julienne-sliced sweet red
    pepper
¼ cup julienne-sliced carrot
¼ cup canned low-sodium
    chicken broth, undiluted
2 tablespoons dry white wine
4 ounces fettuccine, uncooked
2 tablespoons freshly grated
    Romano cheese

Coat a medium nonstick skillet with cooking spray; place over medium-high heat until hot. Add broccoli and next 3 ingredients; sauté 2 minutes. Add zucchini, sweet red pepper, and carrot; sauté 2 minutes or until vegetables are crisp-tender.

Combine chicken broth and wine; add to vegetables in skillet. Cover, reduce heat, and simmer 2 minutes.

Cook pasta according to package directions, omitting salt and fat; drain. Place pasta in a serving bowl. Add vegetable mixture and cheese; toss gently. Serve immediately. Yield: 2 servings.

*Put swordfish fillets on the grill, heat soft breadsticks, and add this fresh vegetable-pasta dish to complete the menu.*

Per Serving:

Calories 265
Calories from Fat 7%
Fat 2.2 g
Saturated Fat 0.6 g
Carbohydrate 51.0 g
Protein 10.7 g
Cholesterol 2 mg
Sodium 54 mg

Exchanges:

3 Starch
1 Vegetable

# FETTUCCINE WITH PESTO

½ cup tightly packed fresh basil
    leaves
1 tablespoon pine nuts
1 tablespoon grated Parmesan
    cheese
1½ tablespoons canned low-
    sodium chicken broth,
    undiluted
1 teaspoon chopped garlic
½ teaspoon olive oil
⅛ teaspoon salt
4 ounces fettuccine, uncooked

Position knife blade in food processor bowl; add first 7 ingredients. Process until smooth, scraping sides of processor bowl occasionally. Set basil mixture aside.

Cook pasta according to package directions, omitting salt and fat; drain. Place pasta in a serving bowl. Add basil mixture, and toss gently. Serve immediately. Yield: 2 servings.

*Capture a taste of Rome when you serve flavorful fettuccine and Italian Beef Rolls (page 83).*

Per Serving:

Calories 279
Calories from Fat 23%
Fat 7.2 g
Saturated Fat 1.4 g
Carbohydrate 44.9 g
Protein 9.6 g
Cholesterol 2 mg
Sodium 206 mg

Exchanges:

3 Starch
1½ Fat

Macaroni and Cheese

# MACARONI AND CHEESE

2 ounces elbow macaroni,
  uncooked
1 tablespoon all-purpose flour
½ cup evaporated skimmed
  milk, divided
2 teaspoons reduced-calorie
  margarine
1½ ounces low-fat loaf process
  cheese spread
Dash of salt
Dash of dry mustard

Dash of pepper
1 tablespoon frozen egg
  substitute, thawed
Vegetable cooking spray
2 teaspoons fine, dry
  breadcrumbs
⅛ teaspoon paprika
Roma tomato slices
  (optional)
Fresh parsley sprigs
  (optional)

Cook macaroni according to package directions, omitting salt and fat; drain
well, and set aside.

Combine flour and 2 tablespoons milk, stirring until smooth. Combine
flour mixture, remaining ¼ cup plus 2 tablespoons milk, and margarine in a
small saucepan, stirring well. Cook over medium heat, stirring constantly,
until mixture is thickened and bubbly. Remove from heat; add cheese and
next 3 ingredients, stirring until cheese melts. Add egg substitute, stirring
constantly.

Combine cooked macaroni and cheese sauce, stirring well. Pour mixture
into a 1½-cup casserole coated with cooking spray. Combine breadcrumbs
and paprika; sprinkle in rows on top of macaroni mixture. Bake, uncovered,
at 350° for 20 to 25 minutes or until bubbly. If desired, garnish with
tomato and parsley. Yield: 2 servings.

**Per Serving:**

Calories 256
Calories from Fat 22%
Fat 6.3 g
Saturated Fat 2.0 g
Carbohydrate 35.4 g
Protein 13.7 g
Cholesterol 14.0 mg
Sodium 550 mg

**Exchanges:**

2 Starch
1 Medium-Fat Meat

# Mostaccioli with Eggplant Sauce

¼ cup crumbled feta cheese
1 tablespoon shredded fresh basil
2 teaspoons red wine vinegar
Olive oil-flavored vegetable cooking spray
2 tablespoons chopped onion
1½ teaspoons minced garlic
1 cup peeled, cubed eggplant
½ cup peeled, seeded, and chopped tomato

½ cup canned no-salt-added chicken broth, undiluted
¼ cup no-salt-added tomato sauce
⅛ teaspoon dried thyme
⅛ teaspoon salt
⅛ teaspoon pepper
2 ounces thin mostaccioli pasta, uncooked

Combine first 3 ingredients in a small bowl; set aside.

Coat a small nonstick skillet with cooking spray; place over medium-high heat until hot. Add onion and garlic; sauté 2 minutes or until tender. Add eggplant and next 6 ingredients; cook, uncovered, over medium heat 10 minutes, stirring frequently. Remove from heat, and keep warm.

Cook pasta according to package directions, omitting salt and fat; drain. Place pasta in a serving bowl. Add eggplant mixture and cheese mixture; toss gently. Serve warm. Yield: 2 servings.

Add a Mediterranean touch to your table with this saucy pasta side dish. Try it with roasted chicken and a Greek salad.

**Per Serving:**

Calories 192
Calories from Fat 20%
Fat 4.3 g
Saturated Fat 2.4 g
Carbohydrate 31.0 g
Protein 7.6 g
Cholesterol 13 mg
Sodium 348 mg

**Exchanges:**

2 Starch
1 Fat

# Creamy Herbed Pasta

1 tablespoon sun-dried tomato
1 tablespoon hot water
1 tablespoon chopped fresh basil
2 tablespoons Neufchâtel cheese, softened
2 tablespoons canned low-sodium chicken broth, undiluted

1 teaspoon chopped fresh oregano
1 teaspoon minced garlic
1 teaspoon lemon juice
⅛ teaspoon dried crushed red pepper
4 ounces orecchiette pasta, uncooked

Combine tomato and water in a small bowl; cover and let stand 15 minutes. Drain well. Chop tomato, and set aside.

Combine basil and next 6 ingredients, stirring well.

Cook pasta according to package directions, omitting salt and fat; drain. Place pasta in a serving bowl. Add chopped tomato and cheese mixture; toss gently. Serve immediately. Yield: 2 servings.

**Per Serving:**

Calories 258
Calories from Fat 16%
Fat 4.5 g
Saturated Fat 2.1 g
Carbohydrate 43.3 g
Protein 9.0 g
Cholesterol 11 mg
Sodium 99 mg

**Exchanges:**

3 Starch
1 Fat

Per Serving:

Calories 111
Calories from Fat 11%
Fat 1.3 g
Saturated Fat 0.2 g
Carbohydrate 21.3 g
Protein 3.9 g
Cholesterol 0 mg
Sodium 257 mg


Exchanges:

1   Starch
1   Vegetable

# MEDITERRANEAN ORZO

| | | | |
|---|---|---|---|
| 1 | tablespoon sun-dried tomato | 1 | tablespoon chopped Greek olives |
| 1 | tablespoon hot water | | |
| ¼ | cup orzo, uncooked | 1 | tablespoon canned low-sodium chicken broth, undiluted |
| | Olive oil–flavored vegetable cooking spray | | |
| 2 | tablespoons chopped sweet red pepper | 2 | teaspoons red wine vinegar |
| | | ⅛ | teaspoon salt |
| 1 | tablespoon chopped green onions | ⅛ | teaspoon pepper |
| 1 | tablespoon chopped fresh parsley | | |

Combine tomato and water in a small bowl; cover and let stand 15 minutes. Drain well. Chop tomato, and set aside.

Cook orzo according to package directions, omitting salt and fat; drain and set aside.

Coat a small nonstick skillet with cooking spray; place over medium-high heat until hot. Add sweet red pepper and green onions; sauté until crisp-tender. Add tomato, parsley, and remaining ingredients to skillet; cook until thoroughly heated, stirring frequently.

Combine vegetable mixture and orzo in a small bowl; toss gently. Yield: 2 servings.

Instead of noodles, serve flavorful orzo pasta as a side for Veal with Sour Cream Sauce (page 87).

# SPAGHETTINI WITH ITALIAN GREEN SAUCE

Per Serving:

Calories 159
Calories from Fat 26%
Fat 4.6 g
Saturated Fat 1.5 g
Carbohydrate 22.9 g
Protein 6.5 g
Cholesterol 5 mg
Sodium 412 mg


Exchanges:

1½ Starch
1   Fat

| | | | |
|---|---|---|---|
| 2 | tablespoons finely chopped fresh flat-leaf parsley | ⅛ | teaspoon pepper |
| | | | Dash of salt |
| 1 | tablespoon chopped green onions | 2 | ounces spaghettini, uncooked |
| 1 | tablespoon lemon juice | 2 | tablespoons freshly grated Asiago cheese |
| 1 | teaspoon minced capers | | |
| 1 | teaspoon olive oil | | |
| ¼ | teaspoon minced garlic | | |

Combine first 8 ingredients in a small bowl, stirring well. Set aside.

Cook pasta according to package directions, omitting salt and fat; drain. Place pasta in a serving bowl. Add parsley mixture, and toss gently. Sprinkle with cheese. Serve warm. Yield: 2 servings.

# TORTELLINI-VEGETABLE TOSS

| | | | |
|---|---|---|---|
| 1 | tablespoon sun-dried tomato | 2 | tablespoons warm canned low-sodium chicken broth, undiluted |
| ¼ | cup hot water | | |
| ¼ | pound fresh asparagus spears (about 9 spears) | ¼ | teaspoon olive oil |
| ¼ | cup julienne-sliced zucchini | | Dash of salt |
| ¼ | cup julienne-sliced carrot | | Dash of freshly ground pepper |
| ½ | teaspoon minced garlic | | |
| 3 | ounces refrigerated cheese tortellini, uncooked | 1½ | teaspoons freshly grated Romano cheese |

Combine tomato and water in a small bowl; cover and let stand 15 minutes. Drain well. Chop tomato, and set aside.

Snap off tough ends of asparagus. Remove scales from stalks with a knife or vegetable peeler, if desired. Cut asparagus diagonally into ½-inch pieces.

Arrange asparagus, zucchini, carrot, and garlic in a vegetable steamer over boiling water. Cover and steam 5 minutes or until vegetables are crisp-tender. Place vegetables in a large bowl. Set aside, and keep warm.

Cook pasta according to package directions, omitting salt and fat; drain well.

Combine chicken broth and next 3 ingredients, stirring well with a wire whisk. Place pasta in a serving dish; add tomato, vegetable mixture, and broth mixture, tossing gently. Sprinkle with Romano cheese, and serve immediately. Yield: 2 servings.

**Per Serving:**

Calories 165
Calories from Fat 18%
Fat 3.3 g
Saturated Fat 1.4 g
Carbohydrate 25.7 g
Protein 9.2 g
Cholesterol 22 mg
Sodium 332 mg

**Exchanges:**

1   Starch
½   Medium-Fat Meat
2   Vegetable

Tortellini-Vegetable Toss

# Fried Rice

Vegetable cooking spray
½ teaspoon sesame oil
¼ cup long-grain rice, uncooked
¾ cup canned no-salt-added beef broth, undiluted
⅛ teaspoon salt
1 tablespoon chopped green onions
1½ teaspoons chopped fresh parsley
1 teaspoon low-sodium soy sauce

Coat a small nonstick skillet with cooking spray; add oil. Place over medium-high heat until hot. Add rice; sauté 4 to 5 minutes or until rice is golden. Add beef broth and salt; bring to boil. Cover, reduce heat, and simmer 20 minutes. Remove from heat; stir in green onions, parsley, and soy sauce. Cover and let stand 5 minutes. Serve immediately.
Yield: 2 servings

Instead of calling out for Chinese food, stir-fry fresh shrimp, and serve with Fried Rice and Spring Rolls (page 220).

Instead of calling out for Chinese food, stir-fry fresh shrimp, and serve with Fried Rice and Spring Rolls (page 220).

# Saffron Rice

Vegetable cooking spray
½ teaspoon vegetable oil
2 tablespoons chopped onion
⅓ cup basmati rice, uncooked
Dash of saffron
1 cup canned low-sodium chicken broth, undiluted
3 tablespoons no-salt-added tomato sauce
⅛ teaspoon salt
⅛ teaspoon pepper
1 tablespoon chopped fresh parsley

Coat a medium nonstick skillet with cooking spray; add oil. Place over medium-high heat until hot. Add onion; sauté 3 minutes. Add rice and saffron; sauté 2 minutes. Add chicken broth, tomato sauce, salt, and pepper; bring to a boil. Cover, reduce heat, and simmer 20 minutes or until rice is tender and liquid is absorbed. Sprinkle with parsley. Yield: 2 servings.

Combine high flavor and rich color by serving Saffron Rice along with Jerk Chicken (page 93) for a memorable low-fat meal.

Combine high flavor and rich color by serving Saffron Rice along with Jerk Chicken (page 93) for a memorable low-fat meal.

# INDIVIDUAL BROWN RICE CASSEROLES

¾ cup water
⅓ cup long-grain brown rice, uncooked
½ cup broccoli flowerets
    Butter-flavored vegetable cooking spray
½ cup chopped fresh mushrooms
2 tablespoons minced onion
2 tablespoons minced celery

¼ cup canned no-salt-added chicken broth, undiluted
2 tablespoons Neufchâtel cheese, softened
⅛ teaspoon salt
⅛ teaspoon pepper
1½ teaspoons lemon juice
2 tablespoons (½ ounce) shredded reduced-fat Cheddar cheese

Bring water to a boil in a small saucepan; add rice. Cover, reduce heat, and simmer 45 minutes or until rice is tender and liquid is absorbed.

Arrange broccoli in a vegetable steamer over boiling water. Cover and steam 4 to 5 minutes or until crisp-tender. Drain.

Coat a small nonstick skillet with cooking spray. Place over medium heat until hot; add mushrooms, onion, and celery. Sauté 3 minutes. Add broccoli, chicken broth, and next 3 ingredients; cook until Neufchâtel cheese melts, stirring occasionally. Stir in cooked rice and lemon juice. Remove from heat; spoon rice mixture evenly into 2 (8-ounce) ramekins coated with cooking spray; sprinkle evenly with Cheddar cheese. Bake at 350° for 10 minutes or until cheese melts. Yield: 2 servings.

**Per Serving:**

Calories 203
Calories from Fat 29%
Fat 6.6 g
Saturated Fat 3.2 g
Carbohydrate 28.9 g
Protein 7.9 g
Cholesterol 15 mg
Sodium 284 mg

**Exchanges:**

2 Starch
1 Fat

# WILD RICE WITH MUSHROOMS AND ALMONDS

¼ cup wild rice, uncooked
1 cup canned low-sodium chicken broth, undiluted
    Butter-flavored vegetable cooking spray
1 teaspoon reduced-calorie margarine
1 tablespoon chopped celery
1 cup sliced fresh mushrooms

1 tablespoon chopped green onions
1 tablespoon chopped water chestnuts
⅛ teaspoon salt
⅛ teaspoon pepper
2 teaspoons slivered almonds, toasted

Combine rice and broth in a saucepan. Bring to a boil; cover, reduce heat, and simmer 50 minutes or until rice is tender, stirring occasionally. Drain; set aside.

Coat a large nonstick skillet with cooking spray; add margarine. Place over medium-high heat until margarine melts. Add celery; cook, stirring constantly, 1 minute. Add mushrooms and next 4 ingredients; cook, stirring constantly, 2 minutes or until vegetables are tender. Add vegetable mixture and almonds to rice; toss gently. Yield: 2 servings.

**Per Serving:**

Calories 152
Calories from Fat 31%
Fat 5.2 g
Saturated Fat 0.7 g
Carbohydrate 22.2 g
Protein 6.3 g
Cholesterol 0 mg
Sodium 206 mg

**Exchanges:**

1½ Starch
1 Fat

Terrific Turkey Pitas (page 163),
Asparagus Vichyssoise (page 148)

# SOUPS 'N' SANDWICHES

Here's the answer for days when you'd rather have a cup of soup than a potful. And don't forget the sandwich to serve with it.

# Asparagus Vichyssoise

½ pound fresh asparagus spears
(about 9 spears)
1 cup canned low-sodium
chicken broth, undiluted
and divided
Vegetable cooking spray
¼ cup finely chopped onion

½ cup peeled, diced potato
½ cup evaporated skimmed
milk
¼ teaspoon salt
Dash of ground white pepper
Lemon rind strips (optional)

Snap off tough ends of asparagus. Remove scales from stalks with a knife or vegetable peeler, if desired. Cut asparagus spears in half crosswise. Bring ¼ cup chicken broth to a boil in a medium saucepan. Add asparagus; cover and cook over medium heat 5 minutes or until crisp-tender. Set aside asparagus in broth.

Coat a small saucepan with cooking spray, and place over medium-high heat until hot. Add onion; sauté until tender. Add remaining ¾ cup broth and potato. Bring to a boil; cover, reduce heat, and simmer 15 minutes or until potato is tender.

Combine potato mixture and asparagus, including broth, in container of an electric blender or food processor; cover and process until smooth. Transfer mixture to a bowl; stir in milk, salt, and pepper. Cover and chill. Stir before serving. Garnish with lemon rind strips, if desired. Yield: 2 servings.

# Corn Chowder

Vegetable cooking spray
2 tablespoons chopped sweet
red pepper
2 tablespoons chopped onion
2 tablespoons diced celery
½ cup diced potato
⅛ teaspoon salt
1 (10½-ounce) can low-
sodium chicken broth

2 tablespoons yellow cornmeal
1 cup skim milk
1 cup frozen whole-kernel
corn, thawed and divided
¼ cup (1 ounce) shredded
reduced-fat sharp Cheddar
cheese

Coat a medium saucepan with cooking spray; place over medium-high heat until hot. Add sweet red pepper, onion, and celery; sauté 1 minute or until tender. Add potato, salt, and chicken broth; bring to a boil. Cover, reduce heat, and simmer 15 minutes or until potato is tender.

Place cornmeal in container of an electric blender; cover and process 1 minute or until powdered. Add milk and ½ cup corn to cornmeal; cover and process until smooth, stopping once to scrape down sides. Add processed corn mixture and remaining ½ cup corn to potato mixture. Cook over low heat until thoroughly heated, stirring frequently.

To serve, ladle soup into individual bowls, and top each serving with 2 tablespoons cheese. Yield: 2 servings.

# Sherried Mushroom and Rice Soup

Vegetable cooking spray
1½ teaspoons reduced-calorie margarine
¾ cup finely chopped celery
¼ cup chopped onion
2 ounces fresh shiitake mushrooms, chopped
2 teaspoons all-purpose flour
1¼ cups evaporated skimmed milk, divided
2 tablespoons dry sherry
⅛ teaspoon pepper
Dash of salt
½ cup cooked long-grain rice (cooked without salt or fat)

Coat a large nonstick skillet with cooking spray; add margarine. Place over medium-high heat until margarine melts. Add celery, onion, and mushrooms; sauté 3 to 4 minutes or until tender.

Combine flour and 2 tablespoons milk, stirring until smooth; add to vegetable mixture. Add remaining milk, sherry, pepper, and salt; cook, stirring constantly, until mixture is thickened. Stir in rice; reduce heat to low, and simmer 10 minutes. Yield: 2 servings.

Serve this rich-tasting mushroom soup as an opener for Fillet of Beef with Peppercorns (page 84), steamed asparagus, and whole wheat rolls.

**Per Serving:**

Calories 233
Calories from Fat 11%
Fat 2.8 g
Saturated Fat 0.2 g
Carbohydrate 38.0 g
Protein 14.6 g
Cholesterol 6 mg
Sodium 337 mg

**Exchanges:**

2 Starch
1 Skim Milk

# Caraway Potato Soup

⅔ pound round red potatoes, peeled and diced
¼ cup chopped onion
¼ cup chopped celery
1 teaspoon chicken-flavored bouillon granules
⅛ teaspoon freshly ground pepper
1 (10½-ounce) can low-sodium chicken broth
⅓ cup evaporated skimmed milk
1 teaspoon reduced-calorie margarine
1 teaspoon caraway seeds

Combine first 6 ingredients in a medium saucepan; bring to a boil. Cover, reduce heat, and simmer 20 minutes. Add milk and margarine, stirring until margarine melts.

Transfer half of potato mixture to container of an electric blender or food processor; cover and process until smooth, stopping once to scrape down sides. Return pureed mixture to saucepan; add caraway seeds. Cook over medium heat until thoroughly heated. Yield: 2 servings.

Warm up a meal of Roast Beef Poor Boys (page 159) with steaming bowls of this hearty potato soup.

**Per Serving:**

Calories 170
Calories from Fat 17%
Fat 3.2 g
Saturated Fat 0.7 g
Carbohydrate 29.5 g
Protein 7.8 g
Cholesterol 2 mg
Sodium 550 mg

**Exchanges:**

2 Starch
½ Fat

# Sweet Potato Soup

1 tablespoon reduced-calorie margarine
¼ cup diced onion
1½ tablespoons all-purpose flour
1 cup canned no-salt-added chicken broth, undiluted
½ cup dry white wine
1 (8-ounce) sweet potato, peeled and diced
½ teaspoon ground ginger
⅛ teaspoon salt
⅔ cup evaporated skimmed milk
1 tablespoon lime juice
2 tablespoons dried cranberries

Melt margarine in a medium saucepan over medium heat. Add onion, and sauté until tender. Sprinkle flour over onion, and cook over low heat, stirring constantly, 1 minute. Gradually add chicken broth and wine; cook over medium heat, stirring constantly, until mixture is thickened and bubbly.

Stir in sweet potato, ginger, and salt. Reduce heat, and simmer, uncovered, 30 minutes or until potato is tender. Stir in milk and lime juice. Transfer sweet potato mixture to container of an electric blender; cover and process until smooth.

To serve, ladle soup into individual bowls, and top each serving with 1 tablespoon cranberries. Yield: 2 servings.

# Roasted Tomato Soup

6 ripe plum tomatoes (about ¾ pound)
Vegetable cooking spray
½ teaspoon dried Italian seasoning
¼ teaspoon freshly ground pepper
1 clove garlic, minced
⅓ cup diced onion
2 tablespoons red wine vinegar
¼ teaspoon salt
1 (13¾-ounce) can no-salt-added beef broth
1 tablespoon crumbled Montrachet goat cheese

Cut tomatoes in half lengthwise; place tomato halves, cut side down, in a 15- x 10- x 1-inch jellyroll pan coated with cooking spray. Coat each tomato half with cooking spray; sprinkle evenly with Italian seasoning, pepper, and garlic. Bake at 500° for 15 to 20 minutes or until tomato skins are charred. Let cool slightly. Position knife blade in food processor bowl; add tomato. Process 3 or 4 times or until slightly chunky.

Coat a medium saucepan with cooking spray; place over medium-high heat until hot. Add onion; sauté until tender. Stir in tomato mixture, vinegar, salt, and beef broth. Bring to a boil; reduce heat and simmer 5 minutes.

To serve, ladle soup into individual bowls, and top evenly with cheese. Yield: 2 servings.

Garden Gazpacho

# GARDEN GAZPACHO

1¼  cups seeded, chopped tomato
1  cup low-sodium vegetable
     juice cocktail
¼  cup chopped cucumber
¼  cup chopped celery
¼  cup chopped green pepper
¼  cup sliced green onions
1  tablespoon lemon juice

1  tablespoon commercial oil-
     free Italian dressing
⅛  teaspoon salt
⅛  teaspoon garlic powder
⅛  teaspoon pepper
⅛  teaspoon hot sauce
     Fresh chive blossoms
     (optional)

Combine first 12 ingredients in a medium bowl. Cover and chill at least
6 hours.

To serve, ladle soup into individual bowls, and garnish with chive blossoms, if desired. Yield: 2 servings.

Gazpacho is a cool way to start a south-of-the-border
meal featuring Chicken Enchiladas (page 94).

**Per Serving:**

Calories 75
Calories from Fat 8%
Fat 0.7 g
Saturated Fat 0.1 g
Carbohydrate 16.3 g
Protein 3.1 g
Cholesterol 0 mg
Sodium 285 mg

**Exchanges:**

1  Starch

# Garden Vegetable-Pasta Soup

Per Serving:

Calories 277
Calories from Fat 7%
Fat 2.3 g
Saturated Fat 0.7 g
Carbohydrate 50.9 g
Protein 11.0 g
Cholesterol 2 mg
Sodium 343 mg

Exchanges:

3  Starch
1  Vegetable

Vegetable cooking spray
½  cup sliced onion
⅓  cup diced celery
¼  cup shredded carrot
1  clove garlic, minced
2  cups canned no-salt-added beef broth, undiluted
½  cup peeled, diced potato
½  cup diced zucchini
½  cup shredded cabbage
¼  teaspoon dried basil
⅛  teaspoon salt
½  cup drained canned cannellini beans
¼  cup chopped plum tomato
2  ounces ditalini (small, tube-shaped) pasta, uncooked
1  tablespoon freshly grated Parmesan cheese

Coat a medium saucepan with cooking spray; place over medium-high heat until hot. Add onion and next 3 ingredients; sauté until tender. Add beef broth and next 5 ingredients. Bring to a boil; cover, reduce heat, and simmer 1 hour.

Add beans, tomato, and pasta to vegetable mixture; cover and cook an additional 15 minutes or until pasta is tender.

To serve, ladle soup into individual bowls, and sprinkle evenly with cheese. Yield: 2 servings.

With Garden Vegetable-Pasta Soup, all you need for a complete meal is a tossed green salad and whole wheat bread.

# Mexican Vegetable-Beef Soup

Per Serving:

Calories 243
Calories from Fat 15%
Fat 4.0 g
Saturated Fat 1.3 g
Carbohydrate 28.0 g
Protein 17.4 g
Cholesterol 35 mg
Sodium 679 mg

Exchanges:

2  Starch
1½ Lean Meat

¼  pound ground round
1  cup frozen mixed vegetables
¾  cup peeled, cubed potato
1  (10-ounce) can diced tomato and green chiles, undrained
1  teaspoon dried marjoram
¼  teaspoon onion powder
¼  teaspoon salt-free herb-and-spice blend
⅛  teaspoon pepper
1  (13¾-ounce) can no-salt-added beef broth

Cook ground round in a medium saucepan over medium heat until browned, stirring until it crumbles. Drain and pat dry with paper towels. Wipe drippings from saucepan with a paper towel.

Return meat to saucepan. Stir in mixed vegetables and remaining ingredients. Bring to a boil; cover, reduce heat, and simmer 30 to 35 minutes or until potato is tender. Yield: 2 servings.

For a no-fuss dinner, take two Chile-Corn Muffins (page 221) from the freezer, and simmer this spicy vegetable-beef soup on the stove.

# GOOD LUCK SOUP

Vegetable cooking spray
½ cup chopped onion
½ cup chopped green pepper
½ cup chopped celery
2 cloves garlic, minced
1 cup frozen black-eyed peas, thawed
¾ cup water
¼ cup diced lean cooked ham
½ teaspoon dried marjoram
⅛ teaspoon salt
⅛ teaspoon hot sauce
1 (13¾-ounce) can no-salt-added beef broth
½ cup sliced fresh okra
½ cup seeded, chopped tomato

Coat a medium saucepan with cooking spray; place over medium-high heat until hot. Add onion and next 3 ingredients; sauté until vegetables are tender. Add peas and next 6 ingredients; bring to a boil. Cover, reduce heat, and simmer 20 minutes. Add okra and tomato; cook, uncovered, an additional 20 minutes or until okra is tender. Yield: 2 servings.

Per Serving:

Calories 207
Calories from Fat 10%
Fat 2.2 g
Saturated Fat 0.5 g
Carbohydrate 33.1 g
Protein 13.1 g
Cholesterol 9 mg
Sodium 419 mg

Exchanges:

2 Starch
1 Lean Meat

# CHINESE NOODLE SOUP

2¼ cups canned low-sodium chicken broth, undiluted
2 tablespoons julienne-sliced carrot
2 tablespoons sliced water chestnuts
2 tablespoons sliced fresh mushrooms
¼ teaspoon peeled, minced gingerroot
1 ounce vermicelli, uncooked
½ cup shredded cooked chicken breast (skinned before cooking and cooked without salt)
8 unpeeled medium-size fresh shrimp
½ cup fresh snow pea pods, trimmed
1 tablespoon low-sodium soy sauce
1 tablespoon sliced green onions

Bring chicken broth to a boil in a medium saucepan. Add carrot and next 3 ingredients; cook, uncovered, 2 minutes.

Break vermicelli into pieces; add vermicelli and chicken to broth mixture. Cook over medium heat 5 minutes, stirring occasionally.

Peel and devein shrimp; chop shrimp. Add shrimp and snow peas to broth mixture. Cook 3 to 5 minutes or until shrimp turns pink. Stir in soy sauce.

To serve, ladle soup into individual bowls, and sprinkle evenly with green onions. Yield: 2 servings.

Celebrate Chinese New Year with bowls of Chinese Noodle Soup, Oriental Green Salad (page 59), teriyaki rice cakes, and fortune cookies.

Per Serving:

Calories 245
Calories from Fat 16%
Fat 4.3 g
Saturated Fat 0.6 g
Carbohydrate 23.1 g
Protein 26.8 g
Cholesterol 98 mg
Sodium 385 mg

Exchanges:

1 Starch
3 Lean Meat
1 Vegetable

# CHICKEN ENCHILADA SOUP

1 (6-inch) corn tortilla
　Vegetable cooking spray
1 teaspoon vegetable oil
1 (4-ounce) skinned, boned
　chicken breast half, cubed
2 tablespoons all-purpose flour
½ cup no-salt-added tomato
　sauce
¼ cup skim milk
1 (13½-ounce) can no-salt-
　added chicken broth

¾ teaspoon chili powder
¼ teaspoon ground cumin
⅛ teaspoon salt
⅛ teaspoon garlic powder
　Dash of ground red pepper
¼ cup seeded, chopped tomato
2 tablespoons (½ ounce)
　shredded reduced-fat sharp
　Cheddar cheese
½ teaspoon minced jalapeño
　pepper (optional)

Cut tortilla into very thin strips; place on a baking sheet. Bake at 325° for 10 minutes or until crisp. Set aside.

Coat a medium saucepan with cooking spray; add oil. Place over medium-high heat until hot. Add chicken; sauté 4 minutes or until lightly browned. Add flour, and cook, stirring constantly, 1 minute. Gradually stir in tomato sauce, milk, and chicken broth. Stir in chili powder and next 4 ingredients. Cover, reduce heat, and simmer 15 minutes, stirring occasionally.

To serve, ladle soup into individual bowls, and top each serving with half of tortilla strips, 2 tablespoons tomato, 1 tablespoon cheese, and, if desired, ¼ teaspoon jalapeño pepper. Yield: 2 servings.

Chicken Enchilada Soup

# White Chili with Fresh Tomatoes

1 (15-ounce) can Great
   Northern beans, drained
   Vegetable cooking spray
½ cup chopped onion
2 cloves garlic, minced
1 (13¾-ounce) can no-salt-
   added chicken broth
¾ cup chopped cooked chicken
   breast (skinned before
   cooking and cooked
   without salt)

1 (4-ounce) can chopped green
   chiles, undrained
½ teaspoon dried oregano
½ teaspoon ground cumin
¼ teaspoon ground coriander
   Dash of ground red pepper
   Dash of ground cloves
¾ cup chopped tomato, divided
⅛ teaspoon salt

Place ½ cup beans in a small bowl; mash and set aside. Reserve remaining whole beans.

Coat a medium saucepan with cooking spray; place over medium-high heat until hot. Add onion and garlic; sauté until tender. Stir in mashed and whole beans, chicken broth, and next 7 ingredients. Bring to a boil; cover, reduce heat, and simmer 15 minutes. Stir in ½ cup tomato and salt; cover and simmer an additional 3 minutes.

To serve, ladle chili into individual bowls, and sprinkle evenly with remaining ¼ cup tomato. Yield: 2 servings.

*Fresh carrot and celery sticks are all you'll need
to serve with this hearty chicken-based chili.*

**Per Serving:**

Calories 334
Calories from Fat 13%
Fat 4.9 g
Saturated Fat 0.8 g
Carbohydrate 40.8 g
Protein 32.7 g
Cholesterol 48 mg
Sodium 542 mg

**Exchanges:**

2½ Starch
3 Lean Meat
1 Vegetable

# Quick Vegetarian Chili

   Vegetable cooking spray
½ cup chopped onion
1 clove garlic, minced
⅓ cup frozen mixed vegetables
1 (15-ounce) can no-salt-added
   kidney beans, drained
1 (10-ounce) can diced tomatoes and green chiles

1 (8-ounce) can no-salt-added
   tomato sauce
2 teaspoons chili powder
½ teaspoon ground cumin
½ teaspoon dried oregano
½ teaspoon brown sugar
   Nonfat sour cream
   alternative (optional)

Coat a medium saucepan with cooking spray; place over medium-high heat until hot. Add onion and garlic; sauté until tender. Add mixed vegetables and next 7 ingredients; bring to a boil. Reduce heat, and simmer, uncovered, 15 minutes.

To serve, ladle chili into individual bowls, and top each serving with sour cream, if desired. Yield: 2 servings.

**Per Serving:**

Calories 305
Calories from Fat 5%
Fat 1.7 g
Saturated Fat 0.2 g
Carbohydrate 55.9 g
Protein 15.5 g
Cholesterol 0 mg
Sodium 659 mg

**Exchanges:**

3 Starch
½ Lean Meat Substitute
2 Vegetable

# Broiled Tomato and Pesto Bagels

3   tablespoons fresh
      basil leaves
1   tablespoon fresh
      parsley leaves
1½  teaspoons water
1   teaspoon pine nuts
1   teaspoon olive oil
1   teaspoon lemon juice
½   teaspoon red wine vinegar
⅛   teaspoon garlic powder
      Dash of salt
2   bagels, split and toasted
4   (½-inch-thick) slices large
      ripe tomato
¼   cup (1 ounce) shredded part-
      skim mozzarella cheese

Position knife blade in miniature food processor bowl; add first 9 ingredients. Process until smooth, scraping sides of processor bowl occasionally.

Spread basil mixture evenly on 4 bagel halves. Top each bagel half with a tomato slice, and sprinkle evenly with cheese.

Place bagel halves on a baking sheet. Broil 5½ inches from heat (with electric oven door partially opened) 1 minute or until cheese melts. Yield: 2 servings.

# Black Bean Burritos

½   cup canned black beans,
      undrained
2   teaspoons salt-free
      herb-and-spice blend
⅛   teaspoon ground cumin
      Dash of ground red pepper
½   cup cooked long-grain rice
      (cooked without salt or fat)
2   green leaf lettuce leaves
2   (8-inch) flour tortillas
¼   cup (1 ounce) shredded
      reduced-fat Monterey Jack
      cheese
2   tablespoons minced green
      onions
2   tablespoons no-salt-added
      mild salsa

Combine first 4 ingredients in a small saucepan, stirring well. Cook over medium heat, stirring constantly, until thoroughly heated. Stir in cooked rice.

Place a lettuce leaf on each tortilla. Spoon bean mixture evenly down center of each tortilla. Top each with 2 tablespoons cheese, 1 tablespoon green onions, and 1 tablespoon salsa. Roll up tortillas, and secure with wooden picks. Yield: 2 servings.

For a change of pace from your usual brown-bag meal, pack meatless burritos, commercial baked tortilla chips, and fresh nectarines.

# SHRIMP SALAD SANDWICHES

| | | | |
|---|---|---|---|
| 3 | cups water | 2 | tablespoons diced sweet red pepper |
| 1 | pound unpeeled medium-size fresh shrimp | 2 | teaspoons nonfat mayonnaise |
| ¼ | cup nonfat cream cheese, softened | 2 | teaspoons lime juice |
| 2 | tablespoons sliced green onions | 1 | teaspoon capers |
| | | ½ | teaspoon dried dillweed |
| | | 2 | (2½-ounce) French rolls |

Bring water to a boil; add shrimp, and cook 3 to 5 minutes or until shrimp turns pink. Drain well; rinse with cold water. Chill. Peel and devein shrimp.

Combine cream cheese and next 6 ingredients, stirring well. Add shrimp, and toss gently. Cover and chill 1 hour.

Cut a ½-inch slice off top of each roll; set tops aside. Hollow out center of rolls, leaving ½-inch-thick shells. Reserve excess bread for another use. Place bread shells and tops, cut sides up, on rack of a broiler pan. Broil 5½ inches from heat (with electric oven door partially opened) 1 to 2 minutes or until lightly toasted. Spoon shrimp mixture evenly into shells; cover with tops. Yield: 2 servings.

**Per Serving:**

Calories 311
Calories from Fat 7%
Fat 2.4 g
Saturated Fat 0.7 g
Carbohydrate 35.0 g
Protein 33.2 g
Cholesterol 228 mg
Sodium 960 mg

**Exchanges:**

2 Starch
3 Lean Meat
1 Vegetable

# TUNA SANDWICH BOATS

| | | | |
|---|---|---|---|
| 4 | (1½-ounce) sourdough French rolls | 1 | tablespoon slivered almonds, toasted |
| 1 | (3¼-ounce) can tuna in water, drained | 1½ | teaspoons grated onion |
| 2 | tablespoons (½ ounce) shredded reduced-fat Cheddar cheese | 1½ | teaspoons sliced pimiento-stuffed olives |
| 1 | tablespoon chopped water chestnuts | | Dash of low-sodium Worcestershire sauce |
| 1 | tablespoon chopped celery | 1½ | tablespoons nonfat mayonnaise |
| 1 | tablespoon chopped green pepper | | |

Cut a ½-inch slice off top of each roll; set tops aside. Hollow out center of rolls, leaving ½-inch-thick shells. Reserve excess bread for another use.

Combine tuna and remaining ingredients, tossing gently. Spoon tuna mixture evenly into shells; cover with tops. Transfer sandwiches to a baking sheet. Bake at 400° for 15 minutes or until thoroughly heated; serve warm. Yield: 2 servings.

Children will love eating tuna in bread boats. Round out a sandwich meal with sliced fresh vegetables, grapes, and White Chocolate Oatmeal Cookies (page 194).

**Per Serving:**

Calories 361
Calories from Fat 19%
Fat 7.8 g
Saturated Fat 1.9 g
Carbohydrate 50.0 g
Protein 20.3 g
Cholesterol 22 mg
Sodium 826 mg

**Exchanges:**

3 Starch
1 Lean Meat
1 Vegetable
1 Fat

Grilled Grouper Sandwiches with Pineapple Salsa

# GRILLED GROUPER SANDWICHES WITH PINEAPPLE SALSA

1   (8¼-ounce) can crushed pineapple in juice
2   tablespoons sliced green onions
1   tablespoon finely chopped red pepper
1   tablespoon lime juice
½   teaspoon sugar
½   teaspoon peeled, minced gingerroot
½   teaspoon dry mustard
    Dash of ground white pepper
2   (4-ounce) grouper fillets (¾ inch thick)
    Vegetable cooking spray
2   green leaf lettuce leaves
2   (2½-ounce) kaiser rolls, split and toasted

Drain pineapple, reserving juice. Combine 2 tablespoons pineapple juice, drained pineapple, green onions, and next 6 ingredients. Set aside.

Place fillets in a grilling basket coated with cooking spray. Place grill rack on grill over medium-hot coals (350° to 400°). Place basket on rack; grill, covered, 5 minutes on each side or until fish flakes easily when tested with a fork, basting frequently with reserved pineapple juice.

Place a lettuce leaf on bottom half of each roll; place fillets on lettuce. Spoon 3 tablespoons pineapple mixture over each fillet; top with remaining roll halves. Using a slotted spoon, serve remaining pineapple mixture with sandwiches. Yield: 2 servings.

# Roast Beef Poor Boys

2 tablespoons nonfat
   mayonnaise
1 tablespoon Creole mustard
1 teaspoon prepared
   horseradish

2 (2½-ounce) French rolls, split
4 ounces thinly sliced cooked
   lean roast beef
1 cup shredded iceburg lettuce
4 (¼-inch-thick) tomato slices

Combine first 3 ingredients in a small bowl, stirring well. Spread 1 table-spoon mayonnaise mixture over bottom half of each roll; top each evenly with roast beef, shredded lettuce, and tomato slices. Spread remaining mayonnaise mixture evenly over top halves of rolls, and place over tomato. Yield: 2 servings.

*Pack a picnic of poor boys, Jalapeño Potato Salad
(page 70), and juicy watermelon wedges.*

**Per Serving:**

Calories 349
Calories from Fat 14%
Fat 5.6 g
Saturated Fat 1.7 g
Carbohydrate 45.8 g
Protein 25.7 g
Cholesterol 50 mg
Sodium 718 mg

**Exchanges:**

3 Starch
2 Lean Meat

# Open-Faced Steak Sandwiches

½ pound lean boneless beef
   sirloin steak
   Vegetable cooking spray
¾ cup sliced fresh mushrooms
¼ cup thinly sliced onion,
   separated into rings
¼ teaspoon minced garlic
1½ tablespoons low-sodium
   Worcestershire sauce

1½ teaspoons cornstarch
½ cup canned no-salt-added
   beef broth, undiluted
⅛ teaspoon dried basil
⅛ teaspoon pepper
   Dash of salt
   Dash of dry mustard
4 (¾-ounce) slices French
   bread, toasted

Partially freeze steak; trim fat from steak. Slice steak diagonally across grain into ⅛-inch-wide strips. Coat a nonstick skillet with cooking spray. Place over medium-high heat until hot. Add steak; cook 3 minutes or until browned. Drain and pat dry. Wipe drippings from skillet with a paper towel.

Coat skillet with cooking spray. Add mushrooms, onion, and garlic; sauté until tender. Combine Worcestershire sauce and cornstarch in a small bowl, stirring until smooth. Stir in beef broth and next 4 ingredients. Add broth mixture to mushroom mixture, and cook over medium heat, stirring constantly, 2 minutes or until mixture is thickened. Add steak, and cook 2 to 3 minutes or until thoroughly heated.

To serve, place 2 bread slices on each serving plate; spoon beef mixture evenly over bread. Serve immediately. Yield: 2 servings.

**Per Serving:**

Calories 361
Calories from Fat 21%
Fat 8.6 g
Saturated Fat 2.9 g
Carbohydrate 35.4 g
Protein 32.8 g
Cholesterol 81 mg
Sodium 466 mg

**Exchanges:**

2 Starch
3 Lean Meat
1 Vegetable

# Greek Gyros

Per Serving:

Calories 377
Calories from Fat 17%
Fat 7.0 g
Saturated Fat 1.8 g
Carbohydrate 48.9 g
Protein 24.1 g
Cholesterol 55 mg
Sodium 357 mg


Exchanges:

3 Starch
2 Lean Meat
1 Vegetable

| | |
|---|---|
| 6 ounces lamb leg cutlets (½ inch thick), cut into strips | ¼ cup plain nonfat yogurt |
| | 3 tablespoons grated peeled cucumber, drained |
| ¼ cup red wine vinegar | ½ teaspoon minced garlic |
| 2 tablespoons chopped fresh parsley | ⅛ teaspoon dried dillweed |
| | Vegetable cooking spray |
| 1 tablespoon minced onion | 2 green leaf lettuce leaves |
| 1 teaspoon minced garlic | 2 (8-inch) pita bread rounds |
| ½ teaspoon dried oregano | ¼ cup seeded, chopped tomato |
| ⅛ teaspoon salt | 1 tablespoon chopped green onion |
| ⅛ teaspoon pepper | |

Place lamb strips in a heavy-duty, zip-top plastic bag. Combine vinegar and next 6 ingredients, stirring well. Pour vinegar mixture over lamb; seal bag, and shake until meat is well coated. Marinate in refrigerator at least 8 hours.

Combine yogurt and next 3 ingredients. Cover and chill. Remove lamb from bag; discard marinade. Coat a nonstick skillet with cooking spray; place over medium-high heat until hot. Add lamb; cook 2 to 3 minutes or until browned, stirring frequently. Drain and pat dry with paper towels.

Place 1 lettuce leaf on each pita round; place half of lamb on each. Top each with 2 tablespoons tomato and half of yogurt mixture. Sprinkle with green onions. Roll up pita rounds and serve. Yield: 2 servings.

# Kibbe Sandwiches

Per Serving:

Calories 371
Calories from Fat 21%
Fat 8.7 g
Saturated Fat 2.1 g
Carbohydrate 50.1 g
Protein 22.3 g
Cholesterol 47 mg
Sodium 602 mg


Exchanges:

3 Starch
2 Medium-Fat Meat
1 Vegetable

| | |
|---|---|
| ⅔ cup boiling water | ⅛ teaspoon salt |
| ½ cup bulgur (cracked wheat), uncooked | ⅛ teaspoon pepper |
| | Dash of ground allspice |
| 5 ounces lean ground lamb | Vegetable cooking spray |
| 3 tablespoons chopped fresh parsley | 1 (8-inch) pita bread round, cut in half crosswise |
| 3 tablespoons finely chopped onion | 4 green leaf lettuce leaves |
| | ½ cup alfalfa sprouts |
| 2 teaspoons pine nuts, chopped | 3 tablespoons fat-free cucumber dressing |
| 1 clove garlic, minced | |

Pour water over bulgur in a small bowl; cover and let stand 15 minutes. Drain thoroughly. Combine bulgur, lamb, and next 7 ingredients in a medium bowl, stirring well. Shape mixture into 10 (1½-inch) meatballs.

Place meatballs on rack of a broiler pan coated with cooking spray. Broil 5½ inches from heat (with electric oven door partially opened) 30 minutes or until done.

Line each pita half with 2 lettuce leaves; place ¼ cup sprouts and 5 meatballs in each. Top evenly with cucumber dressing. Yield: 2 servings.

# GREEK SALAD HEROS

¾ cup thinly sliced fresh
    mushrooms
½ cup thinly sliced cucumber
2 tablespoons sliced ripe olives
1 tablespoon white balsamic
    vinegar
⅛ teaspoon dried oregano
4 cherry tomatoes, thinly
    sliced

2 tablespoons crumbled feta
    cheese
1 clove garlic, minced
2 (2½-ounce) submarine rolls
2 green leaf lettuce leaves
2 ounces thinly sliced reduced-
    fat, low-salt ham
2 ounces thinly sliced cooked
    turkey breast

Per Serving:

Calories 345
Calories from Fat 31%
Fat 12.0 g
Saturated Fat 3.1 g
Carbohydrate 39.3 g
Protein 20.7 g
Cholesterol 58 mg
Sodium 730 mg

Exchanges:

2 Starch
1½ High-Fat Meat
2 Vegetable

Combine first 8 ingredients in a small bowl; toss gently. Let stand 30 minutes, tossing occasionally.

Cut a thin slice off top of each roll; discard slices. Set tops aside. Cut a 2-inch-wide, V-shaped wedge down length of each roll. Reserve bread wedges for another use.

Drain vegetable mixture. Line each roll with a lettuce leaf; top evenly with ham and turkey. Spoon vegetable mixture evenly over meat; cover with bread tops. Yield: 2 servings.

Greek Salad Hero

# GRILLED HAM, CHEESE, AND PINEAPPLE SANDWICHES

Per Serving:

Calories 200
Calories from Fat 26%
Fat 5.8 g
Saturated Fat 1.4 g
Carbohydrate 26.3 g
Protein 14.3 g
Cholesterol 20 mg
Sodium 809 mg


Exchanges:

1   Starch
1½  Lean Meat
1   Fruit

2   teaspoons nonfat mayonnaise
    Dash of ground nutmeg
4   (¾-ounce) slices reduced-
    calorie whole wheat bread
2   (¾-ounce) slices nonfat
    process Cheddar cheese

2   (½-inch-thick) slices fresh
    pineapple
2   (1-ounce) slices reduced-fat
    low-salt ham
    Vegetable cooking spray

Combine mayonnaise and nutmeg in a small bowl, stirring well. Spread mayonnaise mixture evenly over 2 bread slices; top each with a cheese slice, pineapple slice, ham slice, and a remaining bread slice.

Transfer sandwiches to a sandwich press or hot griddle coated with cooking spray. Cook until bread is lightly browned and cheese melts. Yield: 2 servings.

# CILANTRO-GRILLED CHICKEN SANDWICHES

Per Serving:

Calories 270
Calories from Fat 24%
Fat 7.2 g
Saturated Fat 1.3 g
Carbohydrate 20.5 g
Protein 29.1 g
Cholesterol 71 mg
Sodium 331 mg


Exchanges:

1   Starch
3   Lean Meat
1   Vegetable

2   tablespoons chopped fresh
    cilantro
2   tablespoons chopped onion
2   tablespoons chopped sweet
    red pepper
2   tablespoons chopped tomato
    Dash of ground red pepper
1   tablespoon lime juice
1½  teaspoons olive oil
1½  teaspoons low-sodium soy
    sauce

1   clove garlic
2   (4-ounce) skinned, boned
    chicken breast halves
    Vegetable cooking spray
2   green leaf lettuce leaves
4   (½-ounce) slices reduced-
    calorie Italian bread,
    toasted

Position knife blade in food processor bowl; add first 9 ingredients. Process 1 minute or until blended.

Place chicken in a shallow baking dish; spoon 3 tablespoons cilantro mixture over chicken, turning to coat. Reserve remaining cilantro mixture. Cover and marinate chicken at least 4 hours, turning occasionally.

Coat grill rack with cooking spray; place on grill over medium-hot coals (350° to 400°). Place chicken on rack; grill, covered, 4 minutes on each side or until done.

Place a lettuce leaf on each of 2 bread slices. Place chicken breast halves on lettuce; spoon remaining cilantro mixture evenly over chicken, and top with remaining bread slices. Yield: 2 servings.

# Terrific Turkey Pitas

4 ounces sliced cooked turkey
   breast
1 (8-inch) whole wheat pita
   round, halved
2 tablespoons commercial oil-
   free Italian dressing
2 (¾-ounce) slices nonfat
   process Cheddar cheese
¼ cup chopped tomato
½ cup alfalfa sprouts

Place half of turkey in each pita half; spoon dressing evenly over turkey.
Place 1 cheese slice in each pita half. Wrap pitas in foil, and bake at 400°
for 5 to 8 minutes or until cheese melts. Sprinkle pitas evenly with tomato,
and top with alfalfa sprouts. Yield: 2 servings.

Pack a lunch of turkey pitas, Greek Coleslaw (page 65),
and fat-free onion-flavored potato chips.

Greek Coleslaw (page 65)

**Per Serving:**

Calories 256
Calories from Fat 10%
Fat 2.9 g
Saturated Fat 0.6 g
Carbohydrate 27.4 g
Protein 26.5 g
Cholesterol 43 mg
Sodium 515 mg

**Exchanges:**

1½ Starch
2½ Lean Meat
1 Vegetable

# Turkey Reubens

¼ cup white vinegar
1½ tablespoons sugar
½ teaspoon celery seeds
2 cups shredded cabbage
2 tablespoons commercial
   nonfat Thousand Island
   dressing
4 (1-ounce) slices rye bread,
   toasted
4 ounces thinly sliced cooked
   turkey breast
⅓ cup (1.2 ounces) shredded
   reduced-fat Swiss cheese

Combine first 3 ingredients in a small saucepan. Cook over medium heat,
stirring constantly, until sugar dissolves. Place cabbage in a small bowl. Pour
vinegar mixture over cabbage; let stand at least 30 minutes.

Spread dressing evenly over 2 bread slices. Arrange turkey evenly over
dressing. Drain cabbage mixture, and spoon evenly over turkey; sprinkle
with cheese.

Place sandwiches on a baking sheet, and broil 5½ inches from heat (with
electric oven door partially opened) 1 to 2 minutes or until cheese melts.
Top with remaining bread slices. Serve immediately. Yield: 2 servings.

Bake Parmesan Potato Wedges (page 129)
to go with hearty Turkey Reubens.

Parmesan Potato Wedges (page 129)

**Per Serving:**

Calories 381
Calories from Fat 14%
Fat 5.8 g
Saturated Fat 2.4 g
Carbohydrate 54.9 g
Protein 29.6 g
Cholesterol 50 mg
Sodium 656 mg

**Exchanges:**

3 Starch
2 Lean Meat
2 Vegetable

Tiramisú (page 180)

# SOMETHING SWEET

Dessert dilemma solved! Make just enough for two, and spare yourself
tempting extra helpings of delectable desserts.

# CARAMEL APPLE DUMPLINGS

2 tablespoons skim milk
½ teaspoon ground cinnamon
4 caramel candies, unwrapped
2 medium baking apples

2 sheets commercial frozen
   phyllo pastry, thawed
   Butter-flavored vegetable
   cooking spray

Combine first 3 ingredients in a small saucepan. Cook over low heat, stirring constantly, until smooth. Remove from heat, and set aside.

Core apples, cutting to, but not through, the bottom of each apple. Spoon caramel mixture evenly into centers of apples. Place apples in a small baking dish; cover and bake at 400° for 20 to 22 minutes or until apples are tender. Remove from dish, and let cool.

Place 1 sheet of phyllo on a damp towel (keeping remaining phyllo covered). Coat phyllo with cooking spray. Fold phyllo in half crosswise. Place 1 apple on phyllo rectangle. Coat edges of phyllo with cooking spray; bring corners to center, pinching edges to seal. Coat dumpling with cooking spray. Repeat with remaining apple and phyllo.

Place dumplings on a baking sheet coated with cooking spray. Bake at 400° for 5 to 6 minutes or until golden. Yield: 2 servings.

*Be sure to thaw frozen phyllo according to package directions so it won't be too dry to fold.*

# BANANAS WITH RASPBERRY SAUCE

2 cups fresh raspberries,
   divided
1 tablespoon sugar

2 small bananas
1 teaspoon lemon juice

Place 1½ cups raspberries in container of an electric blender; cover and process until smooth. Pour raspberry puree into a wire-mesh strainer; press with back of spoon against the sides of the strainer to squeeze out juice. Discard pulp and seeds remaining in strainer. Combine raspberry juice and sugar, stirring until sugar dissolves.

Peel bananas; slice each banana diagonally into 4 pieces. Place banana in a bowl; add lemon juice, and toss gently. Arrange banana and remaining ½ cup raspberries evenly on 2 dessert plates. Spoon raspberry sauce evenly over fruit. Yield: 2 servings.

# BLUEBERRIES JUBILEE

½ cup unsweetened apple juice
1 tablespoon cornstarch
1 tablespoon sugar
2 teaspoons lemon juice
  Dash of ground cinnamon
1 cup fresh or frozen
    blueberries, thawed
3 tablespoons brandy
1 cup vanilla nonfat ice cream

Combine apple juice and cornstarch, stirring well. Pour apple juice mixture into a medium skillet. Bring to a boil, stirring constantly. Boil 1 minute. Remove from heat; add sugar, lemon juice, and cinnamon, stirring until sugar dissolves. Gently stir in blueberries.

Place brandy in a small saucepan, and heat just until warm. Pour brandy over blueberry mixture, and immediately ignite with a long match. Let flames die down.

Scoop ½ cup ice cream into each of 2 dessert bowls. Spoon blueberry mixture evenly over ice cream. Serve immediately. Yield: 2 servings.

**Per Serving:**

Calories 220
Calories from Fat 2%
Fat 0.4 g
Saturated Fat 0 g
Carbohydrate 52.1 g
Protein 2.7 g
Cholesterol 0 mg
Sodium 29 mg

**Exchanges:**

1 Starch
2½ Fruit

# QUICK PEACH CRISP

1 (16-ounce) can sliced
    peaches in juice, drained
2 tablespoons sugar
1 teaspoon cornstarch
  Vegetable cooking spray
¼ cup low-fat granola without
    raisins

Combine first 3 ingredients in a small bowl. Spoon peach mixture evenly into 2 (10-ounce) custard cups coated with cooking spray.

Place cups on a baking sheet; top each with 2 tablespoons granola. Bake, uncovered, at 400° for 20 to 25 minutes or until peach mixture is thoroughly heated and topping is crisp. Yield: 2 servings.

*This is the dessert to make when you're in a hurry and need a quick-fix sweet.*

**Per Serving:**

Calories 143
Calories from Fat 5%
Fat 0.9 g
Saturated Fat 0 g
Carbohydrate 34.0 g
Protein 1.9 g
Cholesterol 0 mg
Sodium 23 mg

**Exchanges:**

½ Starch
1½ Fruit

# BLUSHING PEARS IN CHOCOLATE SAUCE

Per Serving:

Calories 197
Calories from Fat 4%
Fat 0.9 g
Saturated Fat 0.2 g
Carbohydrate 48.5 g
Protein 1.5 g
Cholesterol 0 mg
Sodium 19 mg


Exchanges:

½ Starch
3 Fruit

2 medium-size firm pears
(about ¾ pound)
1 tablespoon unsweetened
orange juice
1½ cups blush wine
¾ cup cranberry-raspberry
juice cocktail

2 tablespoons powdered sugar
2 teaspoons unsweetened
cocoa
½ teaspoon cornstarch
¼ cup water
½ teaspoon vanilla extract
Orange zest (optional)

Peel each pear; remove core from bottom end, leaving stem end intact. If needed, slice about ¼ inch from base of each pear so that it will sit flat. Brush pears with orange juice.

Combine wine and cranberry-raspberry juice in a medium saucepan; bring to a boil. Place pears, stem end up, in pan. Cover, reduce heat, and simmer 15 minutes or just until pears are tender. Remove pears from liquid with a slotted spoon. Reserve poaching liquid for another use, if desired.

Combine powdered sugar, cocoa, and cornstarch in a small saucepan. Gradually add water, stirring until smooth. Cook, stirring constantly, over medium heat until slightly thickened. Remove from heat, and stir in vanilla.

Spoon 1 tablespoon chocolate sauce into each of 2 dessert dishes; place pears on sauce. Drizzle 1 tablespoon chocolate sauce over each pear. Garnish with orange zest, if desired. Yield: 2 servings.

Blushing Pears in Chocolate Sauce

# RASPBERRY-FILLED MERINGUES

1   egg white
½   teaspoon almond extract
⅛   teaspoon cream of tartar
    Dash of salt
2   tablespoons sugar
1   tablespoon sliced almonds,
        toasted and ground

1   cup fresh raspberries
2   tablespoons dry red wine
1   tablespoon sugar
    Fresh mint sprigs (optional)

Line a baking sheet with parchment paper. Draw 2 (4-inch) circles on paper; turn paper over. Set aside baking sheet.

Beat first 4 ingredients at high speed of an electric mixer until soft peaks form. Gradually add 2 tablespoons sugar, 1 tablespoon at a time, beating until stiff peaks form and sugar dissolves (2 to 4 minutes). Gently fold in almonds.

Pipe egg white mixture onto circles on paper, building up sides to form a shell. Bake at 225° for 1 hour and 20 minutes. Turn off oven. Cool in oven 2 hours with oven door closed. Carefully remove from paper; let cool completely on wire racks.

Combine raspberries, wine, and 1 tablespoon sugar; let stand 1 hour.

Place meringues on 2 dessert plates. Spoon raspberry mixture evenly into meringues. Garnish with mint sprigs, if desired. Yield: 2 servings.

Your meringues won't be as sticky if you bake them on a dry, clear day.

Per Serving:

Calories 149
Calories from Fat 13%
Fat 2.2 g
Saturated Fat 0.2 g
Carbohydrate 28.0 g
Protein 3.1 g
Cholesterol 0 mg
Sodium 102 mg

Exchanges:

1   Starch
1   Fruit

# STRAWBERRY SOUP

2   cups fresh strawberries,
        halved
1   tablespoon chopped pecans
1   (6-ounce) carton vanilla
        nonfat yogurt, divided

2   tablespoons dry red wine
2   teaspoons sugar
    Sliced strawberries (optional)

Combine strawberries and pecans in container of an electric blender; cover and process until smooth, stopping once to scrape down sides. Reserve 1 tablespoon yogurt; add remaining yogurt to strawberry mixture, stirring well. Add wine and sugar; cover and process until blended. Cover and chill.

To serve, ladle soup evenly into 2 dessert bowls. Drizzle 1½ teaspoons yogurt over each serving. Garnish with sliced strawberries, if desired. Yield: 2 cups.

Per Serving:

Calories 123
Calories from Fat 21%
Fat 2.9 g
Saturated Fat 0.3 g
Carbohydrate 17.5 g
Protein 5.7 g
Cholesterol 2 mg
Sodium 67 mg

Exchanges:

1   Fruit
½   Skim Milk
½   Fat

# BLACKBERRY GRANITA

Per Serving:

Calories 262
Calories from Fat 1%
Fat 0.4 g
Saturated Fat 0 g
Carbohydrate 64.6 g
Protein 0.8 g
Cholesterol 0 mg
Sodium 2 mg

Exchanges:

4 Fruit

½ cup sugar
½ cup water
2 tablespoons dry red wine

1½ cups fresh blackberries
Fresh blackberries (optional)
Mint sprigs (optional)

Combine sugar and water in a small saucepan, stirring well. Bring mixture to a boil; cook, stirring constantly, 1 minute or until sugar dissolves. Let cool slightly.

Position knife blade in food processor bowl; add sugar mixture, wine, and 1½ cups blackberries. Process until smooth. Pour blackberry puree into a wire-mesh strainer; press with back of spoon against the sides of the strainer to squeeze out juice. Discard pulp and seeds remaining in strainer. Pour mixture into an 8-inch square pan. Cover and freeze at least 8 hours or until firm.

To serve, scrape mixture with the tines of a fork until fluffy. Scoop into 2 dessert bowls, and serve immediately. If desired, garnish with additional blackberries and mint sprigs. Yield: 2 servings.

For an elegant presentation, serve the granita
in a wine glass or a stemmed compote.

# ORANGE SORBET

Per Serving:

Calories 72
Calories from Fat 1%
Fat 0.1 g
Saturated Fat 0 g
Carbohydrate 17.9 g
Protein 0.9 g
Cholesterol 0 mg
Sodium 0 mg

Exchanges:

1 Fruit

1 large orange
¼ cup unsweetened orange
    juice

1 tablespoon sugar

Cut orange in half crosswise; remove and discard seeds. Clip membrane, and carefully remove pulp. Set pulp aside. Drain orange shells upside down on paper towels.

Position knife blade in food processor bowl; add orange pulp. Process until smooth. Pour puree into a wire-mesh strainer; press with back of spoon against the sides of the strainer to squeeze out juice. Discard pulp remaining in strainer. Combine strained juice, ¼ cup orange juice, and sugar, stirring well. Pour mixture into an 8-inch square pan. Cover and freeze at least 8 hours or until firm.

Position knife blade in food processor bowl; add frozen orange mixture. Process until smooth but not thawed. To serve, scoop into 2 dessert dishes or into orange shells, if desired. Serve immediately. Yield: 2 servings.

# WATERMELON SORBET

3 tablespoons sugar
3 tablespoons water
3 cups cubed, seeded
    watermelon

1 tablespoon lemon juice
   Fresh blackberries (optional)
   Watermelon wedges (optional)

Combine sugar and water in a small saucepan, stirring well. Bring mixture to a boil; cook, stirring constantly, 1 minute or until sugar dissolves. Let cool slightly.

Position knife blade in food processor bowl; add watermelon, sugar mixture, and lemon juice. Process until smooth. Pour mixture into an 8-inch square pan. Cover and freeze at least 8 hours or until firm.

Position knife blade in food processor bowl; add frozen watermelon mixture. Process until smooth but not thawed. To serve, scoop into 2 dessert dishes, and serve immediately. If desired, garnish with blackberries and watermelon wedges. Yield: 2 servings.

Per Serving:

Calories 152
Calories from Fat 6%
Fat 1.0 g
Saturated Fat 0.5 g
Carbohydrate 36.7 g
Protein 1.5 g
Cholesterol 0 mg
Sodium 5 mg

Exchanges:

2½ Fruit

Watermelon Sorbet

# NEOPOLITAN ICE CREAM PIE

⅓ cup chocolate graham
    cracker crumbs
1 tablespoon reduced-calorie
    margarine, melted
    Vegetable cooking spray
½ cup vanilla nonfat ice cream,
    softened

½ cup strawberry nonfat ice
    cream, softened
2 teaspoons chocolate nonfat
    ice cream topping

Combine graham cracker crumbs and margarine in a small bowl. Firmly press crumb mixture evenly into bottom of a 5-inch springform pan coated with cooking spray.

Spoon vanilla ice cream into crust; cover and freeze until set. Spoon strawberry ice cream over vanilla. Cover and freeze until set. Drizzle chocolate topping over ice cream filling; cut into wedges, and serve immediately. Yield: 2 servings.

Per Serving:

Calories 253
Calories from Fat 27%
Fat 7.7 g
Saturated Fat 1.6 g
Carbohydrate 42.3 g
Protein 3.8 g
Cholesterol 0 mg
Sodium 209 mg

Exchanges:

1 Starch
2 Fruit
1½ Fat

# HONEY-NUT PHYLLO SLICES

2 tablespoons honey, divided
2 teaspoons reduced-calorie
    margarine
⅛ teaspoon ground allspice
    Dash of ground cloves
⅛ teaspoon vanilla extract

3 sheets commercial frozen
    phyllo pastry, thawed
    Butter-flavored vegetable
    cooking spray
2 teaspoons ground walnuts

Combine 1½ tablespoons honey, margarine, allspice, and cloves in a small saucepan. Cook over low heat until margarine melts. Remove from heat; stir in vanilla.

Cut each phyllo sheet in half crosswise. Place 1 half-sheet of phyllo on wax paper (keeping remaining phyllo covered). Lightly coat phyllo with cooking spray. Place another half-sheet of phyllo over first sheet; coat with cooking spray. Brush about 2 teaspoons honey mixture over phyllo. Repeat layers twice. Sprinkle top layer with walnuts, leaving a 1-inch margin on long sides.

Roll up phyllo, jellyroll fashion, starting with long side. Place, seam side down, on a baking sheet coated with cooking spray. Brush remaining honey mixture over phyllo. Cut diagonally into 4 slices. Bake at 300° for 30 minutes.

Drizzle remaining ½ tablespoon honey evenly over warm phyllo slices. Let cool. Yield: 4 slices.

*If you happen to have one or two phyllo slices left over, you can store them overnight in a heavy-duty, zip-top plastic bag.*

Per Slice:

Calories 101
Calories from Fat 32%
Fat 3.6 g
Saturated Fat 0.4 g
Carbohydrate 16.6 g
Protein 1.6 g
Cholesterol 0 mg
Sodium 88 mg

Exchanges:

1 Starch
1 Fat

# APPLE PIE BUNDLES

¼ cup plus 2 tablespoons sifted
    cake flour
¼ teaspoon baking powder
¾ teaspoon sugar
1 tablespoon margarine, cut
    into small pieces and chilled
2¼ teaspoons ice water
    Butter-flavored vegetable
    cooking spray

½ cup peeled, chopped apple
1 tablespoon sugar
¾ teaspoon all-purpose flour
⅛ teaspoon ground cinnamon
    Dash of ground nutmeg
½ teaspoon sugar
    Dash of ground cinnamon

Combine first 3 ingredients in a bowl; cut in margarine with a pastry blender until mixture resembles coarse meal and is pale yellow. Sprinkle ice water over surface; toss with a fork until dry ingredients are moistened and mixture is crumbly.

Divide dough in half, and shape into 2 balls. Gently press each ball between 2 sheets of heavy-duty plastic wrap; roll each ball of dough into a 6-inch circle. Place dough rounds in freezer 10 minutes or until top sheet of plastic wrap can be removed easily. Invert and fit each round into a muffin pan cup coated with cooking spray; remove remaining sheet of plastic wrap.

Combine apple and next 4 ingredients in a small bowl, stirring well. Spoon apple mixture evenly into pastry-lined muffin pan cups; fold pastry over apple mixture. Spray pastry with cooking spray. Combine ½ teaspoon sugar and dash of cinnamon; sprinkle evenly over pastry. Bake at 350° for 25 minutes or until golden. Yield: 2 servings.

When you use cake flour instead of all-purpose flour in a
low-fat pastry, you will get a more tender pastry.

**Per Serving:**

Calories 193
Calories from Fat 30%
Fat 6.4 g
Saturated Fat 1.2 g
Carbohydrate 32.8 g
Protein 1.9 g
Cholesterol 0 mg
Sodium 67 mg

**Exchanges:**

1 Starch
1 Fruit
1 Fat

# Berry Good Cobbler

Per Serving:

Calories 314
Calories from Fat 19%
Fat 6.8 g
Saturated Fat 1.0 g
Carbohydrate 62.2 g
Protein 4.2 g
Cholesterol 0 mg
Sodium 55 mg


Exchanges:

2  Starch
2  Fruit
1  Fat

1  cup fresh blackberries
1  cup fresh blueberries
3  tablespoons sugar
1  teaspoon cornstarch
¼  teaspoon grated orange rind
¼  teaspoon ground cinnamon
   Vegetable cooking spray

⅓  cup sifted cake flour
2  teaspoons sugar, divided
¼  teaspoon baking powder
2  teaspoons chilled margarine
1  to 1½ tablespoons skim milk
2  teaspoons sliced almonds

Combine first 6 ingredients in a medium bowl; toss gently. Spoon mixture into a 7- x 5¼- x 1½-inch baking dish coated with cooking spray. Set aside.

Combine flour, 1 teaspoon sugar, and baking powder in a small bowl; cut in margarine with a pastry blender until mixture resembles coarse meal and is pale yellow. Sprinkle milk, 1 teaspoon at a time, over surface of dough; toss with a fork until dry ingredients are moistened and mixture is crumbly. Shape dough into a ball.

Roll dough into a 7½- x 5½-inch rectangle between 2 sheets of heavy-duty plastic wrap. Place in freezer 10 minutes or until top sheet of plastic wrap can be removed easily. Invert dough over berry mixture; remove remaining sheet of plastic wrap. Cut slits in pastry for steam to escape. Sprinkle with remaining teaspoon sugar and almonds. Bake at 375° for 30 minutes or until berry mixture is bubbly and crust is golden. Serve warm or at room temperature. Yield: 2 servings.

Fresh Blueberries

# Coconut Cream Pie

3 tablespoons sifted cake flour
½ teaspoon sugar
⅛ teaspoon baking powder
2 teaspoons chilled margarine
2 teaspoons ice water
   Vegetable cooking spray
2 tablespoons sugar
2 teaspoons cornstarch
⅓ cup skim milk

1 tablespoon frozen egg substitute, thawed
1 tablespoon unsweetened coconut, toasted and divided
½ teaspoon vanilla extract
1 egg white
⅛ teaspoon cream of tartar
1 tablespoon sugar

Combine first 3 ingredients in a small bowl; cut in margarine with a pastry blender until mixture resembles coarse meal and is pale yellow. Sprinkle water, 1 teaspoon at a time, over surface of dough; toss with a fork until dry ingredients are moistened and mixture is crumbly. Shape into a ball.

Roll dough into a 6-inch circle between 2 sheets of heavy-duty plastic wrap. Place in freezer 10 minutes or until top sheet of plastic wrap can be removed easily. Invert and fit dough into a 4-inch pie pan coated with cooking spray; remove remaining sheet of plastic wrap. Fold edges under and flute, if desired. Prick bottom of crust with a fork. Bake at 425° for 7 to 8 minutes or until golden. Let cool on a wire rack.

Combine 2 tablespoons sugar and cornstarch in a small saucepan. Gradually stir in milk and egg substitute. Cook, stirring constantly, over medium-high heat until mixture comes to a boil. Boil 1 minute or until thickened. Remove from heat; stir in 2 teaspoons coconut and vanilla. Spoon filling into cooled pastry.

Beat egg white and cream of tartar at high speed of an electric mixer until foamy. Gradually add 1 tablespoon sugar, beating until stiff peaks form and sugar dissolves (2 to 4 minutes). Spread meringue mixture over coconut filling, sealing to edge of pastry. Sprinkle with remaining 1 teaspoon toasted coconut. Bake at 325° for 20 to 25 minutes or until golden. Yield: 2 servings.

**Check your local kitchen shops or variety stores for 4-inch pie pans.**

Per Serving:

Calories 206
Calories from Fat 25%
Fat 5.8 g
Saturated Fat 2.2 g
Carbohydrate 33.6 g
Protein 4.9 g
Cholesterol 1 mg
Sodium 105 mg

Exchanges:

2 Starch
1 Fat

# GINGERED PEAR PIE

1 teaspoon minced crystallized
   ginger
2 tablespoons water
¼ cup sifted cake flour
⅛ teaspoon baking powder
½ teaspoon sugar
1 tablespoon chilled
   margarine, cut into pieces
1½ to 2 teaspoons ice water

Vegetable cooking spray
1 cup peeled, thinly sliced pear
   (about 1 small pear)
2 tablespoons sugar
2 teaspoons quick-cooking
   tapioca, uncooked
⅛ teaspoon ground cinnamon
⅛ teaspoon ground nutmeg
½ teaspoon sugar

Combine ginger and water in a small saucepan. Bring to a boil; remove from heat. Cover and let stand 1 hour. Drain mixture, reserving liquid.

Combine flour, baking powder, and ½ teaspoon sugar in a small bowl; cut in margarine with a pastry blender until mixture resembles coarse meal and is pale yellow. Sprinkle ice water, 1 teaspoon at a time, over surface of dough; toss with a fork until dry ingredients are moistened and mixture is crumbly.

Divide dough in half. Gently press each half of dough between 2 sheets of heavy-duty plastic wrap into a 4-inch circle. Chill 15 minutes. Roll each half of dough into a 5½-inch circle between sheets of plastic wrap. Set 1 dough circle aside. Remove top sheet of plastic wrap from other circle. Invert dough, and fit into a 4-inch tartlet pan coated with cooking spray. Remove remaining plastic wrap.

Combine reserved ginger liquid, pear, and next 4 ingredients. Spoon mixture into prepared pastry. Remove top sheet of plastic wrap from remaining dough circle. Invert dough over filling. Remove remaining sheet of plastic wrap; fold edges under and flute, if desired. Cut slits in top pastry for steam to escape. Sprinkle with ½ teaspoon sugar. Bake at 400° for 50 minutes or until golden. Let cool slightly before serving. Yield: 2 servings.

Make a holiday meal even more special by ending
with this "just-the-right-size" fruit pie.

**Per Serving:**

Calories 217
Calories from Fat 26%
Fat 6.3 g
Saturated Fat 1.2 g
Carbohydrate 40.2 g
Protein 1.5 g
Cholesterol 0 mg
Sodium 68 mg

**Exchanges:**

1½ Starch
1 Fruit
1 Fat

# Orange-Pumpkin Pies

½  cup gingersnap crumbs
    (about 9 cookies)
1  tablespoon reduced-calorie
    margarine, melted
    Vegetable cooking spray
½  teaspoon all-purpose flour
⅓  cup canned pumpkin
2  tablespoons sugar
2  tablespoons evaporated
    skimmed milk

2  tablespoons frozen egg
    substitute, thawed
1  tablespoon unsweetened
    orange juice
¼  teaspoon ground cinnamon
⅛  teaspoon ground ginger
⅛  teaspoon ground nutmeg
2  tablespoons frozen reduced-
    calorie whipped topping,
    thawed

Combine gingersnap crumbs and margarine, stirring well. Coat 2 (3½-inch) tartlet pans with cooking spray. Sprinkle flour evenly over bottom of each pan. Press crumb mixture on bottom and up three-fourths sides of pans. Bake at 375° for 5 minutes.

Combine pumpkin and next 7 ingredients, stirring well with a wire whisk. Pour evenly into prepared crusts. Bake at 375° for 30 minutes or until set. Let cool completely on a wire rack. Top each pie with 1 tablespoon whipped topping. Yield: 2 servings.

**Per Serving:**

Calories 272
Calories from Fat 33%
Fat 10.0 g
Saturated Fat 2.3 g
Carbohydrate 41.5 g
Protein 5.4 g
Cholesterol 12 mg
Sodium 143 mg

**Exchanges:**

2  Starch
1  Fruit
2  Fat

# Strawberry Fruit Tarts

1  cup sliced fresh strawberries
2  tablespoons sugar, divided
½  cup graham cracker crumbs
1½  tablespoons reduced-calorie
    margarine, melted
    Vegetable cooking spray
2½  tablespoons plain nonfat
    yogurt

2½  tablespoons Neufchâtel
    cheese, softened
1½  tablespoons powdered sugar
½  teaspoon vanilla extract
1  tablespoon apple jelly

Combine strawberries and 1 tablespoon sugar; let stand 10 minutes. Drain strawberries, reserving 2 teaspoons liquid.

Combine remaining 1 tablespoon sugar, strawberry liquid, graham cracker crumbs, and margarine, stirring well. Press crumb mixture evenly into bottoms and up sides of 2 (3½-inch) tartlet pans coated with cooking spray. Bake at 350° for 8 minutes; let cool.

Spread yogurt onto several layers of heavy-duty paper towels; cover with additional paper towels. Let stand 10 minutes. Scrape yogurt into a bowl, using a rubber spatula.

Combine yogurt, Neufchâtel cheese, powdered sugar, and vanilla, stirring well. Spoon mixture evenly into prepared crusts. Cover and chill thoroughly.

Arrange strawberries evenly over yogurt mixture. Place apple jelly in a small saucepan; cook over low heat until jelly melts, stirring occasionally. Drizzle jelly evenly over tarts. Yield: 2 servings.

**Per Serving:**

Calories 322
Calories from Fat 35%
Fat 12.5 g
Saturated Fat 3.9 g
Carbohydrate 49.2 g
Protein 4.6 g
Cholesterol 14 mg
Sodium 329 mg

**Exchanges:**

1½ Starch
2  Fruit
2  Fat

Grasshopper Parfaits

# Grasshopper Parfaits

**Per Serving:**

Calories 302
Calories from Fat 10%
Fat 3.2 g
Saturated Fat 1.7 g
Carbohydrate 59.3 g
Protein 6.7 g
Cholesterol 3 mg
Sodium 140 mg

**Exchanges:**

3   Fruit
1   Skim Milk
½   Fat

¼   cup plus 2 tablespoons sugar
2   teaspoons cornstarch
1   cup skim milk
2   tablespoons frozen egg
      substitute, thawed
1   tablespoon crème de menthe
¼   cup frozen reduced-calorie
      whipped topping, thawed

¼   cup chocolate graham
      cracker crumbs
1   chocolate-covered mint
      wafer candy, cut in half
      diagonally (optional)

Combine sugar and cornstarch in a small saucepan. Gradually stir in milk and egg substitute. Cook, stirring constantly, over medium heat until mixture comes to a boil. Boil 2 minutes or until thickened. Remove from heat; stir in crème de menthe. Let cool; fold in whipped topping.

Spoon 2 tablespoons custard mixture into each of 2 (6-ounce) parfait glasses. Sprinkle about ½ tablespoon graham cracker crumbs over each custard mixture; repeat layers, using remaining custard mixture and crumbs. Garnish with candy, if desired. Cover and chill. Yield: 2 servings.

# Irish Coffee-Caramel Dessert

1 teaspoon unflavored gelatin
2 tablespoons cold water
⅔ cup evaporated skimmed milk
1 tablespoon powdered sugar
2 tablespoons fat-free caramel-flavored syrup

2 tablespoons Irish cream liqueur
½ teaspoon instant coffee granules
2 tablespoons frozen reduced-calorie whipped topping, thawed

Sprinkle gelatin over cold water in a small saucepan; let stand 1 minute. Cook over low heat, stirring until gelatin dissolves, about 2 minutes. Stir in milk and next 4 ingredients.

Pour gelatin mixture evenly into 2 dessert dishes. Cover and chill until set. Just before serving, top each serving with 1 tablespoon whipped topping. Yield: 2 servings.

Keep a container of reduced-calorie whipped topping in the freezer to have on hand. You'll be able to use it in several recipes in this chapter.

**Per Serving:**

Calories 190
Calories from Fat 15%
Fat 3.2 g
Saturated Fat 2.0 g
Carbohydrate 31.2 g
Protein 8.5 g
Cholesterol 3 mg
Sodium 153 mg

**Exchanges:**

2 Starch
½ Fat

# Peaches and Cream Mousse

¾ cup frozen unsweetened peaches, thawed
1½ teaspoons unflavored gelatin
¼ cup plus 2 tablespoons apricot nectar
1½ tablespoons sugar

1½ tablespoons peach schnapps
⅛ teaspoon almond extract
¾ cup frozen reduced-calorie whipped topping, thawed
Fresh mint leaves (optional)

Place peaches in container of an electric blender; cover and process until smooth, stopping once to scrape down sides.

Sprinkle gelatin over apricot nectar in a small saucepan; let stand 1 minute. Stir in pureed peaches and sugar. Cook over medium heat, stirring until gelatin dissolves. Remove from heat; stir in schnapps and almond extract. Chill 1 hour or until consistency of unbeaten egg white.

Gently fold in whipped topping. Spoon mixture evenly into 2 (8-ounce) parfait glasses. Cover and chill until set. Garnish with mint leaves, if desired. Yield: 2 servings.

**Per Serving:**

Calories 185
Calories from Fat 16%
Fat 3.3 g
Saturated Fat 0 g
Carbohydrate 31.3 g
Protein 3.3 g
Cholesterol 0 mg
Sodium 25 mg

**Exchanges:**

1 Starch
1 Fruit
½ Fat

# Tiramisú

Per Serving:

Calories 325
Calories from Fat 26%
Fat 9.4 g
Saturated Fat 5.6 g
Carbohydrate 45.6 g
Protein 13.3 g
Cholesterol 78 mg
Sodium 324 mg

Exchanges:

2   Starch
1   Skim Milk
2   Fat

1   (8-ounce) carton coffee-flavored low-fat yogurt
¼   cup nonfat cottage cheese
¼   cup Neufchâtel cheese, softened
⅓   cup sifted powdered sugar
1½  tablespoons water
2   teaspoons Kahlúa or other coffee-flavored liqueur
4   ladyfingers, split
1   teaspoon grated semisweet chocolate
Chocolate curls (optional)

Place a small colander in a 1-quart glass measure or small bowl. Line colander with 4 layers of cheesecloth, allowing cheesecloth to extend over edges. Spoon yogurt into colander. Cover loosely with plastic wrap; refrigerate at least 4 hours.

Spoon drained yogurt into a small bowl; discard liquid. Place cottage cheese, Neufchâtel cheese, and powdered sugar in container of an electric blender; cover and process until smooth, stopping once to scrape down sides. Add cottage cheese mixture to drained yogurt, stirring well.

Line a 5¾- x 3¼- x 2-inch loafpan with aluminum foil, allowing foil to extend 1 inch from both ends of pan. Set aside.

Combine water and liqueur. Brush cut sides of 4 ladyfinger halves with liqueur mixture; place, cut side down, in bottom of prepared loafpan. Spread half of yogurt mixture over ladyfingers in pan. Repeat layers with remaining ladyfingers, liqueur mixture, and yogurt mixture. Cover loosely with plastic wrap, and chill at least 8 hours. To serve, carefully lift foil out of pan, and cut in half crosswise. Place each half on a dessert plate. Sprinkle evenly with chocolate, and garnish with chocolate curls, if desired.
Yield: 2 servings.

Tiramisú

# GINGER BRÛLÉE

1 tablespoon peeled, minced
   gingerroot
1 tablespoon sugar
¼ cup plus 1 tablespoon water
¾ cup skim milk
½ cup frozen egg substitute,
   thawed

¼ cup sugar
2 tablespoons instant nonfat
   dry milk powder
1 teaspoon vanilla extract
   Vegetable cooking spray
1 teaspoon brown sugar

Combine first 3 ingredients in a small saucepan. Bring to a boil; reduce heat, and simmer, uncovered, 5 minutes or until mixture is reduced by half. Remove from heat, and strain mixture, reserving liquid; discard ginger.

Combine ginger liquid, milk, and next 4 ingredients in a small bowl; beat at medium speed of an electric mixer until blended. Pour mixture evenly into 2 (8-ounce) ramekins coated with cooking spray. Place ramekins in an 8-inch square pan. Add hot water to pan to depth of 1 inch. Bake at 325° for 55 to 60 minutes or until set. Remove ramekins from water, and cool 15 minutes. Cover and chill thoroughly.

Sprinkle ½ teaspoon brown sugar over top of each custard. Place ramekins on a baking sheet. Broil 5½ inches from heat (with electric oven door partially opened) 1 minute or until sugar melts. Serve immediately. Yield 2 servings.

**Per Serving:**

Calories 225
Calories from Fat 2%
Fat 0.4 g
Saturated Fat 0.1 g
Carbohydrate 42.8 g
Protein 11.8 g
Cholesterol 3 mg
Sodium 179 mg

**Exchanges:**

2 Starch
1 Skim Milk

# CREAMY FLAN

2 teaspoons sugar
   Vegetable cooking spray
1 cup skim milk
⅓ cup frozen egg substitute,
   thawed

2 tablespoons sugar
1 teaspoon vanilla extract

Place 2 teaspoons sugar in a small saucepan. Cook over medium heat, stirring constantly, 2 minutes or until sugar melts and turns light brown. Quickly pour hot mixture evenly into 2 (6-ounce) custard cups coated with cooking spray, tilting to coat bottoms of cups.

Combine milk and remaining ingredients; pour evenly into custard cups. Place custard cups in an 8-inch square pan; add hot water to pan to depth of 1 inch. Bake at 325° for 1 hour and 20 minutes or until partially set. Remove custard cups from water, and let cool on a wire rack. Cover and chill 2 hours. To serve, loosen edges of custards with a knife; invert onto serving plates. Yield: 2 servings.

**Per Serving:**

Calories 137
Calories from Fat 3%
Fat 0.4 g
Saturated Fat 0.1 g
Carbohydrate 24.0 g
Protein 8.2 g
Cholesterol 2 mg
Sodium 124 mg

**Exchanges:**

1 Starch
½ Milk

# BANANA-CARAMEL PUDDING

¾   cup skim milk
2   caramel candies, unwrapped
2   tablespoons sugar
2   tablespoons frozen egg
    substitute, thawed
1   tablespoon cornstarch
½   teaspoon vanilla extract

1   medium banana, peeled and
    thinly sliced
8   vanilla wafers, cut in half
2   tablespoons frozen reduced-
    calorie whipped topping,
    thawed
    Banana slices (optional)

Combine milk and caramel candies in a small saucepan. Cook over medium-low heat until candies melt, stirring frequently. Combine sugar, egg substitute, and cornstarch in a small bowl. Gradually stir about one-fourth of hot mixture into egg substitute mixture; add to remaining hot mixture, stirring constantly. Cook over medium heat, stirring constantly, until mixture is thickened. Remove from heat; stir in vanilla.

Layer half of banana slices and half of caramel mixture in 2 (8-ounce) ramekins. Repeat layers with remaining banana slices and caramel mixture. Arrange vanilla wafers around edge of ramekins. Cover and chill thoroughly. Top each serving with 1 tablespoon whipped topping. Garnish with additional banana slices, if desired. Yield: 2 servings.

# CHOCOLATE-AMARETTO PUDDING

3   tablespoons sugar
1½  tablespoons unsweetened
    cocoa
1   tablespoon plus 1 teaspoon
    cornstarch

1   cup 1% low-fat milk
1   teaspoon amaretto
¼   teaspoon vanilla extract
2   teaspoons chopped almonds,
    toasted

Combine first 3 ingredients in a small saucepan. Gradually add milk, stirring with a wire whisk until smooth. Cook over medium-low heat, stirring constantly, 8 to 10 minutes or until mixture is thickened. Remove from heat; stir in amaretto and vanilla.

Spoon mixture evenly into 2 dessert dishes. Cover and chill thoroughly. Just before serving, sprinkle evenly with almonds. Yield: 2 servings.

If you prefer not to use amaretto, simply omit it from the recipe. You'll still get a smooth, rich-tasting chocolate pudding.

# CHOCOLATE-BANANA BREAD PUDDING

⅔ cup evaporated skimmed
    milk
2 (1-ounce) slices French
    bread, cut into ¾-inch
    cubes
¼ cup mashed ripe banana
¼ cup frozen egg substitute,
    thawed

3 tablespoons sugar
1 tablespoon unsweetened
    cocoa
½ teaspoon vanilla extract
1 tablespoon semisweet
    chocolate mini-morsels
Vegetable cooking spray

Combine milk and bread; set aside. Combine banana and next 4 ingredients in a medium bowl, beating with a wire whisk until well blended. Stir in bread mixture and chocolate morsels.

Pour mixture evenly into 2 (10-ounce) custard cups coated with cooking spray. Place cups in an 8-inch square pan. Add hot water to pan to depth of 1 inch. Bake at 350° for 35 minutes or until set in center. Serve warm or at room temperature. Yield: 2 servings.

**Per Serving:**

Calories 313
Calories from Fat 12%
Fat 4.0 g
Saturated Fat 2.0 g
Carbohydrate 56.4 g
Protein 13.4 g
Cholesterol 4 mg
Sodium 310 mg

**Exchanges:**

2 Starch
1 Fruit
1 Low-Fat Milk

# RAISIN BREAD PUDDING WITH WHISKEY SAUCE

⅔ cup evaporated skimmed
    milk
⅓ cup frozen egg substitute,
    thawed
1 tablespoon sugar
½ teaspoon vanilla extract
¼ teaspoon ground cinnamon
3 (1-ounce) slices raisin bread,
    cut into ¾-inch pieces

Vegetable cooking spray
1 tablespoon sugar
2 tablespoons bourbon
1 tablespoon water
2 teaspoons reduced-calorie
    margarine
1 teaspoon cornstarch

Combine first 5 ingredients in a medium bowl, stirring well with a wire whisk. Add bread, stirring gently until bread is coated.

Spoon bread mixture evenly into 2 (6-ounce) custard cups coated with cooking spray. Place cups in an 8-inch square pan. Add hot water to pan to depth of 1 inch. Bake at 350° for 40 minutes or until knife inserted in center comes out clean.

Combine 1 tablespoon sugar and remaining ingredients in a small saucepan. Cook over medium heat, stirring constantly, until mixture is thickened and bubbly. Spoon evenly over puddings. Serve warm. Yield: 2 servings.

**Per Serving:**

Calories 282
Calories from Fat 13%
Fat 4.1 g
Saturated Fat 0.7 g
Carbohydrate 48.0 g
Protein 13.2 g
Cholesterol 5 mg
Sodium 352 mg

**Exchanges:**

3 Starch
½ Skim Milk
1 Fat

# CHILLED LEMON SOUFFLÉ

**Per Serving:**

Calories 269
Calories from Fat 18%
Fat 5.3 g
Saturated Fat 1.7 g
Carbohydrate 48.0 g
Protein 8.9 g
Cholesterol 222 mg
Sodium 84 mg

**Exchanges:**

3  Starch
1  Fat

| | |
|---|---|
| 1 teaspoon unflavored gelatin | ½ teaspoon grated lemon rind |
| 1 tablespoon cold water | 3 tablespoons lemon juice |
| 2 eggs, separated | ¼ cup skim milk |
| ¼ cup plus 3 tablespoons sugar, divided | Dash of cream of tartar |
| | 2 tablespoons water |

Sprinkle gelatin over 1 tablespoon cold water; let stand 1 minute. Combine egg yolks, 3 tablespoons sugar, lemon rind, and lemon juice in a small saucepan. Stir in milk. Cook over medium-low heat, stirring constantly, 20 minutes or until thickened. Add gelatin mixture; stir until gelatin dissolves.

Transfer mixture to a small bowl. Cover and chill 1 hour or until mixture mounds slightly when dropped from a spoon.

Beat egg whites and cream of tartar at high speed of an electric mixer until stiff peaks form.

Combine remaining ¼ cup sugar and 2 tablespoons water in a small saucepan. Bring mixture to a boil; cook, without stirring, until candy thermometer registers 238° (about 7 minutes).

Gradually pour sugar mixture in a thin stream over egg white mixture while beating constantly at high speed. Continue to beat until mixture is cool and set. Fold egg white mixture into lemon mixture. Spoon into a 2½-cup soufflé dish. Cover and chill at least 4 hours. Yield: 2 servings.

# ORANGE SOUFFLÉS

**Per Serving:**

Calories 116
Calories from Fat 23%
Fat 3.0 g
Saturated Fat 0.8 g
Carbohydrate 16.2 g
Protein 3.6 g
Cholesterol 111 mg
Sodium 37 mg

**Exchanges:**

1  Starch
½  Fat

| | |
|---|---|
| Vegetable cooking spray | ¼ teaspoon grated orange rind |
| 2 tablespoons sugar, divided | 1½ teaspoons sifted powdered sugar, divided |
| 1 tablespoon skim milk | ⅛ teaspoon cream of tartar |
| 1 teaspoon all-purpose flour | Orange zest (optional) |
| 1 egg, separated | |
| 1 teaspoon orange extract | |

Coat 2 (6-ounce) soufflé dishes or custard cups with cooking spray. Sprinkle dishes evenly with 1 tablespoon sugar, carefully shaking to coat bottom and sides of each dish; set aside.

Combine 1 tablespoon sugar, milk, and flour in a non-aluminum saucepan, stirring with a wire whisk until blended. Cook over medium heat, stirring constantly, until thickened and bubbly. Remove from heat.

Beat egg yolk until thick and pale. Gradually stir about one-fourth of hot mixture into yolk; add to remaining hot mixture, stirring constantly. Stir in orange extract and orange rind; set aside.

Beat egg white, ½ teaspoon powdered sugar, and cream of tartar in a bowl at high speed of an electric mixer until stiff peaks form. Fold egg white mixture into orange mixture. Spoon into prepared dishes. Bake at 375° for 15 minutes or until puffed. Sift remaining 1 teaspoon powdered sugar over soufflés. Garnish with orange zest, if desired. Serve immediately. Yield: 2 servings.

# GRAND MARNIER SOUFFLÉS

Vegetable cooking spray
2 tablespoons sugar, divided
1 tablespoon skim milk
1 teaspoon all-purpose flour
2 teaspoons Grand Marnier or
   other orange-flavored
   liqueur

1 egg, separated
½ teaspoon powdered sugar
⅛ teaspoon cream of tartar
   Chocolate Sauce

Coat 2 (8-ounce) soufflé dishes or custard cups with cooking spray. Sprinkle dishes evenly with 1 tablespoon sugar, carefully shaking to coat bottom and sides of each dish; set aside.

Combine milk, flour, and remaining 1 tablespoon sugar in a small saucepan. Cook over medium heat, stirring constantly, until mixture is thickened and bubbly. Remove from heat. Stir in liqueur.

Beat egg yolk until thick and pale. Gradually stir hot mixture into egg yolk.

Beat egg white, powdered sugar, and cream of tartar in a medium bowl at high speed of an electric mixer until stiff peaks form. Gently fold egg white mixture into milk mixture. Spoon evenly into prepared dishes. Bake at 375° for 15 minutes or until soufflés are puffed. Spoon Chocolate Sauce evenly over soufflés, and serve immediately. Yield: 2 servings.

## Chocolate Sauce

¼ cup water
1½ tablespoons sugar
1 tablespoon unsweetened
   cocoa

½ teaspoon cornstarch
2 teaspoons Grand Marnier or
   other orange-flavored
   liqueur

Combine first 4 ingredients in a small saucepan, stirring until smooth. Cook over medium heat, stirring constantly, until mixture is thickened and bubbly. Stir in liqueur, and cook, stirring constantly, 1 minute. Let cool. Yield: ¼ cup plus 1 tablespoon.

Per Serving:

Calories 169
Calories from Fat 18%
Fat 3.3 g
Saturated Fat 1.0 g
Carbohydrate 30.9 g
Protein 4.4 g
Cholesterol 111 mg
Sodium 39 mg

Exchanges:

2 Starch
½ Fat

Per Tablespoon:

Calories 24
Calories from Fat 8%
Fat 0.1 g
Saturated Fat 0.1 g
Carbohydrate 5.5 g
Protein 0.3 g
Cholesterol 0 mg
Sodium 1 mg

Exchanges:

¼ Starch

# CHOCOLATE ANGEL FOOD CAKES

½ cup plus 1 tablespoon sifted cake flour
¼ cup plus 2 tablespoons sugar, divided
2 tablespoons unsweetened cocoa
6 egg whites
¾ teaspoon cream of tartar
Dash of salt
¼ cup sugar
½ teaspoon vanilla extract
¼ teaspoon almond extract
Vegetable cooking spray
1½ teaspoons powdered sugar

Sift first 3 ingredients together 3 times into a medium bowl; set aside.

Beat egg whites, cream of tartar, and salt in a large bowl at high speed of an electric mixer until foamy. Gradually add ¼ cup sugar, beating until soft peaks form. Sift flour mixture over egg white mixture, 2 tablespoons at a time; fold in gently after each addition. Fold in flavorings.

Spoon batter evenly into 4 (4-inch) tube pans coated with cooking spray, spreading evenly. Break large air pockets by cutting through batter with a knife.

Bake at 350° for 30 minutes or until cake springs back when lightly touched. Remove cakes from oven; invert pans, and cool completely. Carefully loosen cakes from sides of pans, using a narrow metal knife; remove from pans. Sift powdered sugar over cooled cakes. Yield: 4 cakes.

Chocolate Angel Food Cake

# ICED BANANA CAKES

Vegetable cooking spray
¼ cup all-purpose flour
½ teaspoon baking powder
¼ cup sugar
¼ teaspoon ground cinnamon
3 tablespoons frozen egg substitute, thawed
1 tablespoon water
1½ teaspoons vegetable oil

1 teaspoon vanilla extract
¼ cup mashed ripe banana (about ½ small banana)
2 tablespoons sifted powdered sugar
2 teaspoons Neufchâtel cheese, softened
¼ teaspoon skim milk

Coat 2 (4- x 2½- x 1¼-inch) loafpans with cooking spray; set aside.

Combine flour and next 3 ingredients in a bowl. Combine egg substitute, water, oil, and vanilla, stirring well with a wire whisk. Stir in banana. Add banana mixture to dry ingredients, stirring just until dry ingredients are moistened. Spoon batter into prepared pans. Bake at 350° for 25 to 30 minutes or until a wooden pick inserted in center comes out clean. Cool in pans 10 minutes; remove from pans. Let cool completely on a wire rack.

Combine powdered sugar, Neufchâtel cheese, and milk, stirring well. Spread evenly over tops of cakes. Yield: 2 loaves.

Per Loaf:

Calories 307
Calories from Fat 16%
Fat 5.5 g
Saturated Fat 1.5 g
Carbohydrate 62.8 g
Protein 5.1 g
Cholesterol 4 mg
Sodium 57 mg

Exchanges:

2 Starch
2 Fruit
1 Fat

# CARROT CAKE LOAVES

¼ cup plus 2 tablespoons all-purpose flour
¼ teaspoon baking soda
Dash of salt
½ teaspoon ground cinnamon
Dash of ground allspice
1½ tablespoons brown sugar
1½ tablespoons plain low-fat yogurt
1½ tablespoons unsweetened applesauce
1½ tablespoons frozen egg substitute, thawed

2 teaspoons vegetable oil
1 teaspoon water
¼ cup plus 2 tablespoons shredded carrot
1 tablespoon finely chopped walnuts
¾ teaspoon vanilla extract
Vegetable cooking spray
3 tablespoons powdered sugar
2 tablespoons light process cream cheese product
¼ teaspoon vanilla extract

Combine first 5 ingredients in a bowl; make a well in center of mixture.

Combine brown sugar and next 5 ingredients, stirring well with a wire whisk. Add brown sugar mixture to dry ingredients, stirring just until dry ingredients are moistened. Stir in carrot, walnuts, and ¾ teaspoon vanilla.

Spoon batter into 2 (4-inch) loafpans coated with cooking spray. Bake at 350° for 25 minutes or until a wooden pick inserted in center comes out clean. Cool in pans 10 minutes. Remove from pans, and let cool completely on a wire rack.

Combine powdered sugar, cream cheese, and ¼ teaspoon vanilla, stirring until smooth. Spread evenly over tops of loaves. Yield: 2 loaves.

Per Loaf:

Calories 290
Calories from Fat 31%
Fat 10.0 g
Saturated Fat 2.5 g
Carbohydrate 43.1 g
Protein 6.8 g
Cholesterol 9 mg
Sodium 344 mg

Exchanges:

3 Starch
2 Fat

# Coconut Cheesecake Cups

Vegetable cooking spray
¼ cup graham cracker crumbs
2 teaspoons sugar
2 teaspoons reduced-calorie margarine, melted
¼ cup frozen egg substitute, thawed
3½ tablespoons light process cream cheese product, softened

1 tablespoon sifted powdered sugar
1 teaspoon all-purpose flour
¼ teaspoon coconut extract
1 (6-ounce) carton vanilla nonfat yogurt
1 tablespoon plus 1 teaspoon flaked coconut, toasted and divided

Coat 2 (6-ounce) custard cups with cooking spray. Combine graham cracker crumbs, 2 teaspoons sugar, and margarine; press evenly onto bottoms and 1 inch up sides of cups.

Beat egg substitute and next 5 ingredients at medium speed of an electric mixer until fluffy. Stir 1 tablespoon coconut into cheese mixture. Spoon cheese mixture evenly into prepared cups; sprinkle with remaining 1 teaspoon coconut. Bake at 325° for 30 to 35 minutes or until almost set. Turn off oven, and leave cheesecakes in oven 2 minutes. Partially open oven door; leave cheesecakes in oven 1 hour. Remove from oven; let cool to room temperature on a wire rack. Cover and chill 2 hours or until set. Yield: 2 cheesecakes.

**Per Cheesecake:**

Calories 254
Calories from Fat 36%
Fat 10.1 g
Saturated Fat 4.8 g
Carbohydrate 28.9 g
Protein 11.8 g
Cholesterol 18 mg
Sodium 396 mg

**Exchanges:**

1 Starch
1 Skim Milk
2 Fat

# Kahlúa Cheesecakes

Vegetable cooking spray
2 chocolate wafer cookies, crushed
¼ cup Neufchâtel cheese, softened
¼ cup 1% low-fat cottage cheese
2 tablespoons powdered sugar

2½ tablespoons frozen egg substitute, thawed
2 tablespoons Kahlúa or other coffee-flavored liqueur
½ teaspoon vanilla extract
1 tablespoon fat-free hot fudge topping, warmed

Coat 4 (2½-inch) paper baking cups with cooking spray; sprinkle chocolate wafer crumbs evenly on bottom and up sides of paper cups. Place paper cups in muffin pan cups.

Combine Neufchâtel cheese and next 5 ingredients in container of an electric blender; cover and process until smooth, stopping once to scrape down sides. Spoon cheese mixture evenly over wafer crumbs. Bake at 350° for 20 minutes or until almost set. Remove from oven; let cool to room temperature on a wire rack. Cover and chill.

To serve, remove paper liners, and place on serving plates. Drizzle evenly with hot fudge topping. Yield: 4 cheesecakes.

**Per Cheesecake:**

Calories 134
Calories from Fat 36%
Fat 4.9 g
Saturated Fat 2.7 g
Carbohydrate 16.5 g
Protein 4.9 g
Cholesterol 18 mg
Sodium 171 mg

**Exchanges:**

1 Starch
1 Fat

# ORANGE CHEESECAKES

Vegetable cooking spray
¼ cup graham cracker crumbs
2 teaspoons sugar
2 teaspoons margarine, melted
2 tablespoons powdered sugar
2 tablespoons part-skim ricotta cheese
2 tablespoons plain nonfat yogurt
2 tablespoons frozen egg substitute, thawed
2 tablespoons unsweetened orange juice
1 teaspoon all-purpose flour
Fresh orange slices (optional)

Coat 2 (4-inch) tartlet pans with cooking spray. Combine graham cracker crumbs, 2 teaspoons sugar, and margarine; press evenly onto bottoms and up sides of tartlet pans.

Combine powdered sugar and next 5 ingredients in a small bowl; beat at medium speed of an electric mixer until smooth. Pour mixture evenly into prepared crusts. Bake at 350° for 20 minutes or until set. Turn off oven, and leave cheesecakes in oven 30 minutes. Remove from oven; let cool to room temperature on a wire rack. Cover and chill at least 3 hours. Garnish with orange slices, if desired. Yield: 2 cheesecakes.

You may see several kinds of ricotta cheese in the supermarket, each with a different fat content. Whole milk ricotta contains the most fat, followed by part-skim and then nonfat ricotta. This cheesecake recipe works best with part-skim ricotta rather than the nonfat product.

Per Cheesecake:

Calories 184
Calories from Fat 33%
Fat 6.7 g
Saturated Fat 1.8 g
Carbohydrate 25.8 g
Protein 5.1 g
Cholesterol 5 mg
Sodium 176 mg

Exchanges:

2 Starch
1 Fat

# CHOCOLATE GÂTEAU

Per Serving:

Calories 299
Calories from Fat 22%
Fat 7.3 g
Saturated Fat 3.4 g
Carbohydrate 54.1 g
Protein 5.8 g
Cholesterol 1 mg
Sodium 103 mg

Exchanges:

3½ Starch
1½ Fat

Vegetable cooking spray
1 (1-ounce) square semisweet chocolate, chopped
1 teaspoon margarine
¼ cup frozen egg substitute, thawed
2 tablespoons sugar
2 tablespoons light-colored corn syrup
½ teaspoon vanilla extract
1 tablespoon plus 2 teaspoons all-purpose flour
2 tablespoons sifted powdered sugar
1 tablespoon unsweetened cocoa
2 teaspoons cornstarch
2 tablespoons skim milk
½ teaspoon vanilla extract
Fresh raspberries (optional)
Fresh mint sprigs (optional)

Coat a 6-inch springform pan with cooking spray; line bottom of pan with parchment paper. Coat parchment paper with cooking spray; set pan aside.

Combine chocolate and margarine in a small saucepan; cook over low heat, stirring constantly, until chocolate and margarine melt. Remove from heat; cool slightly. Combine egg substitute and next 3 ingredients, stirring well. Add egg substitute mixture to chocolate mixture, stirring well with a wire whisk. Stir in flour. Pour batter into prepared pan. (Mixture will thinly coat pan.)

Bake at 325° for 20 minutes. Cool in pan on a wire rack 10 minutes. Remove cake from pan; peel off parchment paper, and let cake cool completely on wire rack.

Combine powdered sugar, cocoa, and cornstarch in a small saucepan; gradually stir in milk. Cook over medium heat, stirring constantly, until thickened. Remove from heat; stir in vanilla. Cover and chill thoroughly.

Spread frosting over cake. Cut cake into quarters, forming 4 wedges. Stack 2 wedges to form a layered wedge; repeat with remaining 2 wedges. If desired, garnish with raspberries and mint. Yield: 2 servings.

After an evening at the theater, enjoy this rich-tasting chocolate cake with a cup of espresso.

# Black Forest Brownie Tortes

Vegetable cooking spray
¼ cup all-purpose flour
¼ teaspoon baking powder
¼ cup sugar
2 teaspoons unsweetened cocoa
2 tablespoons frozen egg substitute, thawed
1 tablespoon hot water
2 teaspoons margarine, melted

1 teaspoon vanilla extract
1 cup pitted frozen unsweetened cherries, thawed
1 teaspoon sugar
2 teaspoons cornstarch
1 teaspoon water
1 tablespoon frozen reduced-calorie whipped topping, thawed
Chocolate curls (optional)

Per Serving:

Calories 271
Calories from Fat 17%
Fat 5.0 g
Saturated Fat 1.2 g
Carbohydrate 52.5 g
Protein 4.5 g
Cholesterol 0 mg
Sodium 71 mg

Exchanges:

1½ Starch
2 Fruit
1 Fat

Coat a 6-inch square pan with cooking spray. Combine flour and next 3 ingredients in a small bowl. Stir in egg substitute and next 3 ingredients. Spoon batter into prepared pan. Bake at 350° for 15 minutes or until set in center. Cool in pan 10 minutes; remove from pan. Cool completely on a wire rack.

Combine cherries and next 3 ingredients in a small saucepan. Cook over medium heat, stirring constantly, 3 to 5 minutes or until sauce is slightly thickened. Cool to room temperature.

Cut cooled brownie in half crosswise; cut each half crosswise into thirds, forming 6 rectangular brownie slices. Place 1 brownie slice on a serving plate. Spoon 1 tablespoon cherry mixture over brownie slice. Top with a second brownie slice and 1 tablespoon cherry mixture. Top with a third brownie slice. Repeat procedure with remaining 3 brownie slices and cherry mixture. Dollop evenly with whipped topping; garnish with chocolate curls, if desired. Yield: 2 servings.

**Black Forest Brownie Tortes**

# CHOCOLATE PUDDING CAKE

⅓ cup all-purpose flour
½ teaspoon baking powder
　 Dash of salt
¼ cup sugar
1 tablespoon unsweetened
　 cocoa
3½ tablespoons skim milk
2 teaspoons margarine, melted

½ teaspoon vanilla extract
　 Vegetable cooking spray
1 tablespoon sugar
1½ teaspoons unsweetened
　 cocoa
¼ cup hot water
½ cup vanilla nonfat ice cream

Combine first 5 ingredients in a medium bowl, stirring well. Stir in milk, margarine, and vanilla; stir with a wire whisk until blended. Pour batter into a 1-quart baking dish coated with cooking spray.

　Combine 1 tablespoon sugar and 1½ teaspoons cocoa; sprinkle evenly over batter. Pour hot water over sugar mixture. Bake at 350° for 18 minutes. Remove from oven, and let stand 10 minutes. Spoon cake evenly onto 2 dessert plates. Top each serving with ¼ cup ice cream. Yield: 2 servings.

# GINGER SNACK CAKE

　 Vegetable cooking spray
⅓ cup plus 1 teaspoon
　 all-purpose flour, divided
3 tablespoons sugar
½ teaspoon baking powder
½ teaspoon ground ginger
¼ teaspoon ground cinnamon
⅛ teaspoon ground cloves

3½ tablespoons skim milk
2 tablespoons frozen egg
　 substitute, thawed
1½ teaspoons vegetable oil
1 teaspoon molasses
¼ cup sifted powdered sugar
⅛ teaspoon grated lemon rind
1 teaspoon fresh lemon juice

Coat a 6- x 3- x 2-inch loafpan with cooking spray; dust with 1 teaspoon flour, and set aside.

　Combine remaining ⅓ cup flour, 3 tablespoons sugar, and next 4 ingredients in a medium bowl, stirring well. Combine milk and next 3 ingredients. Add to dry ingredients; stir well. Spoon batter into prepared pan. Bake at 350° for 25 to 30 minutes or until a wooden pick inserted in center comes out clean. Cool in pan on a wire rack 5 minutes; remove from pan. Combine powdered sugar, lemon rind, and lemon juice in a small saucepan; cook over low heat until warm, stirring frequently. Drizzle over cake. Yield: 2 servings.

Sweetheart Shortcakes

# SWEETHEART SHORTCAKES

<table>
<tr><td>1</td><td>cup sliced fresh strawberries</td><td></td><td>Dash of salt</td></tr>
<tr><td>1</td><td>tablespoon sugar</td><td>1</td><td>tablespoon reduced-calorie stick margarine</td></tr>
<tr><td>2</td><td>tablespoons low-sugar strawberry spread, melted</td><td>2½</td><td>tablespoons skim milk</td></tr>
<tr><td>½</td><td>cup plus 2 teaspoons all-purpose flour, divided</td><td></td><td>Vegetable cooking spray</td></tr>
<tr><td>1½</td><td>tablespoons plus 1 teaspoon sugar, divided</td><td>2</td><td>tablespoons frozen reduced-calorie whipped topping, thawed</td></tr>
<tr><td>¾</td><td>teaspoon baking powder</td><td>2</td><td>fresh strawberries (optional)</td></tr>
</table>

Combine sliced strawberries and 1 tablespoon sugar; let stand 20 minutes, stirring occasionally. Stir in melted strawberry spread. Cover and chill.

Combine ½ cup flour, 1½ tablespoons sugar, baking powder, and salt in a bowl; cut in margarine with a pastry blender until mixture resembles coarse meal. Add milk, stirring just until dry ingredients are moistened.

Sprinkle remaining 2 teaspoons flour over work surface. Turn dough out onto floured surface, and knead 4 to 5 times. Divide dough; roll to ½-inch thickness. Cut into 2 hearts with a 3¼-inch heart-shaped cookie cutter (or into rounds with a 3-inch biscuit cutter). Sprinkle with remaining 1 teaspoon sugar. Place on a baking sheet coated with cooking spray. Bake at 400° for 10 minutes or until lightly browned.

Slice shortcakes in half horizontally; spoon strawberry mixture evenly over bottom halves. Place top halves of shortcakes on strawberry mixture. Top each with 1 tablespoon whipped topping. Garnish each with a fresh strawberry, if desired. Yield: 2 servings.

**Per Serving:**

Calories 288
Calories from Fat 16%
Fat 5.1 g
Saturated Fat 0.1 g
Carbohydrate 57.1 g
Protein 4.7 g
Cholesterol 0 mg
Sodium 140 mg

**Exchanges:**

1½ Starch
2 Fruit
1 Fat

# Macaroon Meringue Cookies

1 tablespoon sugar
2 fat-free saltine crackers, finely crushed
1 tablespoon shredded unsweetened coconut, toasted
1½ teaspoons finely chopped pecans

2 teaspoons semisweet chocolate mini-morsels
⅛ teaspoon vanilla extract
1 egg white
1 tablespoon sugar

Line a baking sheet with parchment paper or heavy brown paper; set aside. Combine first 6 ingredients in a small bowl; set aside.

Beat egg white at high speed of an electric mixer until foamy. Gradually add 1 tablespoon sugar, beating until stiff peaks form and sugar dissolves (2 to 4 minutes). Fold in cracker crumb mixture.

Drop mixture by heaping tablespoonfuls, 2 inches apart, onto prepared baking sheet. Bake at 200° for 2 hours. Turn off oven. Cool in oven 1 hour with oven door closed. Carefully remove from paper; let cool completely on wire racks. Yield: 10 cookies.

Go ahead and indulge with these low-fat cookies—5 cookies will count as 1 Starch Exchange and 1 Fat Exchange.

Per Cookie:

Calories 22
Calories from Fat 33%
Fat 0.8 g
Saturated Fat 0.5 g
Carbohydrate 3.7 g
Protein 0.5 g
Cholesterol 0 mg
Sodium 11 mg

Exchanges:

⅕ Starch
⅕ Fat

# White Chocolate Oatmeal Cookies

2 tablespoons brown sugar
1 tablespoon margarine, softened
1 tablespoon frozen egg substitute, thawed
⅛ teaspoon vanilla extract
3 tablespoons all-purpose flour
⅛ teaspoon baking soda

Dash of salt
¼ cup quick-cooking oats, uncooked
2 tablespoons white chocolate mini-morsels
2 tablespoons crisp rice cereal
Vegetable cooking spray

Beat brown sugar and margarine at medium speed of an electric mixer until fluffy; gradually add egg substitute and vanilla, beating well.

Combine flour, soda, and salt; gradually add to margarine mixture. Stir in oats, white chocolate morsels, and cereal.

Drop dough by rounded tablespoonfuls, 2 inches apart, onto a cookie sheet coated with cooking spray. Bake at 350° for 7 to 8 minutes or until lightly browned. Cool on cookie sheet 5 minutes. Remove to wire racks, and let cool completely. Yield: 6 cookies.

Per Cookie:

Calories 102
Calories from Fat 32%
Fat 3.6 g
Saturated Fat 1.3 g
Carbohydrate 15.4 g
Protein 1.8 g
Cholesterol 0 mg
Sodium 117 mg

Exchanges:

1 Starch
1 Fat

# BOURBON TRUFFLES

| | |
|---|---|
| ¼ cup crushed vanilla wafers | 1 teaspoon unsweetened cocoa |
| 1½ tablespoons pureed prunes | ½ ounce semisweet chocolate, melted |
| 1 tablespoon sifted powdered sugar | 1 teaspoon sifted powdered sugar |
| 1 tablespoon bourbon | |

Combine first 6 ingredients in a small bowl. Shape mixture into 4 (1-inch) balls. Roll balls in 1 teaspoon powdered sugar. Cover and chill thoroughly. Yield: 4 truffles.

Instead of pureeing prunes, you can substitute the same amount of baby food prunes.

**Per Truffle:**

Calories 80
Calories from Fat 33%
Fat 2.9 g
Saturated Fat 0.9 g
Carbohydrate 11.1 g
Protein 0.7 g
Cholesterol 0 mg
Sodium 31 mg

**Exchanges:**

1 Starch
½ Fat

# CHOCOLATE TRUFFLES

| | |
|---|---|
| 1½ teaspoons instant nonfat dry milk powder | 1 tablespoon chopped pitted dates |
| 2 teaspoons skim milk | 1 tablespoon finely chopped pecans |
| ½ teaspoon vanilla extract | |
| ¼ cup plus 2 tablespoons chocolate graham cracker crumbs | |

Combine first 3 ingredients in a small bowl; add graham cracker crumbs, stirring with a fork. Stir in dates. Shape mixture into 4 (1-inch) balls. Roll balls in pecans. Cover and chill thoroughly. Yield: 4 truffles.

These truffles can be refrigerated in an airtight container up to a week.

**Per Truffle:**

Calories 63
Calories from Fat 36%
Fat 2.5 g
Saturated Fat 0.5 g
Carbohydrate 9.2 g
Protein 1.1 g
Cholesterol 0 mg
Sodium 38 mg

**Exchanges:**

½ Starch
½ Fat

# LEMON SAUCE

| | | | |
|---|---|---|---|
| 3 | tablespoons sugar | 1 | teaspoon grated lemon rind |
| 2 | teaspoons cornstarch | 2 | tablespoons fresh lemon |
| ⅓ | cup water | | juice |

Combine sugar and cornstarch in a small saucepan, stirring well. Gradually stir in water. Cook over medium heat, stirring constantly, until mixture is thickened and bubbly. Remove from heat; stir in lemon rind and lemon juice. Yield: 2 servings.

*Enjoy warm and tangy Lemon Sauce over slices of commercial fat-free pound cake or angel food cake.*

# BRANDIED PEACH SAUCE

| | | | |
|---|---|---|---|
| 1 | cup frozen sliced peaches, thawed | 2 | teaspoons brandy |
| 2 | teaspoons sugar | 1 | teaspoon unsweetened orange juice |

Combine all ingredients in container of an electric blender; cover and process until smooth, stopping once to scrape down sides. Cover and chill. Yield: 2 servings.

*Serve Brandied Peach Sauce over vanilla nonfat frozen yogurt or nonfat ice cream.*

# RASPBERRY SAUCE

1   cup fresh or frozen
    unsweetened raspberries
2   tablespoons sugar
1   tablespoon red currant jelly,
    melted

2   teaspoons Chambord or
    other raspberry-flavored
    liqueur

Position knife blade in food processor bowl; add raspberries and sugar, and process until smooth. Pour raspberry puree into a wire-mesh strainer; press with back of spoon against the sides of the strainer to squeeze out juice. Discard pulp and seeds remaining in strainer.

Combine melted jelly and liqueur, stirring well. Add to raspberry puree, stirring well. Cover and chill. Yield: 2 servings.

Spoon Raspberry Sauce over slices of commercial
fat-free chocolate pound cake.

Per Serving:

Calories 115
Calories from Fat 2%
Fat 0.3 g
Saturated Fat 0 g
Carbohydrate 27.4 g
Protein 0.6 g
Cholesterol 0 mg
Sodium 4 mg

Exchanges:

2   Fruit

# CHOCOLATE-RUM SAUCE

2½   tablespoons sugar
1½   tablespoons unsweetened
    cocoa
1   tablespoon cornstarch

¼   cup light-colored corn syrup
1½   tablespoons rum
½   teaspoon vanilla extract

Combine first 3 ingredients in a small saucepan. Gradually stir in corn syrup and rum. Cook, stirring constantly, over medium heat until slightly thickened. Remove from heat; stir in vanilla. Yield: 2 servings.

Jazz up angel food cake, nonfat ice cream, or nonfat frozen
yogurt by drizzling with warm Chocolate-Rum Sauce.

Per Serving:

Calories 51
Calories from Fat 2%
Fat 0.1 g
Saturated Fat 0.1 g
Carbohydrate 11.6 g
Protein 0.3 g
Cholesterol 0 mg
Sodium 13 mg

Exchanges:

1   Starch

# MAGIC MEALS

Here's the trick—just cook one extra-sized entrée, and use it as the base for three or four completely different meals.

Spicy Black Beans

# SPICY BLACK BEANS

Cook the entire 1-pound bag of dried beans with some flavorful spices.
Then use these spicy black beans to get a head start on black
beans and rice, black bean soup, salad, or tostados.

1 pound dried black beans
5 (10½-ounce) cans low-
    sodium chicken broth
1 cup chopped onion
½ cup chopped green pepper
½ teaspoon pepper
¼ teaspoon ground cumin

¼ teaspoon ground coriander
¼ teaspoon ground red pepper
2 large cloves garlic, minced
1 bay leaf
½ teaspoon salt

Sort and wash beans; place beans in a large Dutch oven. Cover with water
to depth of 2 inches above beans; let soak overnight. Drain beans. Combine
beans, chicken broth, and next 8 ingredients in Dutch oven; bring to a boil.
Cover, reduce heat, and simmer 2 hours or until beans are tender. Remove
and discard bay leaf. Stir in salt. Spoon 1 cup beans (including liquid) into
each of 6 labeled heavy-duty, zip-top plastic bags. Store in refrigerator up to
1 week or in freezer up to 6 months. Yield: 6 cups.

**Per 1 Cup Beans:**

Calories 307
Calories from Fat 9%
Fat 2.9 g
Saturated Fat 0.9 g
Carbohydrate 53.9 g
Protein 19.4 g
Cholesterol 0 mg
Sodium 284 mg

**Exchanges:**

3½ Starch
1 Lean Meat Substitute

# BLACK BEANS AND RICE
## WITH SPICY BLACK BEANS

Olive oil-flavored vegetable
cooking spray
½ teaspoon olive oil
½ cup chopped tomato
2 tablespoons chopped green
pepper
2 tablespoons chopped onion
1½ teaspoons seeded, chopped
jalapeño pepper
1 teaspoon minced chopped
garlic

1 cup Spicy Black Beans
¼ cup plus 2 tablespoons
canned low-sodium
chicken broth, undiluted
2 teaspoons red wine vinegar
⅛ teaspoon salt
Dash of ground cumin
1 cup cooked long-grain rice
(cooked without salt or fat)

Coat a small nonstick skillet with cooking spray; add oil. Place over
medium heat until hot; add tomato and next 4 ingredients. Sauté 4 minutes. Add Spicy Black Beans and next 4 ingredients. Cook 10 minutes,
mashing beans slightly with the back of a wooden spoon. To serve, spoon
bean mixture over rice. Yield: 2 servings.

**Per Serving:**

Calories 298
Calories from Fat 10%
Fat 3.4 g
Saturated Fat 0.6 g
Carbohydrate 55.6 g
Protein 12.9 g
Cholesterol 0 mg
Sodium 302 mg

**Exchanges:**

3 Starch
2 Vegetable
½ Fat

# BLACK BEAN SALAD
## WITH SPICY BLACK BEANS

1 cup Spicy Black Beans,
drained
¼ cup canned no-salt-added
whole-kernel corn, drained
¼ cup plus 2 tablespoons
chopped zucchini
2 tablespoons chopped sweet
red pepper
1 tablespoon chopped green
onions

1 tablespoon chopped fresh
cilantro
1 teaspoon seeded, chopped
jalapeño pepper
1 teaspoon minced garlic
2 tablespoons white Balsamic
vinegar
½ teaspoon olive oil
⅛ teaspoon pepper

Combine all ingredients in a small bowl, stirring well. Cover and chill at
least 2 hours. Yield: 2 servings.

**Per Serving:**

Calories 188
Calories from Fat 14%
Fat 2.9 g
Saturated Fat 0.6 g
Carbohydrate 32.1 g
Protein 10.7 g
Cholesterol 0 mg
Sodium 147 mg

**Exchanges:**

2 Starch
1 Lean Meat Substitute

# Black Bean Soup
## with Spicy Black Beans

Per Serving:

Calories 330
Calories from Fat 8%
Fat 3.0 g
Saturated Fat 0.9 g
Carbohydrate 56.8 g
Protein 20.8 g
Cholesterol 0 mg
Sodium 445 mg

Exchanges:

4    Starch
1    Lean Meat

2    cups Spicy Black Beans
     (page 200)
¾    cup canned no-salt-added
     chicken broth, undiluted
½    tablespoon no-salt-added
     tomato paste
⅛    teaspoon salt
⅛    teaspoon ground cumin
2    teaspoons dry sherry
1    teaspoon lemon juice
2    tablespoons nonfat sour
     cream alternative

Position knife blade in food processor bowl; add first 5 ingredients. Process until smooth, scraping sides of processor bowl once. Transfer bean mixture to a small saucepan; cook over medium heat just until hot. Stir in sherry and lemon juice. To serve, ladle soup into 2 bowls, and top each serving with 1 tablespoon sour cream. Yield: 2 servings.

# Black Bean Tostados
## with Spicy Black Beans

Per Serving:

Calories 345
Calories from Fat 26%
Fat 10.1 g
Saturated Fat 4.1 g
Carbohydrate 44.8 g
Protein 21.7 g
Cholesterol 19 mg
Sodium 383 mg

Exchanges:

3    Starch
2    Medium-Fat Meat

2    (6-inch) corn tortillas
     Vegetable cooking spray
½    cup (2 ounces) shredded
     reduced-fat Monterey Jack
     cheese
1    tablespoon chopped pickled
     jalapeño pepper
1    cup Spicy Black Beans
     (page 200), drained
1    tablespoon chopped fresh
     cilantro
¼    teaspoon ground cumin
1    cup shredded lettuce
½    cup chopped tomato
1    tablespoon chopped green
     onions
2    tablespoons diced avocado
2    tablespoons nonfat sour
     cream alternative

Place tortillas on a baking sheet coated with cooking spray. Bake at 350° for 6 minutes; turn tortillas, and bake an additional 2 minutes or until crisp. Top evenly with cheese and pepper; bake 2 minutes or until cheese melts.

Coat a small saucepan with cooking spray; add Spicy Black Beans, cilantro, and cumin, mashing beans slightly with the back of a wooden spoon. Cook over medium heat until hot, stirring occasionally. Spoon bean mixture evenly over tortillas. Top evenly with lettuce and remaining ingredients. Yield: 2 servings.

# Hearty Meat Sauce

Simmer a large batch of this versatile meat sauce, and then divide into even portions to be used in the four following recipes.

1¾ pounds ground round
1 cup chopped onion
¾ cup chopped celery
1 large clove garlic, minced
2 (14½-ounce) cans no-salt-added whole tomatoes, undrained and chopped
1 (13¾-ounce) can no-salt-added beef broth

1 (6-ounce) can no-salt-added tomato paste
½ teaspoon pepper
½ teaspoon dried thyme
¼ teaspoon salt
1 large bay leaf
¼ cup chopped fresh parsley

Per ¾ Cup Sauce:

Calories 156
Calories from Fat 28%
Fat 4.9 g
Saturated Fat 1.7 g
Carbohydrate 8.9 g
Protein 18.6 g
Cholesterol 49 mg
Sodium 125 mg

Exchanges:

2 Lean Meat
2 Vegetable

Combine first 4 ingredients in a large Dutch oven; cook over medium-high heat until meat is browned, stirring until it crumbles. Drain and pat dry with paper towels. Wipe drippings from Dutch oven with a paper towel.

Return meat mixture to Dutch oven; add tomato and next 6 ingredients, stirring well. Bring mixture to a boil; reduce heat, and simmer, uncovered, 35 minutes, stirring occasionally. Add parsley; cook 5 minutes. Remove and discard bay leaf.

Spoon 1½ cups sauce into each of 5 labeled heavy-duty, zip-top plastic bags. Store in refrigerator up to 1 week or in freezer up to 3 months. Yield: 7½ cups.

**Hearty Meat Sauce**

# South-of-the-Border Chili
## with Hearty Meat Sauce

**Per Serving:**

Calories 301
Calories from Fat 19%
Fat 6.4 g
Saturated Fat 2.3 g
Carbohydrate 32.9 g
Protein 28.7 g
Cholesterol 52 mg
Sodium 229 mg

**Exchanges:**

2 Starch
3 Lean Meat

1½ cups Hearty Meat Sauce
  (page 203)
 1 cup drained canned low-
  sodium pinto beans
 ¼ cup water
 1 teaspoon ground cumin
 1 teaspoon seeded, chopped
  jalapeño pepper
 ½ teaspoon chili powder

 Dash of salt
 1 tablespoon shredded
  reduced-fat Monterey Jack
  cheese
 1 tablespoon chopped green
  onions
 1 tablespoon chopped fresh
  cilantro

Combine first 7 ingredients in a medium saucepan. Bring to a boil; cover, reduce heat, and simmer 20 minutes, stirring occasionally. To serve, ladle chili into 2 bowls; sprinkle evenly with cheese, green onions, and cilantro. Yield: 2 servings.

# Taco Salad
## with Hearty Meat Sauce

**Per Serving:**

Calories 409
Calories from Fat 27%
Fat 12.3 g
Saturated Fat 4.1 g
Carbohydrate 42.7 g
Protein 32.1 g
Cholesterol 58 mg
Sodium 489 mg

**Exchanges:**

2 Starch
3 Medium-Fat Meat
2 Vegetable

1½ cups Hearty Meat Sauce
  (page 203)
 ½ cup drained canned kidney
  beans
 ½ teaspoon seeded, chopped
  jalapeño pepper
 ½ teaspoon ground cumin
 ¼ teaspoon chili powder
 2 (6-inch) flour tortillas
 3 cups shredded lettuce

 ½ cup chopped tomato
 ¼ cup chopped avocado
 2 tablespoons chopped green
  onions
 ¼ cup (1 ounce) shredded
  reduced-fat Cheddar
  cheese
 2 tablespoons nonfat sour
  cream alternative

Combine first 5 ingredients in a small saucepan. Bring to a boil; reduce heat, and simmer, uncovered, 25 minutes, stirring frequently.

Cut each tortilla into 6 wedges. Place wedges on an ungreased baking sheet. Bake at 350° for 5 minutes on each side or until crisp and golden. Set aside.

Place lettuce evenly on 2 salad plates. Spoon meat mixture evenly over lettuce. Sprinkle ¼ cup tomato, 2 tablespoons avocado, and 1 tablespoon green onions around the edge of each salad. Sprinkle cheese evenly over meat mixture. Top each salad with 1 tablespoon sour cream. Serve with tortilla wedges. Yield: 2 servings.

# SLOPPY JOES
## WITH HEARTY MEAT SAUCE

1½ cups Hearty Meat Sauce
    (page 203)
2 tablespoons finely chopped
    green pepper
2 teaspoons brown sugar

2 teaspoons cider vinegar
1 teaspoon low-sodium
    Worcestershire sauce
2 reduced-calorie whole
    wheat buns

Combine first 5 ingredients in a small saucepan. Bring to a boil; reduce heat, and simmer, uncovered, 20 minutes or until almost all liquid is absorbed, stirring occasionally.

Spoon meat mixture evenly onto bottom halves of buns. Top with remaining halves of buns. Yield: 2 servings.

**Per Serving:**

Calories 254
Calories from Fat 21%
Fat 5.9 g
Saturated Fat 1.8 g
Carbohydrate 28.4 g
Protein 20.7 g
Cholesterol 49 mg
Sodium 356 mg

**Exchanges:**

2 Starch
2 Lean Meat

# PASTA ROLLS
## WITH HEARTY MEAT SAUCE

3 lasagna noodles, uncooked
1 (10-ounce) package frozen
    chopped spinach, thawed
1½ cups Hearty Meat Sauce
    (page 203)
½ cup canned no-salt-added
    tomato sauce
½ cup 1% low-fat cottage
    cheese

1 tablespoon freshly grated
    Romano cheese
⅛ teaspoon dried oregano
⅛ teaspoon dried basil
    Vegetable cooking spray
¼ cup (1 ounce) shredded part-
    skim mozzarella cheese

Cook noodles according to package directions, omitting salt and fat; drain well. Cut noodles in half crosswise. Drain spinach; press between paper towels to remove excess moisture.

Combine Hearty Meat Sauce and tomato sauce in a small saucepan. Bring to a boil; reduce heat, and simmer, uncovered, 20 minutes.

Combine cottage cheese, Romano cheese, oregano, and basil in container of an electric blender or food processor; cover and process until smooth, stopping once to scrape down sides. Transfer cheese mixture to a bowl; add spinach, stirring well.

Spread about 3 tablespoons spinach mixture on each lasagna noodle half, leaving a ¼-inch border around the edge. Roll up each noodle, jellyroll fashion, beginning at narrow end.

Spoon meat sauce into a 1-quart casserole coated with cooking spray. Arrange rolls, seam side down, over sauce. Cover and bake at 350° for 25 minutes. Sprinkle with mozzarella cheese. Bake, uncovered, 5 minutes or until cheese melts. Yield: 2 servings.

**Per Serving:**

Calories 463
Calories from Fat 20%
Fat 10.1 g
Saturated Fat 4.3 g
Carbohydrate 53.3 g
Protein 40.4 g
Cholesterol 63 mg
Sodium 584 mg

**Exchanges:**

3 Starch
4 Lean Meat
1 Vegetable

Savory Pot Roast

# SAVORY POT ROAST

If you love the flavor of old-fashioned pot roast but end up throwing out the leftovers, here's a solution. After enjoying some of the tender meat right after cooking, divide the remainder into 6-ounce portions to use in stew or a beef-potato pie.

**Per Serving:**

Calories 175
Calories from Fat 28%
Fat 5.5 g
Saturated Fat 1.8 g
Carbohydrate 2.8 g
Protein 26.3 g
Cholesterol 65 mg
Sodium 66 mg

**Exchanges:**

3   Lean Meat

1   (2½-pound) lean bottom round roast
    Vegetable cooking spray
2   teaspoons vegetable oil
2   cups canned no-salt-added beef broth, undiluted
2   tablespoons minced garlic
2   tablespoons lemon juice
1   teaspoon pepper
1   (8-ounce) can no-salt-added tomato sauce
2   bay leaves
2   large carrots, scraped and cut into fourths
2   stalks celery, cut into fourths
1   large onion, peeled and cut into fourths

Trim fat from roast. Coat a Dutch oven with cooking spray; add oil. Place over medium–high heat until hot. Add roast; cook until browned on all sides. Add beef broth and next 5 ingredients; bring to a boil. Cover, reduce heat, and simmer 1 hour and 45 minutes. Add carrot, celery, and onion; cook 45 minutes or until meat is tender. Remove and discard bay leaves. Reserve vegetables for other uses, if desired.

Remove meat from broth, and cut into 5 (6-ounce) portions; place in 5 labeled heavy-duty, zip-top plastic bags. Store in refrigerator up to 4 days or in freezer up to 3 months. Strain broth, and reserve for other uses, if desired. Yield: 10 servings.

# Shepherd's Pie
## with Savory Pot Roast

1¼  cups canned low-sodium
    beef broth, undiluted
½  cup sliced carrot
½  cup sliced celery
½  cup cubed turnips
½  cup sliced fresh green beans
    Vegetable cooking spray
½  teaspoon vegetable oil
¼  cup sliced onion
1  tablespoon flour
½  teaspoon low-sodium
    Worcestershire sauce
2  teaspoons no-salt-added
    tomato paste

¼  teaspoon pepper
6  ounces Savory Pot Roast,
    cubed (about 1½ cups)
1½  cups peeled, cubed baking
    potato
3  tablespoons skim milk
1  tablespoon nonfat sour
    cream alternative
⅛  teaspoon salt
1½  teaspoons chopped fresh
    chives, divided
2  tablespoons (½ ounce)
    shredded reduced-fat sharp
    Cheddar cheese

Place first 4 ingredients in a saucepan; bring to a boil, reduce heat, and cook 4 minutes. Add green beans; cook 5 minutes. Coat a nonstick skillet with cooking spray; add oil. Place over medium-high heat until hot. Add onion; sauté 5 minutes. Sprinkle flour over onion; stir. Add broth mixture to onion; stir. Add Worcestershire sauce, tomato paste, and pepper; cook over medium heat until thickened, stirring frequently. Add Savory Pot Roast; cook 2 minutes.

Cook potato in boiling water to cover 10 minutes or until tender. Drain; mash. Add milk; beat at medium speed of an electric mixer until smooth. Stir in sour cream, salt, and 1 teaspoon chives. Spoon beef mixture into 2 (1½-cup) casseroles coated with cooking spray. Spread potato topping over beef mixture; crisscross with tines of fork. Bake, uncovered, at 350° for 20 minutes. Sprinkle with cheese and remaining chives; bake 5 minutes. Yield: 2 servings.

**Per Serving:**

Calories 373
Calories from Fat 20%
Fat 8.4 g
Saturated Fat 2.9 g
Carbohydrate 37.2 g
Protein 35.0 g
Cholesterol 77 mg
Sodium 338 mg

**Exchanges:**

2  Starch
3½ Lean Meat
1  Vegetable

# Beef-Vegetable Stew
## with Savory Pot Roast

2  cups canned low-sodium
    beef broth, undiluted
6  ounces Savory Pot Roast,
    chopped (about 1½ cups)
½  cup cubed potato
½  cup finely shredded cabbage

¼  cup sliced carrot
¼  cup sliced celery
¼  teaspoon salt
¼  teaspoon pepper
½  cup frozen English peas,
    thawed

Combine first 8 ingredients in a medium saucepan; bring to a boil. Reduce heat and simmer, uncovered, 20 minutes. Add peas; cook 12 minutes or until vegetables are tender. Yield: 2 servings.

**Per Serving:**

Calories 255
Calories from Fat 19%
Fat 5.5 g
Saturated Fat 1.9 g
Carbohydrate 16.8 g
Protein 30.4 g
Cholesterol 71 mg
Sodium 408 mg

**Exchanges:**

1  Starch
3½ Lean Meat

# Orange-Baked Ham

Bake a reduced-fat ham in a light orange glaze, and then slice it into 2-ounce portions. You'll be one step ahead in preparing a black-eyed pea salad, a main-dish ham and cheese pasta, and omelets.

Per 2-Ounce Slice:

Calories 103
Calories from Fat 28%
Fat 3.2 g
Saturated Fat 1.0 g
Carbohydrate 5.9 g
Protein 12.1 g
Cholesterol 30 mg
Sodium 683 mg

Exchanges:

2   Lean Meat

1   (2-pound) reduced-fat cooked ham
½   cup frozen orange juice concentrate, thawed and undiluted
¼   cup water
3   tablespoons brown sugar
2   teaspoons white wine vinegar
1   teaspoon dry mustard
½   teaspoon grated orange rind
¼   teaspoon ground ginger
    Vegetable cooking spray
    Whole cloves

Score ham in a diamond design; place in a large heavy-duty, zip-top plastic bag. Combine orange juice concentrate and next 6 ingredients; pour mixture over ham. Seal bag, and shake until ham is well coated. Marinate in refrigerator at least 8 hours, turning bag occasionally.

Remove ham from marinade, reserving marinade. Set aside ½ cup marinade; discard remaining marinade. Place ham on a rack in a roasting pan coated with cooking spray; stud with cloves. Insert meat thermometer into ham, if desired; brush lightly with marinade. Cover; bake at 325° for 1½ hours or until thermometer registers 140°, basting occasionally with marinade.

Slice ham into 16 (2-ounce) portions, and place in a labeled airtight container. Store in refrigerator up to 1 week or in freezer up to 3 months. Remove cloves from ham before serving or using in other recipes.
Yield: 16 (2-ounce) slices.

Orange-Baked Ham

# HAM AND BLACK-EYED PEA SALAD
## WITH ORANGE-BAKED HAM

2 cups water
2 cups frozen black-eyed peas
1 bay leaf
2 ounces Orange-Baked Ham,
   cubed (about ⅓ cup)
½ cup diced celery
¼ cup diced sweet red pepper
3 tablespoons minced green
   onions
2 tablespoons chopped fresh
   parsley

2 teaspoons chopped fresh
   oregano
1 teaspoon minced garlic
¼ cup vinegar
2 teaspoons water
2 teaspoons hot sauce
1 teaspoon vegetable oil
⅛ teaspoon ground red pepper
   Dash of freshly ground black
   pepper

Bring 2 cups water to a boil in a medium saucepan; add peas and bay leaf. Cover, reduce heat, and simmer 30 minutes. Drain. Remove and discard bay leaf. Combine peas, Orange-Baked Ham, and next 6 ingredients in a bowl.

Combine vinegar and remaining ingredients in a small bowl. Stir with a wire whisk until blended. Pour over vegetable mixture; toss gently. Cover and chill at least 2 hours. Yield: 2 servings.

Per Serving:

Calories 320
Calories from Fat 15%
Fat 5.2 g
Saturated Fat 1.3 g
Carbohydrate 49.3 g
Protein 21.4 g
Cholesterol 15 mg
Sodium 417 mg

Exchanges:

3  Starch
1  Medium-Fat Meat
1  Vegetable

# CHEESY DITALI
## WITH ORANGE-BAKED HAM

½ pound fresh asparagus spears
   (about 9 spears)
3 ounces ditali (tube-shaped)
   pasta, uncooked
   Vegetable cooking spray
1 teaspoon reduced-calorie
   margarine
½ teaspoon minced garlic
1 tablespoon all-purpose flour

¼ cup plus 2 tablespoons
   canned no-salt-added beef
   broth, undiluted
¼ cup skim milk
2 ounces Orange-Baked Ham,
   diced (about ⅓ cup)
¼ cup (1 ounce) shredded
   reduced-fat Cheddar cheese
⅛ teaspoon ground white pepper

Snap off tough ends of asparagus. Remove scales from stalks with a knife or vegetable peeler, if desired. Cut spears into 1-inch pieces. Arrange asparagus in a vegetable steamer over boiling water. Cover and steam 3 to 5 minutes or until crisp-tender; drain.

Cook pasta according to package directions, omitting salt and fat; drain well. Set aside, and keep warm.

Coat a medium nonstick skillet with cooking spray; add margarine. Place over medium heat until margarine melts. Add garlic; sauté 30 seconds. Add flour; cook, stirring constantly, 1 minute. Gradually add broth and milk, stirring constantly. Cook over medium heat, stirring constantly, until slightly thickened. Add asparagus, Orange-Baked Ham, cheese, and pepper, stirring until cheese melts. Stir in pasta, and serve immediately. Yield: 2 servings.

Per Serving:

Calories 300
Calories from Fat 19%
Fat 6.5 g
Saturated Fat 2.4 g
Carbohydrate 42.4 g
Protein 18.4 g
Cholesterol 25 mg
Sodium 486 mg

Exchanges:

3  Starch
1  High-Fat Meat

# Ham and Swiss Omelets
## with Orange-Baked Ham

Vegetable cooking spray
2 ounces Orange-Baked Ham (page 208), chopped (about ⅓ cup)
¼ cup chopped green onions
¼ cup peeled, seeded, and chopped tomato
Dash of pepper
2 egg whites
¾ cup frozen egg substitute, thawed
2 tablespoons water
½ teaspoon hot sauce
½ teaspoon dried basil
⅛ teaspoon pepper
¼ cup (1 ounce) shredded reduced-fat Swiss cheese, divided

Coat a 6-inch heavy nonstick skillet with cooking spray; place over medium heat until hot. Add Orange-Baked Ham, green onions, and tomato; cook 2 to 3 minutes or until vegetables are tender. Add dash of pepper. Remove vegetables from skillet; set aside, and keep warm. Wipe skillet dry with a paper towel.

Beat egg whites at high speed of an electric mixer until stiff peaks form; set aside. Combine egg substitute and next 4 ingredients in a small bowl, stirring well. Gently fold egg whites into egg substitute mixture.

Coat skillet with cooking spray; place over medium heat until hot. Pour half of egg white mixture into skillet. Cover, reduce heat, and cook 5 minutes or until golden on bottom. Turn omelet; cover and cook 3 minutes or until puffy and golden. Slide omelet onto a warm serving plate. Spoon half of reserved vegetable mixture over half of omelet; sprinkle with 2 tablespoons cheese, and carefully fold in half. Keep warm. Repeat procedure with remaining egg white mixture, vegetable mixture, and 2 tablespoons cheese. Serve immediately. Yield: 2 servings.

Roasted Turkey Breast

# ROASTED TURKEY BREAST

Go one step beyond leftovers with this roasted turkey breast. You can
slice the meat into 6-ounce portions, and use it as the start of
four more meals for two, including turkey sandwiches,
fruit and turkey salad, and savory gumbo.

1  (4½-pound) turkey breast          ½  teaspoon vegetable oil
   Vegetable cooking spray

Trim fat from turkey. Rinse turkey under cold water, and pat dry. Place
turkey, skin side up, on a rack in a roasting pan coated with cooking spray.
Brush lightly with oil. Insert meat thermometer into meaty part of breast,
making sure it does not touch bone. Bake at 325° for 2 to 2¼ hours or
until meat thermometer registers 170°. Let turkey stand 15 minutes.

Remove and discard skin from turkey. Remove meat from bones, reserving carcass for other recipes, if desired. Slice turkey into 5 (6-ounce) portions, and place in 5 labeled heavy-duty, zip-top plastic bags. Store in
refrigerator up to 1 week or in freezer up to 3 months. Yield: 10 servings.

**Per Serving:**

Calories 142
Calories from Fat 20%
Fat 3.1 g
Saturated Fat 1.0 g
Carbohydrate 0.0 g
Protein 26.4 g
Cholesterol 61 mg
Sodium 57 mg

**Exchanges:**

3½ Lean Meat

# FRUITED TURKEY SALAD
## WITH ROASTED TURKEY BREAST

**Per Serving:**

Calories 209
Calories from Fat 28%
Fat 6.6 g
Saturated Fat 2.1 g
Carbohydrate 9.8 g
Protein 27.0 g
Cholesterol 64 mg
Sodium 411 mg

**Exchanges:**

3½ Lean Meat
1  Vegetable
½  Fruit

| | |
|---|---|
| 6 ounces Roasted Turkey Breast (page 211), cubed (about 1½ cups) | 2 tablespoons nonfat mayonnaise |
| ½ cup sliced celery | 2 tablespoons low-fat sour cream |
| ⅓ cup halved red seedless grapes | 1½ teaspoons chopped fresh dillweed |
| 1 tablespoon coarsely chopped walnuts, toasted | 1 teaspoon cider vinegar |
| | ⅛ teaspoon salt |

Combine first 4 ingredients in a small bowl. Combine mayonnaise and remaining ingredients, stirring well. Add mayonnaise mixture to turkey mixture, and toss gently to combine. Cover and chill. Yield: 2 servings.

# TURKEY-AVOCADO SANDWICH
## WITH ROASTED TURKEY BREAST

**Per Serving:**

Calories 330
Calories from Fat 32%
Fat 11.6 g
Saturated Fat 2.0 g
Carbohydrate 23.6 g
Protein 35.2 g
Cholesterol 64 mg
Sodium 432 mg

**Exchanges:**

1½ Starch
4  Lean Meat

| | |
|---|---|
| ¼ cup nonfat cream cheese | 4 (¾-ounce) slices reduced-calorie whole wheat bread, toasted |
| 1 tablespoon plus 1 teaspoon shredded fresh basil | 6 ounces Roasted Turkey Breast (page 211), sliced |
| 1 tablespoon plus 1 teaspoon lemon juice | ½ medium avocado, thinly sliced |
| 2 teaspoons chopped fresh oregano | ½ cup shredded lettuce |
| ½ teaspoon coarsely ground pepper | ¼ cup alfalfa sprouts |
| ½ teaspoon minced garlic | 1 medium tomato, sliced |

Combine first 6 ingredients in a small bowl, mixing well. Spread cheese mixture evenly on 2 bread slices. Place sliced Roasted Turkey Breast evenly on each prepared bread slice, and top evenly with avocado and remaining ingredients. Top with remaining 2 bread slices. Yield: 2 servings.

# TURKEY GUMBO
## WITH ROASTED TURKEY BREAST

1 turkey carcass
5 cups water
1 stalk celery
1 small carrot, scraped
4 peppercorns
  Vegetable cooking spray
2 teaspoons vegetable oil
1 tablespoon all-purpose flour
1½ tablespoons finely chopped
  onion
1½ tablespoons finely chopped
  celery
½ cup sliced fresh okra

6 ounces Roasted Turkey
  Breast (page 211), cubed
  (about 1½ cups)
½ cup canned no-salt-added
  whole tomatoes, drained
  and chopped
½ cup frozen whole-kernel
  corn, thawed
¼ teaspoon pepper
¼ teaspoon hot sauce
⅛ teaspoon salt
1 fresh sprig of thyme
1 bay leaf

Place turkey bones in a large Dutch oven; add water, celery, carrot, and peppercorns. Bring to a boil; cover, reduce heat, and simmer 1½ hours. Strain broth through a cheesecloth- or paper towel-lined sieve; discard bones, vegetables, and peppercorns. Cover broth, and chill thoroughly. Skim and discard fat from top of broth. Reserve 1¾ cups broth, and set aside.

Coat a small saucepan with cooking spray; add oil. Place over medium heat until hot. Add flour; cook, stirring constantly, 6 minutes or until lightly browned.

Add onion and celery to saucepan; cook 2 minutes, stirring frequently. Add 1¾ cups reserved broth and okra; bring to a boil, reduce heat, and simmer, uncovered, 10 minutes. Add cubed Roasted Turkey Breast and remaining ingredients; bring to a boil. Reduce heat, and simmer, uncovered, 20 minutes. Remove and discard bay leaf. Yield: 2 servings.

**Note**: You can use 1¾ cups undiluted no-salt-added chicken broth instead of making a broth from the turkey carcass.

Per Serving:

Calories 278
Calories from Fat 30%
Fat 9.2 g
Saturated Fat 2.2 g
Carbohydrate 18.8 g
Protein 30.1 g
Cholesterol 59 mg
Sodium 282 mg

Exchanges:

1 Starch
3 Lean Meat
1 Vegetable

Stone-Ground Wheat Bread

# STONE-GROUND WHEAT BREAD DOUGH

One recipe—and at least eight ways to use it. When you start with this master dough recipe, you can bake one loaf, or you can divide the dough into four equal portions and make four different breads. Store any of the baked breads in your freezer. Or freeze or refrigerate the dough until you're ready to bake.

2¼ cups unbleached all-purpose
    flour, divided
3 tablespoons sugar
1 teaspoon salt
1 package active dry yeast
1 cup plus 2 tablespoons water
2 tablespoons vegetable oil

1¼ cups stone-ground wheat
    flour
1 tablespoon unbleached all-
    purpose flour
    Vegetable cooking spray
1 egg white, lightly beaten
1 tablespoon cold water

Combine 1½ cups all-purpose flour, sugar, salt, and yeast in a large mixing bowl; stir well. Combine water and oil in a small saucepan; heat until very warm (120° to 130°). Gradually add warm water and oil to flour mixture,

Per ½-Inch Slice:

Calories 117
Calories from Fat 16%
Fat 2.1 g
Saturated Fat 0.3 g
Carbohydrate 21.8 g
Protein 3.4 g
Cholesterol 0 mg
Sodium 151 mg

Exchanges:

1½ Starch

beating well at low speed of an electric mixer. Beat an additional 2 minutes at medium speed. Gradually add remaining ¾ cup all-purpose flour, beating 2 minutes at medium speed. Gradually stir in stone-ground wheat flour to make a soft dough.

Sprinkle 1 tablespoon all-purpose flour evenly over work surface. Turn dough out onto floured surface, and knead until smooth and elastic (about 10 minutes). Place in a large bowl coated with cooking spray, turning to coat top. Cover tightly, and refrigerate 8 hours or up to 3 days, or cover and let rise in a warm place (85°), free from drafts, 1 hour or until doubled in bulk.

Punch dough down, and divide into 4 equal portions, if desired. Place each portion in a labeled heavy-duty, zip-top plastic bag or in a labeled airtight container. Store in refrigerator up to 3 days or in freezer up to 1 month. Let dough thaw at room temperature, and proceed with recipes as directed.

To make a loaf, punch dough down, and roll entire recipe of dough into a 14- x 7-inch rectangle. Roll up dough, jellyroll fashion, starting at short side, pressing to eliminate air pockets; pinch ends to seal. Place dough, seam side down, in an 8½- x 4½- x 3-inch loafpan coated with cooking spray. Cover and let rise in a warm place, free from drafts, 30 minutes or until doubled in bulk.

Combine egg white and 1 tablespoon water in a small bowl, stirring well. Brush egg white mixture over loaf. Bake at 350° for 35 to 45 minutes or until bread sounds hollow when tapped. Remove from pan immediately; cool on a wire rack. Yield: 1 (8-inch) loaf.

# Cloverleaf Rolls
## with Stone-Ground Wheat Bread Dough

| | |
|---|---|
| ¼ Stone-Ground Wheat Bread Dough (page 214) Butter-flavored vegetable cooking spray | 1 egg white 1 tablespoon cold water |

Divide Stone-Ground Wheat Bread Dough into 12 equal portions; shape each into a ball. Coat 4 muffin pan cups with cooking spray; place 3 balls in each cup. Cover and let rise in a warm place (85°), free from drafts, 25 minutes or until doubled in bulk. Combine egg white and water, stirring well. Brush rolls with egg white mixture, and bake at 350° for 20 minutes or until lightly browned. Yield: 4 rolls.

**Per Roll:**

Calories 123
Calories from Fat 17%
Fat 2.3 g
Saturated Fat 0.3 g
Carbohydrate 21.9 g
Protein 4.3 g
Cholesterol 0 mg
Sodium 164 mg

**Exchanges:**

1½ Starch

# ORANGE-NUT ROLLS
## WITH STONE-GROUND WHEAT BREAD DOUGH

¼ Stone-Ground Wheat Bread Dough (page 214)
1½ teaspoons reduced-calorie margarine, melted and divided
1 tablespoon chopped pecans
½ teaspoon grated orange rind
Butter-flavored vegetable cooking spray
2 teaspoons brown sugar
2 teaspoons powdered sugar
½ teaspoon orange juice

Roll Stone-Ground Wheat Bread Dough into a 7½- x 6-inch rectangle. Brush dough with ½ teaspoon margarine, leaving a ½-inch border. Sprinkle with pecans and orange rind. Roll up, starting at short side, pressing firmly to eliminate air pockets; pinch seam to seal (do not seal ends). Cut into 4 (1½-inch) slices.

Place rolls in muffin pan cups coated with cooking spray, pressing down slightly. Brush tops of rolls evenly with remaining 1 teaspoon margarine, and sprinkle evenly with brown sugar.

Cover and let rise in a warm place (85°), free from drafts, 40 minutes or until doubled in bulk. Bake at 375° for 15 to 18 minutes or until lightly browned.

Combine powdered sugar and orange juice, stirring well. Drizzle orange glaze over rolls. Yield: 4 rolls.

# RAISIN-CINNAMON BREAD
## WITH STONE-GROUND WHEAT BREAD DOUGH

¼  Stone-Ground Wheat Bread
   Dough (page 214)
½  teaspoon reduced-calorie
   margarine, melted
2  teaspoons sugar
1  teaspoon ground cinnamon

2  tablespoons raisins
   Butter-flavored vegetable
   cooking spray
1  egg white, lightly beaten
1  tablespoon cold water

Roll Stone-Ground Wheat Bread Dough into a 6½- x 5½-inch rectangle.
Brush dough with margarine, leaving a ½-inch border. Sprinkle with sugar,
cinnamon, and raisins. Roll up, starting at short side, pressing firmly to
eliminate air pockets. Pinch seam and ends to seal. Place, seam side down,
on a baking sheet coated with cooking spray. Cover and let rise in a warm
place (85°), free from drafts, 30 minutes or until doubled in bulk.

   Combine egg white and water, stirring well. Brush dough with egg
white mixture. Bake at 350° for 20 to 25 minutes or until loaf sounds
hollow when tapped. Yield: 1 (6-inch) loaf.

Per 1-Inch Slice:

Calories 98
Calories from Fat 16%
Fat 1.7 g
Saturated Fat 0.3 g
Carbohydrate 18.6 g
Protein 2.9 g
Cholesterol 0 mg
Sodium 113 mg

Exchanges:

1  Starch

# CHEESY JALAPEÑO BRAID
## WITH STONE-GROUND WHEAT BREAD DOUGH

¼  Stone-Ground Wheat Bread
   Dough
2  tablespoons (½ ounce) finely
   shredded reduced-fat sharp
   Cheddar cheese
1  teaspoon drained, chopped
   pickled jalapeño pepper

   Butter-flavored vegetable
   cooking spray
1  egg white
1  tablespoon cold water

Divide Stone-Ground Wheat Bread Dough into 3 equal portions. Roll
each portion into a 7-inch rope; flatten slightly. Sprinkle ropes evenly with
cheese and pepper, pressing in slightly. Braid ropes together, pinching ends
to seal; tuck ends under. Place braid on a baking sheet coated with cooking
spray. Cover and let rise in a warm place (85°), free from drafts, 20 minutes
or until doubled in bulk.

   Combine egg white and water, stirring well. Brush braid with egg white
mixture. Bake at 350° for 20 to 25 minutes or until braid sounds hollow
when tapped. Yield: 1 (6-inch) braid.

Per 1½-Inch Slice:

Calories 128
Calories from Fat 20%
Fat 2.9 g
Saturated Fat 0.7 g
Carbohydrate 22.0 g
Protein 5.3 g
Cholesterol 2 mg
Sodium 209 mg

Exchanges:

1½ Starch
½ Fat

Bayou Red Beans and Rice (page 230)

# FROZEN ASSETS

You'll reap dividends when you invest time in cooking big-batch recipes to divide and freeze. Cash in on days you're too busy to cook.

# SPRING ROLLS

Per Egg Roll:

Calories 98
Calories from Fat 11%
Fat 1.2 g
Saturated Fat 0.2 g
Carbohydrate 16.5 g
Protein 5.3 g
Cholesterol 13 mg
Sodium 197 mg

Exchanges:

1   Starch
½   Lean Meat

6   ounces unpeeled
      medium-size fresh shrimp
1   (10-ounce) package frozen
      chopped spinach
1   teaspoon sugar
1   teaspoon cornstarch
1   teaspoon oyster sauce
1   teaspoon low-sodium soy
      sauce
    Vegetable cooking spray
2   teaspoons peanut oil
1   cup chopped celery

1¼  cups fresh bean sprouts
½   cup chopped fresh
      mushrooms
½   cup chopped green onions
½   cup chopped bamboo shoots
¼   cup chopped water chestnuts
8   (1-ounce) slices reduced-fat,
      low-sodium ham, chopped
18  egg roll wrappers
⅓   cup frozen egg substitute,
      thawed

Peel and devein shrimp; chop shrimp.

Cook spinach according to package directions, omitting salt. Drain well.
Combine sugar and next 3 ingredients, stirring well.

Coat a wok or a large nonstick skillet with cooking spray; drizzle oil
around top of wok, coating sides. Heat at medium-high (375°) until hot.
Add celery; stir-fry 2 minutes. Add spinach, bean sprouts, and next 4 ingredients; stir-fry 1 minute. Add shrimp; stir-fry 2 minutes or until shrimp
turns pink. Add soy sauce mixture and ham; stir-fry 1 minute. Remove
vegetable mixture from wok; let cool 10 minutes.

Mound ¼ cup vegetable mixture in center of each egg roll wrapper. Fold
one corner of wrapper over filling. Lightly brush exposed sides and corners
of wrapper with egg substitute. Fold left and right corners over filling. Push
filling toward center of wrapper. Tightly roll filled end of wrapper toward
exposed corner; gently press corner to seal securely. Brush egg rolls with
egg substitute. Place egg rolls on a baking sheet coated with cooking spray.
Bake at 400° for 10 minutes; turn rolls, and bake an additional 10 minutes
or until lightly browned. Yield: 18 appetizer egg rolls.

**To Freeze:** Place unbaked egg rolls in labeled heavy-duty, zip-top plastic
bags. Freeze up to 1 month.

**To Serve Two:** Place 6 frozen egg rolls on a baking sheet coated with
cooking spray. Bake at 425° for 12 minutes; turn rolls, and bake an additional
10 to 12 minutes or until lightly browned.

# Chile-Corn Muffins

1 cup yellow cornmeal
1 cup all-purpose flour
2 teaspoons baking powder
1 teaspoon baking soda
½ teaspoon salt
1 tablespoon sugar
1 teaspoon chili powder
1 (8-ounce) carton plain
    nonfat yogurt
⅓ cup skim milk

¼ cup frozen egg substitute,
    thawed
2 tablespoons vegetable oil
⅛ teaspoon hot sauce
1 (8¼-ounce) can no-salt-
    added whole-kernel corn,
    drained
1 (4-ounce) can chopped green
    chiles, drained
  Vegetable cooking spray

Combine first 7 ingredients in a medium bowl; make a well in center of mixture. Combine yogurt and next 4 ingredients; add to dry ingredients, stirring just until dry ingredients are moistened. Stir in corn and chiles.

  Spoon into muffin pans coated with cooking spray, filling three-fourths full. Bake at 400° for 16 to 18 minutes or until lightly browned. Remove from pans immediately. Yield: 14 muffins.

**To Freeze:** Place baked muffins in labeled heavy-duty, zip-top plastic bags or wrap in heavy-duty aluminum foil. Freeze up to 1 month.

**To Serve Two:** Remove 2 muffins from zip-top bags or foil; place frozen muffins on an ungreased baking sheet. Bake at 400° for 25 minutes or until thoroughly heated. Or place 2 frozen muffins in microwave oven; defrost 1 minute. Microwave at HIGH 1 minute or until thoroughly heated.

**Per Muffin:**

Calories 115
Calories from Fat 20%
Fat 2.6 g
Saturated Fat 0.4 g
Carbohydrate 19.2 g
Protein 3.6 g
Cholesterol 0 mg
Sodium 230 mg

**Exchanges:**

1 Starch
½ Fat

# Freezer Slaw

6 cups shredded cabbage
1 cup chopped green pepper
½ cup shredded carrot
1 cup white wine vinegar
½ cup sugar

¼ cup water
1 teaspoon celery seeds
½ teaspoon salt
½ teaspoon dry mustard

Combine cabbage, green pepper, and carrot in a large bowl. Combine vinegar and remaining ingredients in a small saucepan. Bring to a boil; cook 1 minute. Pour vinegar mixture over cabbage mixture; toss well. Cover and chill. Yield: 8 servings.

**To Freeze:** Spoon slaw evenly into 4 labeled heavy-duty, zip-top plastic bags. Freeze up to 1 month.

**To Serve Two:** Thaw 1 (2-serving) bag in refrigerator. Serve with a slotted spoon.

**Per Serving:**

Calories 78
Calories from Fat 3%
Fat 0.3 g
Saturated Fat 0 g
Carbohydrate 18.0 g
Protein 1.1 g
Cholesterol 0 mg
Sodium 166 mg

**Exchanges:**

1 Starch

# GARDEN VEGETABLE SOUP

**Per 1½-Cup Serving:**

Calories 122
Calories from Fat 3%
Fat 0.4 g
Saturated Fat 0.1 g
Carbohydrate 25.1 g
Protein 4.1 g
Cholesterol 0 mg
Sodium 330 mg

**Exchanges:**

1 Starch
2 Vegetable

2 quarts canned no-salt-added beef broth, undiluted
3 cups chopped tomato
2 cups diced potato
2 cups chopped cabbage
1 cup frozen whole-kernel corn
½ cup chopped carrot
½ cup chopped onion
½ cup chopped zucchini
½ cup chopped fresh green beans
1 teaspoon salt
1 teaspoon dried Italian seasoning
½ teaspoon pepper
½ teaspoon hot sauce
1 (6-ounce) can no-salt-added tomato paste
1 bay leaf

Place beef broth in a large saucepan; bring to a boil. Add tomato and remaining ingredients. Reduce heat, and simmer, uncovered, 1 hour, stirring occasionally. To serve, remove and discard bay leaf. Yield: 3 quarts.

**To Freeze:** Place 3 cups soup in each of 4 labeled airtight containers. Freeze up to 1 month.

**To Serve Two:** Thaw 1 (3-cup) container in refrigerator or microwave oven. Place soup in a medium saucepan. Cover and cook over medium heat until thoroughly heated, stirring occasionally.

Garden Vegetable Soup

# Brunswick Stew

4 (4-ounce) skinned, boned chicken breast halves
2 cups water
2 tablespoons chopped fresh parsley
½ teaspoon salt
2 teaspoons minced fresh thyme
2 bay leaves
1½ cups cubed potato
1 cup sliced celery
1 cup chopped onion
1 (14½-ounce) can no-salt-added whole tomatoes, undrained and chopped
1 (10-ounce) package frozen lima beans, thawed
1 (10-ounce) package frozen whole-kernel corn, thawed
2 teaspoons low-sodium Worcestershire sauce
¾ teaspoon pepper
¼ teaspoon garlic powder
¼ teaspoon hot sauce

Combine first 6 ingredients in a large Dutch oven. Bring to a boil; cover, reduce heat, and simmer 20 minutes or until chicken is tender.

Remove chicken from broth; skim fat from broth, reserving broth. Remove and discard bay leaves. Shred chicken, and return to Dutch oven. Add potato and next 5 ingredients to Dutch oven, stirring well. Add Worcestershire sauce and remaining ingredients. Bring to a boil; cover, reduce heat, and simmer 2 hours, stirring occasionally. Yield: 2 quarts.

**To Freeze:** Place 2 cups stew in each of 4 labeled heavy-duty, zip-top plastic bags. Freeze up to 1 month.

**To Serve Two:** Thaw 1 (2-cup) bag in refrigerator or microwave oven. Place stew in saucepan, and cook over medium heat until thoroughly heated, stirring occasionally.

Per 1-Cup Serving:

Calories 186
Calories from Fat 9%
Fat 1.9 g
Saturated Fat 0.5 g
Carbohydrate 24.1 g
Protein 18.5 g
Cholesterol 36 mg
Sodium 255 mg

Exchanges:

1 Starch
1½ Lean Meat
2 Vegetable

# LOUISIANA GUMBO

**Per Serving:**

Calories 271
Calories from Fat 8%
Fat 2.5 g
Saturated Fat 0.4 g
Carbohydrate 40.0 g
Protein 20.7 g
Cholesterol 84 mg
Sodium 540 mg

**Exchanges:**

2   Starch
1½ Lean Meat
2   Vegetable

2   (6-ounce) skinned chicken
      breast halves
5   cups water
½   cup all-purpose flour
      Vegetable cooking spray
2   cups chopped onion
1   cup chopped green pepper
1   cup chopped celery
1   clove garlic, minced
¾   cup chopped lean cooked
      ham
1   tablespoon dried parsley
      flakes
1½ teaspoons low-sodium
      Worcestershire sauce
½   teaspoon paprika
¾   teaspoon salt

¼   teaspoon garlic powder
¼   teaspoon pepper
⅛   teaspoon dried thyme
⅛   teaspoon ground red pepper
⅛   teaspoon ground cloves
⅛   teaspoon hot sauce
1   (10-ounce) package frozen
      cut okra
½   (6-ounce) can no-salt-added
      tomato paste
2   bay leaves
1   pound unpeeled medium-
      size fresh shrimp
4   cups cooked long-grain rice
      (cooked without salt or fat)
      Gumbo filé (optional)

Combine chicken and water in a Dutch oven; bring to a boil. Cover, reduce heat, and simmer 30 minutes or until chicken is done.

Spread flour evenly in a 15- x 10- x 1-inch jellyroll pan. Bake at 350° for 30 minutes or until lightly browned, stirring every 10 minutes. Remove from oven, and set aside.

Remove chicken from broth; skim fat from broth, reserving broth. Bone chicken, and shred. Set aside.

Coat Dutch oven with cooking spray; place over medium-high heat until hot. Add onion, green pepper, celery, and minced garlic; sauté until tender. Stir in browned flour. Gradually stir in reserved chicken broth, shredded chicken, ham, and next 13 ingredients. Bring to a boil; cover, reduce heat, and simmer 45 minutes, stirring occasionally.

Peel and devein shrimp. Add shrimp to vegetable mixture; cook 3 to 5 minutes or until shrimp turns pink. Remove and discard bay leaves. For each serving, place ½ cup rice in individual bowls. Ladle 1 cup gumbo over each serving. Sprinkle with gumbo filé, if desired. Yield: 8 servings.

**To Freeze:** Place 2 cups gumbo (without rice) in each of 4 labeled airtight containers. Freeze up to 1 month.

**To Serve Two:** Thaw 1 (2-cup) container in refrigerator or microwave oven. Place gumbo in a medium saucepan, and cook over medium-low heat 15 minutes or until thoroughly heated, stirring occasionally. Serve over ½-cup portions of rice. Sprinkle with gumbo filé, if desired.

# Chunky Beef Chili

| | | | |
|---|---|---|---|
| 1⅓ | cups dried pinto beans | 2 | (8-ounce) cans no-salt-added tomato sauce |
| 2 | pounds ground round | | |
| 3 | cups chopped onion | 2½ | tablespoons chili powder |
| 1 | cup chopped green pepper | 1 | teaspoon salt |
| 3 | cloves garlic, minced | 1 | teaspoon pepper |
| ½ | cup reduced-calorie ketchup | | |
| 1 | (14½-ounce) can no-salt-added tomatoes, chopped | | |

Sort and wash beans; place in a Dutch oven. Cover with water to depth of 2 inches above beans; let soak 8 hours. Drain; cover with fresh water. Bring to a boil; cover, reduce heat, and simmer 1 hour or until tender.

Cook beef and next 3 ingredients in a Dutch oven over medium heat until meat is browned, stirring until it crumbles. Drain; pat dry with paper towels. Wipe drippings from Dutch oven. Return meat mixture to Dutch oven. Add beans, ketchup, and remaining ingredients. Bring to a boil, reduce heat, and simmer, uncovered, 30 minutes. Yield: 3 quarts.

**To Freeze:** Place 3 cups chili in each of 4 labeled airtight containers. Freeze up to 3 months.

**To Serve Two:** Thaw 1 (3-cup) container in refrigerator or microwave oven. Place chili in a medium saucepan, and cook over medium heat until thoroughly heated.

**Per 1½-Cup Serving:**

Calories 340
Calories from Fat 20%
Fat 7.7 g
Saturated Fat 2.6 g
Carbohydrate 34.6 g
Protein 32.9 g
Cholesterol 70 mg
Sodium 399 mg

**Exchanges:**

2  Starch
3½ Lean Meat
1  Vegetable

# French Bread Pizza

| | | | |
|---|---|---|---|
| | Vegetable cooking spray | ⅛ | teaspoon pepper |
| ½ | cup chopped green pepper | 2 | (6-inch) French rolls, split lengthwise |
| 1 | tablespoon chopped onion | | |
| 1 | teaspoon minced garlic | 3 | ounces thinly sliced Canadian bacon |
| 1 | (8-ounce) can no-salt-added tomato sauce | | |
| | | 1 | cup (4 ounces) shredded part-skim mozzarella cheese |
| ½ | teaspoon dried oregano | | |
| ½ | teaspoon dried Italian seasoning | | |

Coat a saucepan with cooking spray; place over medium-high heat until hot. Add green pepper, onion, and garlic; sauté until tender. Stir in tomato sauce and next 3 ingredients. Cook over medium heat until heated.

Spread sauce over cut side of rolls. Top with bacon and cheese. Place on a baking sheet. Bake at 400° for 6 minutes or until heated. Yield: 4 pizzas.

**To Freeze:** Wrap each unbaked pizza in heavy-duty aluminum foil. Freeze up to 2 weeks.

**To Serve Two:** Unwrap 2 frozen pizzas, and place on a baking sheet. Bake at 375° for 25 minutes or until thoroughly heated.

**Per Pizza:**

Calories 247
Calories from Fat 25%
Fat 7.0 g
Saturated Fat 3.6 g
Carbohydrate 29.0 g
Protein 15.7 g
Cholesterol 28 mg
Sodium 671 mg

**Exchanges:**

2  Starch
1½ Medium-Fat Meat

Mexican Chicken Pizza

# MEXICAN CHICKEN PIZZA

3    (4-ounce) skinned, boned
     chicken breast halves
1    green chile pepper
6    plum tomatoes, divided
¼    cup fresh basil leaves
1    tablespoon olive oil
¼    teaspoon salt
⅛    teaspoon ground white pepper
2    cloves garlic
     Vegetable cooking spray
⅔    cup chopped onion
½    cup chopped fresh cilantro
1    jalapeño pepper, seeded and
     minced
1    teaspoon chili powder

½    teaspoon ground cumin
2    cloves garlic, minced
1    (10-ounce) package
     commercial pizza crust
1    cup (4 ounces) shredded
     part-skim mozzarella
     cheese
1    cup (4 ounces) shredded
     reduced-fat Monterey Jack
     cheese
⅓    cup sliced green onions
2    tablespoons Parmesan cheese
1    teaspoon dried oregano

Place chicken in a medium saucepan; add water to cover. Bring to a boil; cover, reduce heat, and simmer 20 minutes or until chicken is done. Drain and shred chicken. Set aside.

Cut chile pepper in half lengthwise; remove and discard seeds and membrane. Place pepper, skin side up, on a baking sheet; flatten with palm of hand. Broil 3 inches from heat (with electric oven door partially opened) 5 minutes or until charred. Place in ice water until cool; peel and discard skin.

Place chile pepper, 2 plum tomatoes, basil, and next 4 ingredients in container of an electric blender; cover and process until smooth, stopping once to scrape down sides. Set aside.

Coat a nonstick skillet with cooking spray; place over medium-high heat until hot. Add onion and next 5 ingredients; sauté until tender. Set aside.

Unroll pizza crust, and cut into 4 equal portions; place on 2 baking sheets coated with cooking spray. Pat each portion into a 6½-inch circle, forming a rim around edges. Spread pureed tomato mixture evenly over crusts. Sprinkle evenly with mozzarella and Monterey Jack cheeses. Slice remaining plum tomatoes, and arrange evenly on pizzas. Top evenly with shredded chicken, onion mixture, green onions, Parmesan cheese, and oregano. Bake at 425° for 18 minutes. Yield: 4 pizzas.

**To Freeze:** Place unbaked pizzas on baking sheets, and freeze 4 hours or until pizzas are firm. Transfer each frozen pizza to a sheet of heavy-duty aluminum foil; seal tightly and label. Freeze up to 1 month.

**To Serve Two:** Preheat a baking sheet coated with cooking spray at 425° for 3 minutes. Remove 1 pizza from foil, and place on baking sheet. Bake at 425° for 20 minutes.

# SPICY LONDON BROIL

| | |
|---|---|
| 1 (1-pound) lean flank steak | 3 tablespoons low-sodium soy |
| Vegetable cooking spray | sauce |
| ⅔ cup chopped onion | 1½ tablespoons red wine vinegar |
| 1 clove garlic, minced | 1 teaspoon brown sugar |
| ½ cup canned no-salt-added | ½ teaspoon ground allspice |
| beef broth, undiluted | ½ teaspoon ground ginger |

Trim fat from steak. Score steak on both sides. Place steak in a heavy-duty, zip-top plastic bag.

Coat a small nonstick skillet with cooking spray; place over medium-high heat until hot. Add onion and garlic; sauté until tender. Add beef broth and remaining ingredients, and bring to a boil; boil 1 minute. Let cool. Pour marinade over steak; seal bag, and shake until steak is well coated. Marinate steak in refrigerator 8 hours, turning bag occasionally.

Remove steak from bag, and discard marinade. Place steak on rack of a broiler pan coated with cooking spray. Broil 5½ inches from heat (with electric oven door partially opened) 6 to 7 minutes on each side or to desired degree of doneness. Let stand 10 minutes. Cut steak diagonally across grain into ¼-inch-thick slices. Yield: 4 servings.

**To Freeze:** Slice steak in half before marinating. Place half of steak and half of marinade in each of 2 labeled heavy-duty, zip-top plastic bags. Freeze up to 3 months.

**To Serve Two:** Thaw 1 package of steak in refrigerator or microwave oven. Follow broiling instructions above.

Per Serving:

Calories 232
Calories from Fat 50%
Fat 13.0 g
Saturated Fat 5.5 g
Carbohydrate 4.1 g
Protein 22.1 g
Cholesterol 60 mg
Sodium 365 mg

Exchanges:

3 Medium-Fat Meat

# Hot-and-Spicy Pork Burritos

¼ cup lime juice
2½ tablespoons dried crushed red pepper
1 tablespoon chili powder
1 tablespoon hot chili powder
1½ teaspoons dried oregano
1 teaspoon ground cumin
½ teaspoon garlic powder
¼ teaspoon salt
¼ teaspoon ground red pepper (optional)
1 (10½-ounce) can low-sodium chicken broth
2 pounds lean, boneless center-cut loin pork chops (⅓ inch thick)
16 (6-inch) flour tortillas
2 cups shredded lettuce
1 (8-ounce) carton plain nonfat yogurt

Combine first 10 ingredients in a 13- x 9- x 2-inch baking dish, stirring well. Trim fat from chops. Add chops to marinade, turning to coat. Cover and marinate in refrigerator 8 hours, turning chops occasionally.

Bake chops in marinade, covered, at 325° for 1 hour, basting occasionally with marinade. Uncover and bake an additional hour or until most of the liquid is absorbed and meat is saucy. Let cool slightly, and shred.

Spoon 3½ tablespoons shredded pork down center of each tortilla. Roll up tortillas, and secure with wooden picks, if necessary. Place 2 tortillas on each plate, and top with ¼ cup shredded lettuce and 1 tablespoon yogurt. Yield: 16 burritos.

**To Freeze:** Divide shredded pork evenly among 4 labeled heavy-duty, zip-top plastic bags or airtight containers. Freeze up to 3 months.

**To Serve Two:** Thaw 1 (2-serving) bag in refrigerator or microwave oven. Cook pork in a nonstick skillet over medium heat, stirring frequently, 4 minutes or until thoroughly heated, adding 2 tablespoons water, if necessary. Spoon pork mixture evenly down centers of 4 tortillas. Roll up tortillas, and secure with wooden picks, if necessary. Place 2 tortillas on each plate, and top with ¼ cup lettuce and 1 tablespoon yogurt.

# Marinated Pork Tenderloins

½ cup unsweetened pineapple
    juice
3 tablespoons minced onion
2 tablespoons low-sodium soy
    sauce
1 tablespoon peeled, minced
    gingerroot

2 cloves garlic, minced
½ teaspoon dry mustard
¼ teaspoon ground red pepper
2 (¾-pound) pork tenderloins
    Vegetable cooking spray

Combine first 7 ingredients, stirring well.

Trim fat from tenderloins. Place tenderloins in a large heavy-duty, zip-top plastic bag. Pour marinade over tenderloins; seal bag, and shake until meat is well coated. Marinate in refrigerator 24 hours, turning bag occasionally.

Remove tenderloins from marinade. Insert a meat thermometer into thickest part of 1 tenderloin, if desired. Coat grill rack with cooking spray; place on grill over medium-hot coals (350° to 400°). Place tenderloins on rack; grill, covered, 20 to 25 minutes or until meat thermometer registers 160°, turning frequently and basting with reserved marinade. Let pork stand 10 minutes. Cut diagonally across grain into thin slices. Yield: 6 servings.

**To Freeze:** Cut raw tenderloins crosswise into 3 (8-ounce) portions; place in 3 labeled heavy-duty, zip-top plastic bags. Pour ¼ cup marinade into each bag; seal bags, and shake until meat is well coated. Freeze up to 3 months.

**To Serve Two:** Thaw 1 (8-ounce) bag in refrigerator 24 hours. (Do not marinate further after thawing.) Follow grilling instructions above.

Per Serving:

Calories 168
Calories from Fat 24%
Fat 4.5 g
Saturated Fat 1.5 g
Carbohydrate 3.8 g
Protein 26.0 g
Cholesterol 83 mg
Sodium 191 mg

Exchanges:

3 Lean Meat

# BAYOU RED BEANS AND RICE

| | |
|---|---|
| 1 pound dried kidney beans | 2 teaspoons Cajun seasoning |
| 6 ounces lite smoked sausage, cut into ¼-inch-thick pieces and halved | 1 teaspoon dried oregano |
| | 1 teaspoon pepper |
| 6 cups water | 2 teaspoons low-sodium Worcestershire sauce |
| Vegetable cooking spray | |
| 1½ cups chopped onion | ½ teaspoon salt |
| 1½ cups chopped celery | ½ teaspoon ground red pepper |
| ¾ cup chopped green onions | 2 bay leaves |
| ⅔ cup chopped green pepper | 4 cups cooked long-grain rice (cooked without salt or fat) |
| 3 cloves garlic, minced | |
| 1 tablespoon minced fresh parsley | Fresh oregano sprigs (optional) |
| 1 tablespoon plus 1 teaspoon hot sauce | |

Sort and wash beans; place in a Dutch oven. Cover with water to depth of 2 inches above beans; let soak 8 hours. Drain and rinse beans.

Combine beans, sausage, and 6 cups water in Dutch oven. Bring to a boil; cover, reduce heat, and simmer 1 hour, stirring occasionally.

Coat a large nonstick skillet with cooking spray; place over medium-high heat until hot. Add onion and next 5 ingredients; sauté 5 minutes or until tender. Add vegetable mixture, hot sauce, and next 7 ingredients to beans, stirring well. Bring to a boil; reduce heat, and simmer, uncovered, 1½ hours or until beans are tender. Remove and discard bay leaves. Serve over ½-cup portions of rice. Garnish with oregano sprigs, if desired. Yield: 8 servings.

**To Freeze:** Spoon bean mixture (without rice) evenly into 4 labeled heavy-duty, zip-top plastic bags. Freeze up to 1 month.

**To Serve Two:** Thaw 1 (2-serving) bag in refrigerator or microwave oven. Place bean mixture in a medium saucepan. Cook over medium heat, stirring frequently, until thoroughly heated. Serve over ½-cup portions of rice.

# CHEESY CHICKEN SPAGHETTI

1 (3-pound) broiler-fryer,
   skinned and cut up
8 cups water
¼ cup chopped celery
1 medium onion, quartered
1 medium carrot, sliced
8 ounces spaghetti, uncooked
   Vegetable cooking spray
1½ cups sliced fresh mushrooms
1 cup chopped onion
½ cup chopped green pepper
½ cup chopped celery
2 cloves garlic, minced

1 (14-ounce) can no-salt-added
   stewed tomatoes
½ cup no-salt-added tomato
   paste
¼ cup sliced ripe olives
1 tablespoon chopped parsley
1 teaspoon dried Italian
   seasoning
2 teaspoons low-sodium
   Worcestershire sauce
⅛ teaspoon ground red pepper
1½ cups (6 ounces) shredded
   reduced-fat Cheddar cheese

Combine first 5 ingredients in a Dutch oven. Bring to a boil; cover, reduce heat, and simmer 45 minutes or until chicken is done. Remove chicken from broth, and set aside; remove and discard celery, onion, and carrot. Skim fat from broth. Add water, if necessary, to broth to equal 8 cups. Set aside 2 cups broth. Bone chicken; cut into bite-size pieces.

Bring broth in Dutch oven to a boil; add spaghetti. Cook 10 minutes. Drain.

Coat a nonstick skillet with cooking spray; place over medium-high heat until hot. Add mushrooms and next 4 ingredients; sauté until tender. Add reserved 2 cups broth, tomatoes, and next 6 ingredients. Bring to a boil; reduce heat, and simmer, uncovered, 40 minutes. Add tomato mixture and cheese to spaghetti; toss. Spoon into 3 (1-quart) casseroles coated with cooking spray. Cover and bake at 350° for 30 minutes. Yield: 6 servings.

**To Freeze:** Cover unbaked casseroles with heavy-duty aluminum foil, and label. Freeze up to 1 month.

**To Serve Two:** Thaw 1 (1-quart) casserole in refrigerator or microwave oven. Bake, covered, at 350° for 30 minutes or until thoroughly heated.

Cheesy Chicken Spaghetti

**Per Serving:**

Calories 457
Calories from Fat 26%
Fat 13.0 g
Saturated Fat 5.1 g
Carbohydrate 43.4 g
Protein 39.4 g
Cholesterol 92 mg
Sodium 357 mg

**Exchanges:**

3 Starch
4 Lean Meat

# TURKEY LASAGNA

Vegetable cooking spray
½ pound freshly ground raw turkey breast
¾ cup chopped onion
½ cup chopped green pepper
1 teaspoon minced garlic
1 (14½-ounce) can no-salt-added whole tomatoes, undrained and chopped
1 (6-ounce) can no-salt-added tomato paste
½ cup water
¼ cup chopped fresh basil
1 tablespoon plus 1 teaspoon chopped fresh oregano
1 clove garlic, crushed
¼ teaspoon salt
¼ teaspoon pepper
1 cup lite ricotta cheese
¼ cup frozen egg substitute, thawed
4 cooked lasagna noodles (cooked without salt or fat)
1 cup (4 ounces) shredded part-skim mozzarella cheese, divided
2 tablespoons freshly grated Parmesan cheese, divided

Coat a large nonstick skillet with cooking spray; place over medium-high heat until hot. Add turkey, onion, green pepper, and minced garlic; cook until turkey is lightly browned, stirring until it crumbles. Drain turkey mixture, and pat dry with paper towels. Wipe drippings from skillet with a paper towel.

Return turkey mixture to skillet. Add tomato and next 7 ingredients. Bring to a boil; reduce heat to medium, and cook, uncovered, 20 minutes or until thickened, stirring occasionally. Remove from heat, and set aside.

Combine ricotta cheese and egg substitute in a small bowl, stirring well.

Coat 2 (7- x 5¼- x 1½-inch) baking dishes with cooking spray. Cut each noodle in half crosswise. Place 2 cooked noodle halves lengthwise in a single layer in bottom of each dish. Top each with one-fourth of turkey mixture and one-fourth of ricotta cheese mixture. Sprinkle each with ¼ cup mozzarella cheese and 1½ teaspoons Parmesan cheese; repeat layers with remaining noodle halves, turkey mixture, ricotta cheese mixture, and mozzarella and Parmesan cheeses. Bake, uncovered, at 325° for 30 to 35 minutes or until thoroughly heated. Let stand 10 minutes before serving. Yield: 4 servings.

**To Freeze:** Cover unbaked lasagna with heavy-duty aluminum foil, and label. Freeze up to 1 month.

**To Serve Two:** Thaw 1 lasagna in refrigerator or microwave oven. Bake, uncovered, at 325° for 35 to 40 minutes or until thoroughly heated. Let stand 10 minutes before serving.

# SEAFOOD CASSEROLE

½ pound unpeeled medium-
    size fresh shrimp
1 teaspoon olive oil
½ cup diced celery
¼ cup chopped green pepper
¼ cup sliced green onions
1 clove garlic, minced
2 cups sliced fresh mushrooms
¼ pound bay scallops
¼ pound fresh lump crabmeat,
    drained
2 tablespoons sherry
2 teaspoons lemon juice
1 (2-ounce) jar diced pimiento,
    drained
½ cup skim milk

¼ cup plus 2 tablespoons
    nonfat mayonnaise
¼ cup frozen egg substitute,
    thawed
2 tablespoons instant nonfat
    dry milk powder
2 teaspoons low-sodium
    Worcestershire sauce
⅛ teaspoon ground red pepper
1 cup cooked long-grain rice
    (cooked without salt or fat)
1 cup cooked wild rice
    (cooked without salt or fat)
2 tablespoons slivered almonds
    Vegetable cooking spray
¼ cup fine, dry breadcrumbs

**Per Serving:**

Calories 439
Calories from Fat 11%
Fat 5.5 g
Saturated Fat 0.8 g
Carbohydrate 61.5 g
Protein 33.3 g
Cholesterol 109 mg
Sodium 624 mg

**Exchanges:**

4 Starch
3 Lean Meat

Peel and devein shrimp; set aside.

Heat olive oil in a large nonstick skillet over medium-high heat until hot. Add celery, green pepper, green onions, and garlic; sauté 3 minutes. Add mushrooms; sauté 1 minute. Stir in shrimp and scallops; sauté 3 minutes or until shrimp turns pink and scallops are opaque. Remove from heat; stir in crabmeat and next 3 ingredients.

Combine milk and next 5 ingredients in a large bowl; stir in seafood mixture, rices, and almonds. Spoon mixture evenly into 2 (7- x 5¼- x 1½-inch) baking dishes coated with cooking spray; sprinkle evenly with breadcrumbs. Bake, uncovered, at 350° for 20 to 25 minutes or until hot and bubbly. Yield: 4 servings.

**To Freeze:** Cover unbaked casseroles with heavy-duty aluminum foil, and label. Freeze up to 1 month.

**To Serve Two:** Thaw 1 casserole in refrigerator or microwave oven. Bake, uncovered, at 350° for 20 to 25 minutes or until hot and bubbly.

# Recipe Index

238 • Recipe Index

# SUBJECT INDEX

# ACKNOWLEDGMENTS

Oxmoor House wishes to thank the
following merchants:

Annieglass, Santa Cruz, CA
Antiques & Gardens, Birmingham, AL
Barbara Eigen Arts, Jersey City, NJ
Bridges Antiques, Birmingham, AL
Bridgewater/Boston International, Newton, MA
Bromberg's, Birmingham, AL
Cassis & Co., New York, NY
Christine's, Birmingham, AL
Computrition, Inc., Chatsworth, CA
Frankie Engel Antiques, Birmingham, AL
Gien, New York, NY
Goldsmith/Corot, Inc., New York, NY
Izabel Lam, Long Island City, NY
Lamb's Ears Ltd., Birmingham, AL
Le Crueset of America, Inc., Yemassee, SC
Maralyn Wilson Gallery, Birmingham, AL
Martin & Son Wholesale Florist, Birmingham, AL
Palais Royale, Charlottesville, VA
Pillivuyt, Salinas, CA
Swid Powell, New York, NY
Table Matters, Birmingham, AL